A FIRST COURSE IN MARKETING

Frank Jefkins

BSc (Econ), BA (Hons), MCAM, ABC,
FIPR, FAIE, FLCC, FInstSMM, MCIM

DP PUBLICATIONS LTD.
Aldine Place, 142/144 Uxbridge Road
Shepherds Bush Green, London W12 8AA
1989

A CIP catalogue record for this book is available from the British Library

ISBN 1 870941 28 4

First published 1989

Copyright F. Jefkins© 1989

Printed in Great Britain by
The Guernsey Press Company Ltd
Braye Road, Vale
Guernsey, Channel Islands

Acknowledgements

The author wishes to express his gratitude to

 The London Chamber of Commerce

 The Royal Society of Arts

for their kind permission to reproduce questions from their past examination papers, and to

 The Advertising Standards Authority

 Broadcasters' Audience Research Board Ltd and AGB

 National Newspapers' Mail Order Protection Scheme

for their permission to reproduce relevant material, and to all those who assisted the author with information for this book.

Dedication

This book is dedicated to my wife Frances

PREFACE

AIM

1.   Marketing is an important subject which is sometimes regarded as too philosophical and theoretical. This book aims to show marketing as a practical business subject which is full of interest and, in many respects, is part of everyday life. It is very much to do with relations between manufacturers and suppliers and their customers. We are all customers. Products, shops, advertising and sales promotion are part of our daily lives.

This book provides an introduction to the main elements of marketing.

In particular, it provides comprehensive coverage for examinations such as the Royal Society of Arts Background To Business, the London Chamber of Commerce Third Level certificate in Marketing and the Marketing paper in the CAM Certificate in Communications Studies.

NEED

2.   While there are many books on Marketing this book has been specially prepared for those with no prior knowledge of the subject, and who need to get to grips with the subject in a simple and straightforward manner.

APPROACH

3.   The nature of marketing is first explained and defined. The book then proceeds to analyse the 12 elements of the marketing mix, and then in subsequent chapters to discuss the main elements in more detail. The product life cycle is shown to have a number of interesting variations which are not always found in one book, but which are often the subject of examination questions. The examples given throughout are up-to-date. They include many recent innovations so that the book is modern and topical.

At the end of each chapter actual examination questions are quoted with comments and model answers. They bring out examples of how candidates can introduce ideas, facts and examples drawn from their readings of trade journals, observation of the daily marketing scene, and his or her own experiences. This is important because examiners welcome intelligent application of knowledge, rather than just the memorising of textbook and lecture material. Thus, the book familiarises students with examination requirements and the way questions are asked. When they sit for an examination they will know what to expect.

NOTE FOR LECTURERS

At most chapter-ends is an additional exercise for use in the classroom situation. Outline solutions are provided to lecturers requesting them, from DP Publications, on departmental headed notepaper.

(iv)

CONTENTS

Part 1: The Nature of Marketing

INTRODUCTION

We begin by setting the scene. Much of marketing thought originated from the USA. Moreover, the USA had the advantage of developing marketing during the Second World War 1939-1945 when goods were rationed in Britain, marketing was stagnant and advertising hardly existed. However, from the 50s onwards marketing has developed rapidly in Britain, and for obvious reasons such as different geography, the size of the country and our kinds of advertising media, marketing has been adapted to suit British economic, social and political requirements. It will be noticed how the British Chartered Institute of Marketing definition in Chapter 1, differs from the American.

In Chapter 2, we examine the basis of much marketing planning, the marketing mix. Again, this has American origins, but times have changed and a more flexible approach is suggested here. This helps the student to see the marketing mix as an onward flow of closely related activities. The 4Ps formula is useful as a first approach to the marketing mix, but then we have to think of the mix as it really is in practice - like the mix of ingredients needed to bake a cake.

Chapter 3 discusses the effect of competition on the marketing strategy, and shows that marketing is a highly offensive sales battleground.

In Chapter 4 we take a very interesting look at the product life cycle which is sometimes limited to the standard life cycle with its inevitable decline and death of a product. But this happens to only some products: the majority have more complicated or continuous product life cycles and so all the variations on the PLC will be found in this chapter.

1. What is marketing?

INTRODUCTION

In this introductory chapter the foundations will be laid for the more specialised and analytical chapters which follow.

Marketing will be defined, and also distinguished from barter. The differences between a marketing and a product oriented business will be explained, together with some background history of marketing. The chapter will also discuss and clarify confusing terms like marketing concept and market theory, international and global marketing, market forces and strategic marketing. Also considered will be the constraints on marketing in developing countries.

MARKETING DEFINED

The most widely accepted British definition is that of the Chartered Institute of Marketing which says:

Marketing is the management process responsible for identifying, anticipating and satisfying customers' requirements profitably.

This is quite different from barter in which there is simply an exchange of goods which the two sides agree are of equal value. That does not mean necessarily that they are of equal value in money terms, and barter existed long before there was money. People were prepared to exchange what was of less value to them for goods which were of more value, such as wool for meat. Barter still takes place as when one country will exchange goods with another, no money being involved. A modern form of barter is countertrade when two countries buy from each other, using a currency to which both have access, e.g. US dollars.

The definition also differentiates between a marketing oriented company and a product oriented one. The first finds out what the market will buy at a price that will show a profit, the second seeks to sell what it has produced without first finding out whether anyone is likely to buy it and whether it can be sold at a profit.

The second - that is, selling rather than marketing - may sound foolish but it took place for centuries and it still occurs with badly managed companies. That is why the Chartered Institute of Marketing definition refers to a 'management process', and why it has been very critical of management for its poor marketing skills. It is therefore worth analysing the definition. There are certain key words which should be remembered.

A management process means that marketing is not something left to the sales side of the business, but should start at the top as part of management responsibility. Management should not be just about financial policy but about what the organisation is selling to whom and why and whether it will be a business success. This also enhances the status of the marketing function itself, and in marketing oriented companies the head of marketing will be a board director.

Consequently, marketing management has developed from sales management. Significantly, the original name for the Chartered Institute of Marketing was the Institute of Sales Management.

Identifying means finding out what people want. They may actually say what they want by making complaints or suggestions, but more often it is necessary to conduct research to find out what they really want. Do they prefer sweet or dry drinks, blue or white sewing machines, tinned or bottled fruit, a sun roof or a CD player? It is no use guessing or assuming: to be wrong is to suffer financial disaster. People do get it wrong as has been seen with the failure of at least four new newspaper launches in recent years.

Anticipating. Sometimes people do not know what they want, but the likelihood of their being willing to buy if the good or service was available can be investigated. It may not be a guarantee, but it is better than assuming there is a profitable market. Concept research is conducted to discover how people respond to new ideas. It may not be a guarantee, but it is better than assuming there is a profitable market. Concept research is conducted to discover how people respond to new ideas. It may be that the market will have to be prepared, such as by using public relations methods known as market education, before there can be a launch. This will be explained more fully in Chapter 12.

Profitability. There is no point in marketing a product unless it will make a profit, even if profitability takes time to achieve. This will be related to a number of contributory factors such as raw material, labour and production costs, distribution costs, price and likely volume of sales. Price also has to cover taxes, interest to share-holders and the financing of credit such as bank loans to buy or lease machinery. Profit can be a very small part of price so profitability is a major factor in what, in accepting the definition, can be described as the *marketing concept*. This concept, in the words of the late David Malbert, can be defined yet again as *producing and selling at a profit goods that satisfy customers*. That is a simpler definition of marketing as a business philosophy.

The *marketing concept* is sometimes confused with *market theory*, but there is a difference between the process of marketing and the market which is where sales take place. Market theory can be defined as:

Market theory holds that goods will tend to be produced where it is most efficient to do so.

When the Industrial Revolution was developing it was necessary to locate industries close to raw materials or power (such as water) or at ports which received foreign goods (e.g. Port Sunlight where Lever Brothers set up a soap factory using the fat from cattle imported from America). The modern counterpart has been the American aircraft industry which has benefited from having a large domestic market for aircraft. Similarly, it is more efficient to produce cotton goods where cotton is grown, and electronic components where there is cheap labour.

EXCHANGE PROCESSES

While 'exchange' is implicit in the Chartered Institute of Marketing definition, it is stated outright in another popular definition from Philip Kotler:

Marketing is human activity directed at satisfying needs and wants through exchange processes.

This definition is more specific about 'customers' requirements' and divides them into 'needs' and 'wants'. *Needs* are the economic necessities of life, namely food, clothes and shelter. *Wants* are additional goods and services which may be required when they become available such as holidays, cameras, or motor cars, or entirely new things that come on the market like a TV set capable of receiving satellite television. *Exchange processes* are the means of effecting both the sale and purchase of goods and services. These can include money, credit cards, hire purchase, shops, advertising and sales promotion. The exchange has to be mutually satisfying. From the suppliers point of view, satisfaction must be a profitable one. The Kotler definition is less clear about profitability than that of the Chartered Institute of Marketing which emphasises this.

HISTORICAL BACKGROUND

First, there was mechanical and mass production allied with the growth of towns with shops - urbanisation - to provide a market, and the developments of transport by canal, road, railway and eventually air to move goods from factories to distant customers. This was further aided by the emergence of popular media which made it possible to advertise mass produced goods to a mass market. As an example of this, the *Daily Mail* has been a popular newspaper for about 100 years.

There was little marketing in the modern sense in this process of production, distribution and exohange. There was a very different economic situation in pre-Second World War days. Labour and raw material costs were low, prices were low, taxes were low and on the whole profits were proportionately high. Much of this was due to Britain enjoying the resources of the British Empire. For example, Indian independence cost Britain a vast fortune.

There were some early applications of marketing in Britain in the 30s when the government set up marketing boards to promote the sales of fruit and vegetables. The post-Second World War years produced new economic situations such as high employment with very often two adult wage-earners in a family; high taxes to pay for government services; and a huge range of new products or first-time purchases such as plastics, foreign holidays, central heating, refrigerators, television, private houses, motor-cars, and petrol. The post-war years opened up market possibilities unheard of before in Britain, although well established in the USA some twenty years earlier.

Marketing research had arrived in Britain from the USA in 1939, but war set back the development of marketing in Britain until controls and rationing began to disappear in the early 50s. Thus, Britain was some ten years behind America, but quickly adopted American marketing ideas as wartime shortages were remedied. Increased spending power, new types of retailer like the supermarket, greater mobility of shoppers, new means of advertising such as television, new goods and services, and a more intensely competitive marketing situation followed by new credit facilities all created a marketing rather than a selling world. It has been a distribution revolution in which many things discussed in this book, such as the whole span of marketing communications and marketing research, have made marketing a major force in the economy.

From this it will be seen that economics and marketing go hand in hand since economics is the study of scarcities, and in marketing there is no limitless quantity of anything. The above remarks may imply that marketing is a comparatively recent concept, but it is more the development of techniques that is new. As long ago as 1776, in his famous book *Wealth of Nations*, Adam Smith wrote 'Consumption is the sole end of production'. Modern marketing is about producing and selling at a profit what people will consume. The number of consumers, the variety of goods and services, and the costs to be met before a profit is possible, are far greater, more complicated and sophisticated than they were some 200 or so years ago. Now that we are entering the post-Industrial Revolution, marketing has to meet the fresh demands of a high-technology age.

As this book will show, marketing initiatives have been very clever during the past thirty years, and walking round a store today it is easy to take them for granted. They extend from the huge range of product choices (many in a variety of colours hitherto unknown), numerous convenience products, plus methods of selling from sales promotion schemes to literally shopping without shops as seen with direct response marketing. Nowadays, goods and services are marketed, not sold.

INTERNATIONAL AND GLOBAL MARKETING

Marketing is an international activity, intensified by the arrival of satellites which are revolutionising news coverage, entertainment, publishing, television, and advertising. The Euromarket does not have to wait for the single market of 1992 or the opening of Eurotunnel for it is here already. But is there *global* marketing and how does this differ from *international* or export marketing?

International, or export marketing, means selling overseas by exporting, licensing foreign companies to produce one's goods, or setting up manufacturing plants in other countries. This is not necessarily global marketing. With global marketing the same product bearing the same brand name is sold world-wide. This happens with Coca-Cola, Kodak, HP Sauce, Canon, Rolls-Royce and Honda. But some products have to be made or packed differently or given different names to those sold in the home country. The British American Tobacco Company, for instance, sells brands of cigarettes abroad which are never sold in Britain. Some brand names cannot be used in other countries because they have different meanings.

With global marketing the likelihood is that the product can be sold anywhere in the world without change except, perhaps, translated labels or instructions. With much international or export marketing each country or region has to be dealt with separately as with a combine harvester which has to reap different crops under different conditions in various countries.

MARKET FORCES

This is a term often used by Conservative politicians who believe that a government should not interfere but should leave supply and demand and prices to the vagaries of market forces, and not intervene with controls.

Market forces can be unpredictable and uncontrollable, especially as the world begins to 'shrink' and an event on the other side of the world (e.g. a coffee crop destroyed by frost) can effect the price of, say, Nescafé.

Market forces can be defined as:

Various forms which affect attitudes, wants, needs of customers and their satisfaction.

They can include the weather, politics, natural disasters, foreign competition, revolutions and wars, world prices, labour disputes, elections and so on.

STRATEGIC MARKETING

This has become a popular term associated with the marketing plan and is best defined by Alfred D. Chandler as follows:

The determination of the basic long-term, goals and objectives of an enterprise, and the adoption of courses of action and the allocation of resources necessary for carrying out these goals.

This calls for an audit, or appreciation, of the current situation. What are the strengths and weaknesses of the marketing organisation? Similarly, what are the strengths and weaknesses of the competition? And to what extent can the influence of market forces be estimated?

Then comes the planning stage, which extends through the marketing mix which will be discussed in the next chapter. To this will be added the forecast of expected or desired sales, and the objective of the strategy which may be to sell to a new segment or section of the market, or to secure more retail outlets, or to gain a higher share of the market.

The tactics to be employed come next and they will concern the deployment of the sales force, the use of advertising, and perhaps whether or not to use a sales promotion scheme.

Finally, the strategy has to be evaluated, either as an ongoing exercise, or at the completion of the campaign, using marketing research services such as dealer audit or a consumer panel.

The above is a sketch of strategic marketing, a step-by-step scheme to achieve certain objectives, and its different elements will be the subjects of later chapters.

CONSTRAINTS IN DEVELOPING COUNTRIES

Attempts are sometimes made to import Western marketing concepts into Third World countries. This is seldom wise because conditions are totally different. While the industrialised countries are already leaving the Industrial Revolution behind, most developing countries are still largely agricultural ones on the threshold of the Industrial Revolution.

Labour is abundant so there is no justification for automation or robotics, and there is only limited use of computers. Intermediate technology is more appropriate, e.g. mechanical rather than electronic typewriters.

There may be few cities or large towns, and they may be separated by large distances. Roads and transportation may be poor so that distribution is difficult, and the climate may present problems such as flooding.

The cash economy may be limited for two reasons: young people under 15 years of age will predominate, and probably half the population will have no spending power. The majority of the people may be illiterate and difficult to reach by Western-style media which will concern only the elitist educated urban minority.

Marketing relies on marketing research but this is often handicapped by lack of statistics, such as reliable population figures, or because of the resistance of people who are suspicious of researchers asking questions.

Added to this may be communication problems arising from multi-racial societies with many ethnic groups, languages, dialects and social or religious customs.

To apply standard marketing ideas to such different and often complicated societies is seldom practical, and a sales-oriented and seller's market situation is likely to exist.

This is not to say that modern marketing techniques cannot be applied to these countries, but it will take a long time before they enjoy the conditions which made it possible for the marketing concept to be adopted in industrialised countries fifty years ago.

A further complication is that many of these countries have immense overseas debts and suffer from a lack of foreign exchange. This has not been helped by industrialised countries, in the past, selling expensive sophisticated equipment such as armaments to these countries, and so impoverishing them still further with foreign debts. However, out of this have come efforts to develop indigenous industries capable of reducing the need for imports, and here lie opportunities for use of marketing techniques.

This brings us back to the economics of marketing which were very well expressed by the American economist of several decades ago, Irving Fisher, in his equation of exchange $mv = pt$. This says that the quantity of money and its velocity or movement effects the level of prices and the volume of sales. Money is the root of all marketing, and the growth of marketing (as shown earlier in the example of post-war Britain), depends on the ability of people to buy and for manufacturers and other suppliers to make a profit out of satisfying demand. Marketing is the agent of a prosperous economy. The opposite is rationing, often compounded by a black market in scarcities.

SUMMARY

In this chapter marketing has been defined, and the differences between a sales and a marketing oriented business have been explained. The historical background of marketing has been described, with mention of why it was a later development in Britain than in America. The strong association of marketing research has been stressed, and this has occurred again when considering the constraints of marketing in developing countries.

Needs and wants are also defined, and exchange processes are referred to when discussing the definitions of marketing from the Chartered Institute of Marketing and Philip Kotler.

The marketing concept and marketing theory, and international and global marketing, have been clarified at this early stage.

There has been discussed of the influence of market forces, and what they are. Strategic marketing has also been introduced. All this is bound up with the broad marketing concept of producing and selling at a profit goods and services that satisfy customers.

PAST EXAMINATION QUESTIONS

Compulsory Question 1, LCC Series 4 1987

'Marketing is human activity devoted to satisfying needs and wants through exchange processes', says Philip Kotler. This is a limited concept of marketing compared with the Chartered Institute of Marketing's definition which refers to profitability. Discuss the scope and limitations of marketing with special reference to 'exchange processes' and 'profitability'.

Comment

This is a typical compulsory question in the London Chamber of Commerce Third Level marketing paper. It calls for a discussion running to about 1½-2 pages of the A4 size answer book. Marks are given for the quality of the argument and answers will vary according to each candidate's application of knowledge. The answer is well covered by the interpretations of the definitions to be found in this chapter.

There is no harm in the candidate disputing that Kotler's definition is a limited concept of marketing, especially since it is more specific than the CIM definition about needs and wants. The candidate may also quite logically argue that an exchange process is a broad term for buying and selling and that the seller expects to make a profit.

Examiners welcome good intelligent argument, and in this case a model answer would not necessarily be the expected answer.

Compulsory Question 1, LCC Autumn 1985

*(i)   What is the **marketing concept** and how does it differ from the **sales concept**?*

(ii)   Discuss the two major principles of the marketing concept, and illustrate your answer with a definition of marketing which emphasises these principles.

Comment

This is not only the compulsory question - and unless this question is answered the rest of the paper will not be marked - but it is in two parts. In LCC exam questions parts (whether 2, 4, 5, 10 or 20) are given equal marks. To fail to answer a part is to sacrifice the proportion of marks awarded to that part.

Part (i) refers to market-oriented and sales-oriented companies. The marketing concept is concerned with making a profit out of selling consumer goods which research has identified they are likely to buy, whereas the sales concept is confined to seeking to sell goods without first finding out the requirements of the market. The latter may, of course, succeed as can be seen in a street market, but the former is concerned with satisfying buyers.

Part (ii) refers to the two principles of identifying what people will buy and then giving them satisfaction. A motor-car manufacturer may identify wants, e.g. do people want a hatch-batch, a sun roof, low petrol consumption, safety factors, and then product a vehicle which satisfies market demand. The two principles are set out in the Chartered Institute of Marketing definition which candidates should be able to quote.

Question 6, LCC Series 4, 1987

Discuss the main market forces which control the feasibility of a marketing strategy.

Comment

This is a discussion question calling for about $1\frac{1}{2}$ pages which should be set out clearly by numbering each market force and then commenting on its effects on the feasibility and practicality of the marketing strategy. This is a deceptively short question which requires quite a long thoughtful answer. It is useless having a marketing strategy if external market forces can make its attainment impossible or even unlikely.

The main market forces are therefore:

1. **Political.** Is government policy against the idea? A company's proposals could require import of raw materials or of a complete product when the government wishes to reduce imports or to encourage home production. Or does the government favour your proposals?

2. **Economic.** Is the economic situation good or bad, such as low or high unemployment, prosperity or recession?

3. **Competition.** What is the state of competition? Are there many similar products on the market or have you a monopoly?

4. **Legal.** Are there any legal problems concerning your product, e.g. hire purchase regulations, food and drug labelling requirements, limitations on sales and so on?

5. **Customs and taboos.** Are there any social or religious objections to the product or service? In particular, this could affect exports.

6. **Distribution.** Will the trade adopt the new product, or will it resist yet another brand? Supermarkets have limited shelf space allocated to brands on their acceptance list, and some of these are being de-listed in favour of 'own-label' brands. If the supermarkets will not take the product, volume production and mass sales will be impossible.

The candidate may think of other valid market forces, but the above are standard ones which can be developed into an interesting and intelligent answer.

Compulsory Question 1, LCC Series 2 1988

Is global marketing possible, or is it only possible to take each foreign market separately and to plan international marketing accordingly? Illustrate your answer with real or imaginary products.

Comment

This is an 'it depends what you mean' question, and candidates should be aware that questions often call for a balanced debate rather than for a one-sided argument. The examiner expects a thoughtful answer, weighing up the pros and cons. Global marketing is a very loosely used expression, and is often used when international or export marketing would be more correct. These topics have been discussed in this chapter. A possible answer might be:

Model answer

Global marketing is possible when a product or service is acceptable world-wide, but this is true only of some products. Even then, it may be necessary to modify the specifications, or the package, or supply only certain sizes or models to particular countries. It may be necessary to use a different kind of container, or change the colour of the label. For example, a sewing machine in blue casing would not sell to the Chinese in countries like Hong Kong, Singapore and Malaysia, although the product was basically the same.

The best examples of products which are sold unchanged throughout the world, and are true of global marketing, are drinks such as Coca-Cola and Scotch whiskies, camera films like Kodak and Fuji, and equipment like cameras, tape recorders and typewriters.

Some products may be similar up to a point, but will require variations for some countries or regions of the world. A VCR will have to accept a compatible system, unless it is an expensive universal model. Guinness is a familiar beer, but it is labelled differently in some countries.

Not every product is lucky enough to have a name like Coca-Cola, Ford, Kodak or even HP Sauce which is acceptable anywhere. Some products have to be given different names when sold in other countries because the name has an unfortunate meaning abroad. This is already the problem with Euromarketing, where it is not always possible to have a Eurobrand. This promises to be a major problem with advertising on satellite television.

For example, Irish Mist whisky and the Rolls-Royce Silver Mist car have had their troubles at exhibitions in Germany where the words 'mist' in German means dung.

Packaging poses certain snags. A product which melts can be sold in paper or a waxed carton in the Northern hemisphere and it can be kept in a refrigerator. For hot countries it may have to be packed in a tin.

Detergents are sold in monster cartons in Europe, but in developing countries people can afford to buy only small packages, while in some very poor countries such products have to be packed in re-usable containers such as pails.

With a great many products, national or regional requirements need to be researched. A motor-car may need a heater for some countries but an air-conditioner for others. Industrial goods also have their variations such as Arabic, Chinese, Japanese characters for a type-setting machine, or different fittings for farm equipment if it is to sow or reap rice or wheat.

In other words, a great deal of market research is necessary, and some problems are not easily recognised in the country of origin. The Baby Milk Scandal was provoked because exporters of milk powder did not realise that mothers in rural areas had no means of measurement, sterilisation or refrigeration. As a result, babies fed on powdered milk often suffered from malnutrition.

Consequently, with a great many products - and even services like banking and insurance - it may be necessary to look at each region and often each country to see whether or not it has marketing potentials. Perhaps modifications are necessary. Sometimes, neighbouring countries like Singapore and Malaysia, Bahrain and Saudi Arabia, Jordan and Israel have very different requirements, likes and dislikes, customs and taboos. You cannot sell short skirts in a Muslim country, but you can in the Caribbean.

The above answer is not as hard to write as may at first be supposed. Everything in it has been published in popular textbooks which are widely available, and quite a lot of the examples will be found in this book. Candidates should always read more than one book. They do not always have to be bought but can be found in college and public libraries. But candidates can also use their brains: the car heater or air conditioner example is common sense. If the 'mist' story is unknown it is possible to say that a brand name could have a rude meaning in another country and that would be perfectly acceptable to an examiner.

EXERCISE

An insurance company is planning to market a new kind of insurance policy to cover repairs to equipment such as domestic appliances or office machinery which are out-of-guarantee or are not covered by a service agreement. Consider the market forces which could make this a practical or impractical proposition.

2. What is the marketing mix?

INTRODUCTION

The marketing mix (or strategy) and its components will be discussed in this chapter. It forms a foundation for a number of succeeding chapters which elaborate on individual components. E. J. McCarthy's 4Ps will be considered, but also whether it is better to think of the mix as a recipe of components which have to be mixed rather than separated. The subject of *marketing communications* is also introduced in this chapter because it complements those of the marketing mix.

DEFINITION

An omnibus definition of the marketing mix comes from Philip Kotler:

> The marketing mix is the set of controllable variables that the firm can use to influence the buyer's response.

The originator of the marketing mix was Professor Neil Borden of the Harvard Business School, defining it thus:

> The marketing mix refers to the apportionment of effort, the combination, the designing, and the integration of the elements of marketing into a program or 'mix' which on the basis of an appraisal of the market forces, will best achieve the objectives of an enterprise at a given time.

These are omnibus generalisations, but what exactly are the 'variables' and the 'elements'? Practice does need to be applied to the theory. Some typical items are:

Marketing research	Distribution
New product development	Advertising
Pricing	Sales promotion
Packaging	After-sales
Selling	service

Is this list complete? Does it apply to every industry or business? What about branding? Surely the *naming* of the product or service, and also of the company, is a vital element in the mix? It is very difficult to advertise an unidentified good or service. Even a store's own label brand bears the name of the store: it's Sainsbury's or Tesco's baked beans in order to compete with Heinz and Crosse & Blackwell's. And where does *public relations* fit in? As will be shown, public relations is not just an additive but is as ever-present as the air we breathe.

E. J. McCarthy had the notion of putting the elements into boxes labelled the 4Ps. This was so ingenious that almost every writer on marketing has adopted the formula which is as follows:

Product: the product range or mix; characteristics; quality; packaging

Price: determinants of price; discounts; credit policy; pricing strategies

Promotion: selling; advertising; sales promotion, publicity

Place: channels of distribution; warehousing and transport; stock levels.

This may seem a very neat association of the variables or elements under suitable headings. But what has happened to marketing research, or is it supposed to service the 4Ps? And where is public relations? Marketing writers and teachers tend to be shy of public relations, and mostly they follow Kotler's lead of disguising it as publicity, as a kind of 'free advertising'. Publicity is an unfortunate word. Basically, it means making known. That could apply to the name of a street or a newspaper report about a political assassination. As will be shown in Chapter 12, public relations is not limited to publicity or necessarily publicity at all, and in its communicative role of creating understanding it pervades the whole marketing mix.

The trouble with the 4Ps is that like many models it is a form of shorthand that needs to be transcribed into more meaningful words. It can become a dangerous over-simplification when learned parrot fashion by students who use it in the examination room as an excuse for an answer, or try to apply it indiscriminately to irrelevant questions.

The marketeer does not talk about price today and packaging tomorrow. He is more likely to have to consider whether this or that form of packaging will affect the price; or, if it is proposed to change a certain price, what kind of packaging can be afforded. With many expensive gift or status products like perfumes and gold pens the cost of the package forms a large part of the price. And so it goes on. Real workaday marketing does not operate in 4P boxes.

Moreover, the 4Ps do not take into consideration the logical flow or chronological sequence of planning the marketing strategy. It is therefore more sensible to think of a recipe of elements which make up the mix. Some elements like marketing research and public relations may be associated with all or many stages of the mix.

A more apt definition of the marketing mix is:

The marketing mix consists of every element of marketing from product development to the after market.

ELEMENTS OF THE MARKETING MIX

1. Research and product development
2. Marketing research
3. Public relations
4. Naming and branding
5. Packaging
6. Pricing
7. Distribution
8. Selling
9. Advertising
10. Sales promotion
11. Test marketing
12. The after-market

These twelve elements will be described briefly, although most of them will be discussed more fully in later chapters. But, first, another term should be considered since it embraces several of the above elements. This is *Marketing Communications*.

MARKETING COMMUNICATIONS

This has become a subject on its own. The name is incorporated in a number of marketing and public relations agency or consultancy business names, and job titles. It is sometimes used in a narrow sense to cover only promotional communications such as selling, advertising and sales promotion.

Marketing management has to communicate at all times. The brand name and the label or the package, and also marketing research, are all forms of marketing communications in the broadest practical sense. So, too, is public relations no matter who the publics are - employees, distributors, consumers and many others. Therefore, marketing communications are an important aspect throughout the marketing mix, ranging from complaints or suggestions which may influence product development to instruction manuals which belong to the after-market and could influence future sales.

Marketing communications complement the marketing mix, and the following analysis will show how they extend beyond the conventional idea of the subject consisting only of promotional communications.

1. Names of companies and branding of products or services.

2. Labelling, packaging, instructions and 'stuffers' like the information leaflet packed with a film.
3. Price - which can communicate so much about the character or value of the product or service and pinpoint its market segment.
4. Management-employee relations since these can effect productivity.
5. The sales force - incentive schemes, sales contests, conferences, bulletins.
6. Dealer relations - dealer house magazines, works visits, trade press relations, training retail staff.
7. Customer relations - dealing with complaints, media relations, customer house journals.
8. Market education - preparing the market for the launch of new products, especially technical ones or totally new product ideas.
9. The after-market - after-sales service, spares, instruction manuals.
10. Advertising - press, radio, TV, cinema, outdoor, exhibitions, point-of-sale etc.
11. Sales promotion - special short-term promotional efforts.
12. Direct response marketing (formerly known as mail order).
13. Public relations - which is an integral part of other items in this list.
14. Sponsorships for advertising, marketing and public relations purposes.
15. Marketing research - which applies to many of the above items.

Marketing communications are therefore a continuous process and the relevance and importance of this will be seen in the following analysis of the marketing mix itself.

ANALYSIS OF THE 12 ELEMENTS OF THE MARKETING MIX

These elements apply to most products or services, but they may be applied differently according to the nature of what is being marketed and, as already noted, at different times in the progress of the product life cycle. Although we start below with research and development (R & D), and while this may be continuous to improve a product or service, or it may be the starting point of a marketing strategy, a marketing plan may be required annually for a long-established standard product like a box of matches which itself may not have changed.

1. Research and product development
What product or service is to be marketed? Some products are totally new, like new medicines, new generations of computers, or new aircraft. They may have required years of research, design and tests. Many 'new' products are innovations like the electric typewriter, the electronic typewriter and the word processor, evolving from the original manual typewriter which itself went through many modifications. Or the company may be a bank, insurance company or building society which, as a result of new laws, has been able to extend its range of services. A business cannot afford to stand still. Even the manufacturer of a standard product or service may diversify. Rentokil, for instance, is not only concerned with pest control but offers hygiene services and has a company which supplies tropical plants to offices.

Under this heading can be included:
1. New products or services
2. Modified or new models
3. Diversification into a new product or service area.

2. Marketing research
Market research studies the market, but *marketing research* covers every kind of research concerning the marketing mix from product concept to evaluating results. The idea of a new product, choice of brand name, price, packaging, advertisements, media, what consumers buy and the share of the market held by a brand, response to advertising and conversion into sales are all topics for different marketing research techniques. They will be explained in Chapter 7.

This is a subject which sometimes confuses students, but it is not necessary to delve into the sociological and statistical aspects of marketing research. The important thing is to understand what needs to be researched, and the methods which can be used to obtain the required information. A lot of research is a kind of insurance to avoid making mistakes.

For example, who actually buys clocks? One survey showed a clock manufacturer that the majority of buyers were middle-aged women who bought clocks as presents. It is no use trying to guess this sort of thing: it has to be found out. To take another example, an advertising agency may think it has a splendid idea for an advertisement or commercial, but pre-testing may show they are completely wrong. Better to find out before it is too late!

Marketing research is therefore a very interesting subject, but examiners complain that candidates are often poorly informed and confused about it.

3.   Public relations

Since public relations is concerned with creating understanding through knowledge which in turn leads to goodwill and reputation, it is inherent throughout the marketing mix. It is probably one of the most misunderstood aspects of the marketing world when it should be appreciated as an asset. Much of public relations is about effecting change and, as will be explained in Chapter 12, its role is often that of overcoming negative marketing situations such as hostility, prejudice, apathy and ignorance which can hinder a marketing programme. Some examples of its range of purposes and techniques will be found in the analysis of marketing communications given earlier in this chapter.

Another side to public relations in marketing is when mis-uses of marketing communications can create ill-will which is bad public relations or bad relations with the public. This can include a brand name which is difficult to pronounce or remember, an exces-sive price which is resented, an advertisement which misleads or offends, a sales promotion scheme which disappoints, or a poor after-sales service. If we accept for a moment the 'publicity' interpretation of public relations, these calamities can provoke bad publicity. Public relations is not about pretending things are better than they are, and it can be about admitting that something has gone wrong as with the recall of a faulty product.

4. Naming and branding

Here is another example of marketing communications which parallels the marketing mix. The name of the company, and the name of the brand, convey images of the manufacturer or supplier and of the product or service. Their choice calls for great skill. So many names already exist, so many are similar, and yet it is necessary to strive for something which is original, distinctive, appropriate, and easy to say, spell and remember. It also needs to lend itself to display and advertising.

Short names are often excellent, but a name consisting of three syllables and the use of vowels trips easily off the tongue. Good examples of short names are Oxo, Daz and Shell while three syllable ones are Texaco, Winalot and Ferodo.

Finding the right name is often the subject of research to discover which name people prefer. It is also necessary to check that proposed names are not already legally registered and protected by rival companies.

Another consideration is whether or not the name is acceptable overseas. This was touched on in the model answer on global marketing in the first chapter.

It is also necessary to remember that a name needs to be permanent. If a name is changed it may infer that the newly named product is different or inferior, and the long task of establishing a new name has to be undertaken. A company invests its reputation in a brand name as was seen throughout the Second

World War when Stork margarine was continuously advertised so that it was not forgotten even though it was unobtainable.

Once a product is branded it can be advertised. Branding and advertising go hand in hand, and that applies to the package which has to identify itself on the supermarket shelf where there is no shop assistant to sell it.

One of the secrets of advertising is repetition, and repetition of a brand name is an essential part of advertising. This is also linked to habit buying, the customer being persuaded to always buy the same brand. One of the cleverest slogans ever created was *Player's Please* which was exactly what the customer was expected to say when making the purchase.

5. Packaging

Shape, size, design, colour and material all contribute to successful packaging, whether it be the immediate container like a sauce bottle or a carton in which the container may be packed as with toothpaste. Thus there may be one or two packages for the same product, and there may also be a label.

Packaging has several tasks to perform:

1. It has to hold or contain quantities of the product such as tablets or liquids.

2. It has to protect the product - when transported, when stored or displayed, when taken home by the customer, and while in the customer's possession. Some of this is bound up in 'convenience' such as keeping a clothing product clean as when shirts are packed in plastic bags.

3. It has to identify the product - as when advertised or displayed. 'Pack recognition' is often a feature of advertisements and commercials.

4. It may be necessary to the actual use of the product as with an aerosol or other dispenser.

5. It may be necessary for the protection of the customer as with razor blades.

6. It may have another convenience factor in providing a correct measure of the product such as a sachet of shampoo, a tea-bag or a packet of soup.

7. It may be a means of pre-packaging items which are less easily sold when loose, as with many hardware items like nails, screws and cup hooks.

8. It can be a way of displaying and protecting many fresh foods, such as with plastic trays and stretched film covering, or waxed cartons for refrigerated items.

As will be seen from the above, a lot of ingenuity goes into packaging. It has a utility value, but with modern retailing it is a promotional aid while at the same time making an important contribution to customer satisfaction.

The shape - like some whisky and brandy bottles - will instantly identify the brand. The size may be important, either that it is conveniently small or that it is a bargain monster or economy size as with cartons of cereals or two-litre bottles of soft drinks.

Colour is a big factor in both attracting attention and distinguishing identity. Colour can also suggest characteristics, bold colours standing out and pastel shades receding. Two makes of camera film are quickly identified by the colour of the packs, the yellow Kodak and the red and green Fuji. White suggests hygiene, black (like Black Magic) an air of mystery and intrigue. Colour can also link with the corporate identity as when a company uses a special colour like Marks and Spencer's green or Woolworths red, which may be represented in store packaging like paper bags and carrier bags.

Finally, there is the material and packages may be made of paper, card, wood, metal, glass or various plastic materials. Which material works best in satisfying the eight tasks listed above? Should mustard be in a tin, a tube, a jar or a plastic-squeezy bottle? Which is cheapest, most impressive, most protective or preferred by customers? Packaging poses a lot of questions, but nowadays the packaging industry provides a remarkable array of answers.

There are even ecological considerations. Does a package create waste disposal problems? Milk is still packed in glass bottles because disposable plastic ones would have caused a massive pollution problem.

6. Pricing

The theory of pricing and types of pricing are explained in Chapter 6. Getting the price right, and getting one's price, are essential to both customer satisfaction and profitability. A long time ago Beecham said his pills were 'worth a guinea a box' although they cost only a fraction of a penny to produce. The huge modern Beecham empire was founded on them.

There are two ways of looking at price? It is what the market has to pay so that the producer recovers his costs and earns a living or makes a profit, and it is also what the buyer thinks is worth paying. The exchange process means that each side makes a sacrifice for a higher reward - what the other has it more valuable than what each has.

Getting the price right is therefore a critical task calling for strict budgeting. Sometimes a product has to be made to meet a price, and if it cannot be made and sold at that price a profit cannot be made and there is no point in making the product or supplying the service. The margin - the difference between cost and profit - can be very small as with packaged holidays. Or there can be a point, as with airliners, when there is a capacity point - say 60 per cent of seats filled - which shows a profit, and the rest of the seats can be sold more cheaply.

It also depends on volume of sales, product capacity, and turnover what sort of price can be charged. If millions of items are sold daily, as with fast moving consumer goods (fmcgs), the profit margin will be small per unit, but with goods sold infrequently like motor-cars or jewellery the price and the profit will be high.

To arrive at an *economic* price which recovers costs and makes a profit - but other kinds of price are discussed in Chapter 6 - the following costs may have to be recovered.

Components of price

Raw materials
Labour - perhaps a major cost
Production costs, e.g. machinery, power
Overheads - rates, light, heat
Packaging - both for distribution and of
  individual products
Warehousing and depots
Delivery transport or carriage by other
  means
Sales force - commission, salaries,
  expenses, training
Wholesalers' profit   )
Retailers' profit   ) trade terms
Office administration - sales office,
  accounts department
Bank loans, leasing of equipment
Marketing research
Advertising - production, media, fees
Sales promotion, e.g. purchase of
  merchandise for special offers
Public relations - consultancy fee
Services such as accountants, lawyers,
  test houses.

All these costs have to be paid for by the customer in the price, including profit out of which have to be paid taxes, dividends to shareholders, and cash for re-investment.

It is a formidable list! Sometimes labour can be 60 per cent of price, while all the distribution costs such as warehousing, delivery, trade discounts and promotion can be a very large part of price. A product may cost little to produce but a lot to sell.

The customer may say if there was less advertising the price could be reduced. This is a false argument because the price may be *as low as it is* because advertising permits volume production which in turn keeps the price down. This is called economy of scale.

There is also valued added tax (VAT) to consider which may be included in the price or added to it if the goods or services are rated for VAT.

7. Distribution

Distribution will be discussed in Part 3, including ways in which distribution has changed in recent years. Direct response marketing or shopping without shops has brought about many changes. For instance, whereas insurance was largely sold by brokers or door-step salesmen, much of it is now sold by mail.

Physical distribution (i.e. apart from aids to distribution like advertising) includes warehousing and depots, wholesalers, retailers, agents, brokers, markets and so on which make up the *channels of distribution*. These are the routes by which goods or services travel between the producer and the consumer. For example, a hotel may sell its facilities to a tour operator like Thomson Holidays (virtually a wholesaler) who sells holidays through retailers (travel agents). But some goods like fresh produce go through importers, markets (and sometimes both national and local ones), before arriving at the butchers, greengrocers or supermarket.

The question is, how best can distribution be effected? Control can be lost if supply is through wholesalers instead of direct to retailers. On the other hand, it would be uneconomic to sell paper clips direct to stationers and better to use wholesalers Or it may be even more economic to have one's own retail outlets. Cutting out the middleman may

help to both keep prices down and to have a closer relationship with the ultimate consumer.

Another factor may be that it is a technical product requiring skilled retailers able to both explain the product and service it, and so appointed dealers, perhaps monopolising sales of one make, will be used as with main dealers for motor-cars.

8. Selling

The company may employ a sales force which sells to wholesalers, retailers or direct to customers. The size, organisation (e.g. regions with regional sales offices and sales managers), calibre, training and method of remuneration all have to be planned. This may be different from one company to another, even though similar products or services are sold. One insurance company may have a field sales force while another will sell through brokers only, and a third may sell by post. Telephone selling is another method, as used by newspapers to sell advertisement space.

The quality of the sales force is therefore an important feature of the marketing mix, and the whole strategy will depend on its effectiveness. The effectiveness - that is, ability to obtain orders, meet sales targets, gain and keep customers - will depend on skilled sales management. This, in turn, will depend on recruitment, training, incentives and supervision.

The sales manager is not just a drill sergeant ordering his staff about, but a director of human resources. A perennial problem is that the salesman can be a lonely, isolated individual who operates a long way from base, yet he must feel part of a team allied along to head office. Salesmanship is a competitive, demanding, frustrating yet rewarding occupation. Good marketing communications need to operate here, both between the sales manager and his sales representatives and between them and their clients or customers. This calls for the supply of information from head office, and the submission by salesmen of regular reports on calls and results.

Selling may not only occur in the field. Retail store groups, building societies and banks have groups of sales staff at numerous branches and the branch manager is virtually their sales manager. A bank teller may seem to be more of a clerk than a shop assistant yet this person works so closely with customers that he or she is often responsible for selling the bank's services. Similarly, a waitress in a restaurant does not just take orders but advises on the menu and asks 'is there anything else?'

9. Advertising

Where would marketing be without advertising? It is to marketing what petrol is to a motor-car. Advertising is the means of making known in order to sell, and it is no accident that in this analysis it follows selling. Few things cannot be sold unless they are advertised, even a second-hand bicycle or pram. The card in the corner shop window saying *Room To Let* is just as much an advertisement as the brash commercial on prime time television. The saying 'it pays to advertise' is true enough. When the salesman tries to sell the new brand of cat food the buyer, whether he works for a 1000 store supermarket chain or is the village grocer, inevitably asks 'Will it be advertised?' And preferably on television! This subject is dealt with more extensively in Chapter 11 but it will be helpful here to distinguish between *above-the-line* and *below-the-line* advertising media, and between *primary* and *secondary* media since the two pairs of terms are sometimes confused.

Above-the-line media are also referred to as media advertising, and consist of the five media which are handled by advertising agencies under the commission system. They are press, radio, television, cinema and outdoor (including transportation such as London Underground). Traditionally, these media give agencies commission on purchases of space,

airtime or site rental.

The various trade bodies representing newspapers, magazines, ITV and ILR companies grant recognition on the basis of credit worthiness (ability to pay bills) and acceptance of the British Code of Advertising Practice. Recognition does not imply approval of an agency's abilities, so it is of no advantage to a client that an agency is recognised. A la carte creative agencies, which undertake creative work only, do not need recognition as they buy no media.

Below-the-line media are all other types of media such as exhibitions, direct mail, catalogues, sales literature, point-of-sale display material, and so on including novelties, give-aways and anything else used for advertising purposes. It does not include public relations since that is not a form of advertising nor an advertising medium.

Primary media are the first line media used by an advertiser to spearhead a campaign.

Secondary media are supporting media.

Either may be above or below-the-line media.

A brewer may use television and press as his primary media, supported by outdoor and point-of-sale displays including beer mats in pubs.

A direct response marketeer may use catalogues and direct mail as primary media supported by occasional press advertising.

NB: **The word media is the plural of medium**. The press is *a* medium, the press and television *are* media. It is therefore incorrect to say that the press is a good media. In an advertising agency the person responsible for planning media schedules is called the media planner, and the one who buys space or airtime is called a space or airtime buyer or media buyer.

10. Sales promotion

In the UK sales promotion refers to short term promotional schemes such as special offers and competitions, and is regarded as a form of marketing rather than as an advertising medium. This is stressed because in America sales promotion is another name for below-the-line advertising, and even in the UK it is sometimes regarded as advertising although more often it is used as an alternative to advertising. At one time, and still in some circles such as commercial television, it was called merchandising. The subject is covered more thoroughly in Chapter 13.

Forms of sales promotion have changed in recent years, as may be observed by noticing schemes announced in the popular press, delivered on the doormat, and to be seen in the shops. Many offers can be obtained or redeemed at the point-of-sale instead of having to write away for them. Modern developments have been a cross between direct response marketing and sales promotion with gift-cum-mail order catalogues whereby customers can obtain offers partly with coupons with purchases and partly with cash.

Great ingenuity has entered into sales promotion with specialist agencies devising schemes, specialist firms creating promotional gimmicks or supplying merchandise for offers, and a growth in third-party and multi-party schemes. One charity scheme involved eight firms collaborating by putting tokens on their packs which could be collected in favour of the Save the Children Fund.

Manufacturers like sales promotion schemes because they give them closer contact with their customers, and create a relationship which is impossible with the more distant forms of media advertising.

Sales promotion is one of the oldest marketing aids, and is older than marketing itself with a history extending over the past century. One of the most popular sales promotion schemes was the set of 50 cigarette cards given in packets of Players and Wills cigarettes in the 30s.

11. Test marketing

This has been separated from general marketing research because in a way it is the research to end all research before a product 'goes national'. Test marketing is not to be confused with product pre-testing, a common mistake with examination candidates.

Test marketing takes place when the product or service is ready to hit the market, after all research has been completed regarding name, package, price, media, copy and so on, and now the complete strategy is to be put to the ultimate test. Will it work in practise?

To do this it is necessary to select a town or region which is a reasonable miniature of the national market. It has to have a cross-section of the same kind of people and shops, and be covered by representative advertising media such as regional commercial television and local or regional editions of the sort of newspapers or magazines which would be used in a national campaign.

The test also needs time to prove itself and this will depend on how frequently the product is bought or if there are repeat purchases. The test occupies three stages, the pre-test when there are zero sales for the new line but certain shares of the market are held by existing lines; the initial test when the product is launched; and the post-test which accounts for the way repeat sales are producing a reliable share of the market percentage. (These 'shares' are discovered by dealer audit research which is usually based on regional ITV areas and conducted by firms like A.C. Nielsen. Invoices and stocks are checked regularly at a panel of retailers, thus showing the shares of the market held by each brand.)

The sponsor of the test will usually expect to gain a desired percentage of the market during the test, otherwise the new product will be abandoned. But such is the state of competition that many products that succeed under test marketing conditions fail when launched on the broadscale. Not to test market at all could be, however, a costly gamble.

The problem with test marketing is how to avoid distorting the results. The selling, display and advertising effort can be so concentrated in a small area that it is very impactive and enjoys a novelty effect. A national campaign can be more dispersed and therefore weaker so that the new product does not catch on quite so quickly as in the test situation. Results should be interpreted very critically, with allowance for a generous margin of error. Nevertheless, one manufacturer set a test market target of 15 per cent of the market but scored 17½ per cent and knew he had a winner.

12. The after-market

The after-market is not limited to after-sales service but includes everything following completion of a sale which will influence enjoyment of the benefits of the product or service. Customer satisfaction is very much bound up in this. It does not include methods of payment, carrier bags or delivery service, although it could include the way in which a company deals with unpaid debts, as when a building society has to increase its mortgage interest rates.

Some products will not sell unless there is promise of after-sales service or availability of spare parts. A problem with many modern technical products is that their life expectancy is short by comparison with, say, a manual typewriter or a cylinder lawn mower. A combination of plastic instead of metal materials and sophisticated electronic gadgetry makes the newer equipment subject to greater wear and tear. Added to this, manufacturers operate strict computerised inventory control and it can be uneconomic to make and store parts for models beyond a certain age. Customers do not understand this, expecting products like clocks, electric razors, domestic

appliances and so on to last for ever. There is, therefore, a conflict of consumer and manufacturer interests. It can be a bad public relations situation which may have to be resolved by, say, generous trade-in terms on a new model.

The after-market has many public relations aspects. One is that if customers *are* satisfied they will recommend the product or service. That is the most powerful form of promotion because it effectively breaks down sales resistance. A customer who makes recommendations is a friend for life. This can be encouraged by offering gifts in return for recommendations as occurs with much direct response marketing.

Instruction leaflets, books and manuals can be an important part of the after-market. Are they so well written, designed, illustrated and printed that the customer gets maximum value for his money and is able to understand the product and benefit from it? These publications may be used instantly in order to know, for instance, how and when to use a weedkiller, but maybe at some distant date as with the manual for a camera, office copier or a motor-car. It may not be possible to use the product unless the instructions are read and understood, or the instructions may be resorted to only in an emergency.

Attention to the after-market may be as simple as putting a small leaflet in the package giving an address to contact if the product is found to be unsatisfactory, or a note to the effect on the wrapper itself. A receipt often counts as a guarantee for a given period, or there is a detailed printed guarantee form or card, but some companies give an open promise that they will refund or replace if the product fails to satisfy.

There are thus many ways or taking care of the customer after the money has been rung up in the till. These methods can also be excellent ways of maintaining goodwill and protecting the manufacturer's (and very often the suppliers!) good name.

In fact, market education may have to continue into the after-market period, helping people to make the best use, or make other uses, of a product. This happens with many food ingredients by means of recipe leaflets and booklets, cookery demonstrations, or cookery articles in the press.

SUMMARY

The chapter began with definitions of the marketing mix and comments on their strengths and weaknesses, bringing out discussion of terms such as 'variables' and 'elements'. It was noted that the original list of elements was incomplete.

An historical introduction was given with references to the early approaches to the marketing mix made by Neil Borden, E.J. McCarthy and Philip Kotler. The popular 4Ps concept was set out and its possible shortcomings discussed in the light of professional marketing realities rather than academic theories. A more chronological approach was suggested.

Before analysing the elements of this chronological approach there was a discussion of marketing communications, which were shown in a broader context than the conventional one of regarding only promotional communications as marketing communications. It was pointed out that the marketeer has to be a good communicator at all times, and that many aspects of the marketing mix from branding and labelling to instructions are forms of marketing communications.

Marketing communications were introduced at this point because there are so many parallels between them and the elements of the marketing mix and their sequence of application.

The twelve elements of the marketing mix, although not necessarily a conclusive list nor applicable to every product or service, were then analysed one by one. This analysis also served as an introduction to a number of subjects given their own comprehensive chapters later in the book.

PAST EXAMINATION QUESTIONS

Since the marketing mix covers a number of subjects, not all of which have their separate chapters later on, a variety of relevant questions will now be considered. Up until 1986 the LCC paper contained 14 questions, mainly to provide questions for overseas candidates, but since 1987 there have been only 10 questions in LCC papers. The syllabus has also been re-arranged more clearly. LCC questions now tend to be omnibus ones, ranging over many parts of the syllabus. This makes it very difficult to offer model answers, and there is always the danger students will try to memorise such answers and offer them in an examination, not realising that the question in the new paper is different from those set previously.

The following are three past questions on the marketing mix.

Question 11, LCC Autumn 1982

Choose a well-known product and analyse its marketing strategy as far as you are aware of it, bringing in as many elements of the marketing mix as you can.

Comment

This is a particularly good example of a question where it would be unrealistic to offer a model answer since every answer to the question will be individual and different. It is unlikely that many candidates will choose the same product.

Purely as an example, suppose the chosen product was a chocolate bar, known in the trade as a countline. Its marketing strategy would probably involve security so that the launch had the maximum degree of surprise for competitors, and test marketing would be out of the question. The sales force would need to sell in quickly, followed up by good deliveries, so that when advertising broke - probably on television - there would be adequate distribution, i.e. ample stocks available to meet demand. Factory production would have to be planned not only to achieve adequate initial distribution, but to keep apace of re-ordering. The strategy would therefore be urgent when selling and advertising took place. Sales promotion is more likely to be something for the future.

All this would be preceded by new product development, branding, packaging, pricing, followed by distribution, selling, and advertising. Marketing research can be applied to many of the elements. If the company already has a splendid reputation as a confectionary manufacturer this will help both with selling in to the trade and selling out to consumers.

Noticeably, the above notes indicate that this answer calls for an analytic approach to the marketing mix, and to quote the 4Ps would not be helpful because it would handicap the flow of the marketing mix which should resemble the links in a chain rather than the division of the mix into isolated compartments.

Question 10, LCC Spring 1983

Your company is an international drinks manufacturer. (You may choose either an alcoholic or a soft drink.) The company plans to make this product under licence in a foreign country. (You may choose any country with which you are familiar.) Such a drink has not previously been imported into nor manufactured in that country: it is therefore largely unknown except to those who have visited the country of origin.

Consider the special conditions relating to the state of the economy and any ethnic, religious, language or other conditions which may effect the naming, packaging, labelling, advertising, public relations, market acceptance of the product and likely volume of sale.

What are the marketing implications in relation to the marketing mix?

Comment

The question has been carefully worded so that it is capable of being answered anywhere in the world. A variety of answers is invited by such a broad-based question. A 4Ps approach would be inadequate. In fact, dependant on the country in which the drink is being introduced, some elements of the marketing mix may be irrelevant. Marketing research and test marketing may be different or impossible, as with a country with a large rural population and a minority of town dwellers. Media may be scarce. Perhaps only those in the towns will have money for buying such a product. Alternatively, if there is a tourist industry the product could sell well in cafes, restaurants and hotels. Distribution may be limited. These are all possibilities which mean that the marketing mix has to be considered very differently from the way it is considered in a wealthy industrialised country.

The other aspects of naming, packaging and labelling may require care over the possibility of an offensive brand name; packaging that is suitable for the country (e.g. glass or plastic bottle, can, waxed paper carton and so on); and the wording of the container or label which must be comprehensible.

Public relations methods suitable for the country, and using appropriate local media, may be needed to educate the market about the new drink.

This is therefore a question which calls for a very practical understanding of the marketing mix, and its application to circumstances as they exist in different countries. But it could apply just as much to the import of cranberry juice into Britain as to the introduction of cider into Indonesia.

Question 2, LCC Spring 1984

(i) What is the marketing mix?

(ii) List and explain the components of the marketing mix, from the creation of a new product to after-sales service.

Comment

The first part calls for a definition such as one of those given at the beginning of this chapter. A good definition is usually a one sentence explanation, not a rambling paragraph.

The second part deliberately uses the word 'list' which implies a chronological sequence of elements. A 4Ps answer would not be a list. It is important to follow the examiner's instructions.

Question 8, LCC Autumn 1982

If you were seeking a name for a new product what would be your five most important considerations? Give examples of five products whose names obey your criteria.

Comment

There are two parts to this question. (In later years LCC questions have been more carefully divided into numbered parts.)

There are more than five possible important considerations, but good answers should contain five of the following: distinctive, original, characteristic, short, easy to pronounce, easy to spell, easy to remember, or acceptable overseas.

Five products whose names obey five of the

above considerations could be Oxo, Elf, Shell, Coca-Cola, Kodak, Ford, Honda, Nissan and Lipton.

Question 11, LCC Spring 1983

How does test marketing differ from marketing research?

Comment

This is another deceptively short question, but it is capable of a 1½ page essay in which the two subjects are analysed in sufficient detail to demonstrate how they differ. Both are discussed in this chapter, and marketing research has a chapter to itself. The mistake has to be avoided of confusing test marketing with product pre-testing: test marketing is a final test of the whole campaign in a representative miniature of the national market. Marketing research techniques can be used throughout the marketing mix, and also before, during and after a marketing campaign.

Question 11, LCC Spring 1985

(i) Distinguish between above-the-line and below-the-line advertising media, and between primary and secondary media.

(ii) Suggest the primary and secondary media for (a) a toothpaste, and (b) a mail order trader.

Comment

The question is well covered in this chapter in the Advertising section of the analysis of the marketing mix. They are examples of the terminology or jargon of marketing. This 'language of the trade' has to be learned if lectures, textbooks and examination questions are to be understood. Jargon changes and increases all the time. The second part of the answer brings out the candidate's understanding and application of the terms.

Model answer

Q.11(i)   Above-the-line advertising media or media advertising cover press, radio, television, cinema and outdoor (including transportation). These are the advertising media which are handled by full service advertising agencies under the 'recognition' and 'commission system' whereby the media owners recognise agencies so that they are entitled to claim commission on media purchase. This also applies to the media independents, agencies which plan and buy media but do no creative work.

Below-the-line advertising refers to all other media, most of which do not give agency commission. It is not usually handled by full-service agencies, except perhaps on a fee basis, but there are specialist agencies, and there are also 'through-the-line' agencies which handle any media appropriate to a campaign. More often, below-the-line advertising is handled by the in-house advertising or product manager.

Below-the-line media consist of exhibitions, direct mail, door-to-door mail drops, point-of-sale display material, catalogues, sales literature, aerial advertising such as balloons and airships or banner-trailing aircraft, body media such as hats and T-shirts, sponsorships, calendars, and various give-aways and gimmicks. It does not include public relations.

Primary media are those chosen to spearhead an advertising campaign, and secondary media are those used in support of primary media. The two are not necessarily the same as above-the-line and below-the-line media.

Q.11(ii)   For a toothpaste, primary media might be television and women's magazines, and secondary media could be posters and point-of-sale displays.

For a mail order trader, primary media might be catalogues, sales literature and direct mail, and secondary media could be occasional press advertising to obtain new customers or enquiries for inclusion in future mailing lists.

(**NB**. A common error is to place poster advertising among below-the-line media, and to include public relations which is not an advertising medium. Another fault is to assume that below-the-line media are inferior to above-the-line, but part (ii) of the question disproves this.)

EXERCISE

Assemble the marketing mix for (a) a consumer product and (b) a consumer service. Then consider the marketing communications aspects of each element in the two mixes.

3. How does competition affect marketing strategy?

INTRODUCTION

First, the two kinds of competition, perfect and imperfect, will be defined in economic terms. Then, following a review of the contradictions between supply and demand theory and marketing effectiveness, the three kinds of competition identified by J.M. Clark will be discussed.

Whether or not competition is a good or bad thing will be considered, together with the causes of competition.

The chapter will then concentrate on three specific areas of competition as they affect the marketing strategy, namely: the competitive effects of a rival product or service; the means of competing; and the special causes of competition.

Finally, there will be a discussion on what happens, or can be done, when excessive competition becomes uneconomic and unprofitable.

PERFECT AND IMPERFECT COMPETITION DEFINED

Perfect competition occurs when there are so many manufacturers or suppliers that none can dominate the price structure.

Ideally, perfect competitions means that the products from competitors are the same, as are the selling conditions. Perfect competition also requires that full information is available to buyers.

In these circumstances there will be a variety of prices for similar goods or services, although they will be subject to two forces: the effects of supply and demand, and what consumers are prepared to pay. Pricing policies and kinds of price will be dealt with in Chapter 6.

Imperfect competition occurs when, as with a monopoly, price rings or with state controlled prices, control of supplies permits control of prices.

Monopoly exists when there is only one supplier or one company dominates by controlling one third of the market (Monopolies and Restrictive Practices Act, 1945). The Monopolies and Mergers Commission investigates cases of monopoly. Duopoly refers to domination of the market by only two suppliers as happens in British radio and television with the BBC and the IBA (or whoever may in future control commercial broadcasting). Price rings exist when, say, a trade organisation seeks to set fixed prices, although this is usually discouraged or made illegal.

However, in reality imperfect competition is subject to the variables which exist in prosperous societies where most people have purchasing power over and above the cost of essentials or subsistence needs. This applies even to young people's pocket money, while pensioners are not absolutely poor.

Perfect and imperfect competition are therefore extremes which seldom exist except, perhaps, that there is perfect competition at a stock or commodity exchange or there is imperfect competition in a wartime situation of state controlled monopoly and rationing. In between we have mixed economies of state and private enterprises, with varying buying situations and differing states of knowledge of what is available.

Moreover, competition is less about price than about product differences, or different sales appeals put out in advertising, or additional benefits as projected by sales promotion schemes. Thus, there is a move away from purely economic arguments of supply and demand to the influence of marketing devices upon demand.

It is even possible to turn classical economic theory on its head, as when demand can actually be increased by a higher price! There is the excellent example of the cheap British-made Smiths watch which customers spurned in favour of more expensive foreign ones, although in fact the British watch was superior and the prices of the foreign watches were actually inflated by import duty. Equally, people will buy a more expensive German motor-car because it is more reliable than a cheaper British one, and once again price fails to control demand and supply and demand theory is abandoned.

THREE KINDS OF COMPETITION

Differentiated competition, substitution competition and alternative purchase competition are three kinds of competition suggested by J. M. Clark in his book *Competition as a Dynamic Process*. Adopting his ideas very broadly they can be developed as follows:

Differentiated competition exists when there are differences between the lines in a product group which allow them to compete with each other. In advertising terms this can be what has been called the unique selling proposition which enables one, say, brand of tea to be sold because it has this or that competitive advantage over another. There may actually be no difference between the products as has been shown with some branded petrols which originate from the same source!

Substitution competition exists when completely different products or services serve the same purpose. If one wishes to travel from England to France one can go by car, coach, train, aircraft, ferry or hovercraft. Central heating may be provided by solid fuel, gas,

electricity or oil. These are all forms of substitution competition.

Alternative purchase is based on opportunity cost. The opportunity to buy, say, a holiday is foregone in favour of, say, new furniture of similar cost. A choice has to be made between buying one or the other. This is related to the spending of discretionary income, that is money left over after buying essentials. There is intense competition for the sale of these expensive items, the more so as a country becomes more prosperous and people have more discretionary income. This can be affected by a rise or fall in taxation or interest rates.

THE NATURE OF COMPETITION

Competition exists when there is abundance and the consumer has a choice. A virtue of competition (which includes advertising) is that the consumer enjoys a choice between various goods, services or brands. He or she can choose between buying one of many newspapers or magazines, which is an advantage not enjoyed by those living in some Third World countries where there are few publications.

When goods are in short supply, or are even rationed as in wartime, there is scarcity and lack of choice. Competition also encourages low prices or at least one competitor can offer lower prices than another. This may not be limited to the price itself but to what the customer gets for the price as with free credit facilities when buying one make of motor-car rather than another.

A very interesting situation occurs from the manufacturer's point of view. If there is only one such product or service on the market it is sometimes less easy to sell it than if there are competitors. Monopoly can be a bad thing whereas if there is a product group each brand can help to sell the others because there is greater publicity all round. For example, if six travel firms are selling holidays in Greece more people are likely to be attracted by the idea of a Greek holiday than if there was only one operator. Competition can thus be healthy for a whole trade, industry or product group. Competition does not necessarily have to be feared.

Competition can arise because an existing product is rivalled by a newcomer with a special selling point. It may be a variation or a modification, or something which serves the same purpose differently, more economically or more efficiently. Thus, an umbrella is not just an umbrella of which there can only be one standard kind, anymore than all ballpoint or felt-tip pens are the same.

Competition stimulates the market, increases choice, and boosts sales. In the marketing mix, new product development is often the starting point. If a business is to survive it has to learn new tricks. All this calls for imagination, but not just hunches, and new ideas need testing before money is invested in their production, distribution and promotion.

SPECIFIC AREAS OF COMPETITION

It is fatal to assume everlasting popularity and sales success. Many products which were based on this false assumption have long since disappeared. The market changes as society changes. Some things have made the market change, such as the aeroplane. Years ago people were content to take their holidays in Blackpool or Brighton: now they seek holidays further and further afield in places like Miami or Penang. Pre-war houses had no garage: today every new house has a garage. Foreign restaurants were once found only in city centres: now they have almost put the village fish-and-chip shop out of business.

Competition thrives on change. These changes may also be in simple things like the way aspirins, garden seeds or deodorants are packed. In the latter case, aerosols are going out of favour and roll-on packs are more popular, no doubt because of the outcry about the effect of chlorofluorocarbons on the ozone.

Three specific areas of competition will now be analysed:

1. The competitive effects of a rival

Rival manufacturers, servicing companies or retailers may use the following forms of competition.

(a) **Products**. There may be entirely new products like new brands of confectionery, or extensions to the product range or mix like new shades of paint. There may be new shapes or versions of product like the hatch-back motor-car, the hover mower, the electric toothbrush, the compact disc (and CD player), the camcorder, the wine box, the diet soft drink, the non-alcoholic beer, and unleaded petrol.

(b) **Materials**. Products may be made of different materials which make them lighter, smaller, stronger, quieter, cheaper, more attractive-looking, or more up-to-date. Or people may be willing to pay extra for the benefits provided by new materials. But it may be necessary for conventional materials to fight back as with the 'brick is beautiful' campaigns.

Plastics have played a big part in this, even with fairly ordinary items like the bottles for whisky and gin sold as duty free items on airliners. In a similar way it is possible to sell large quantities of liquids because they are packed in two litre plastic bottles. Or products like ice cream are packed more conveniently in plastic boxes instead of waxed paper cartons. Convenience, and eventual home storage in refrigerators or freezers, can be a very competitive factor.

(c) **Prices**. Even though maintained prices are illegal, nevertheless competitive price advantages can compete by way of money-off vouchers, price cuts (e.g. 5p off) flashed on packages, banded and jumbo packs, cash refunds and so on.

(d) Advertising. If a competitor launches a new advertising campaign, and especially one that is highly original and impactive, this can cause serious competition.

(e) Sales promotion. Very competitive is the short, sharp sales promotion scheme which encourages consumers to switch to another brand, especially one which requires the purchase of several items which effectively block sales of other brands until the special offer items are exhausted.

2.   The means of competing

Conversely, the above five methods can be used in order to compete or to recover lost sales. Perhaps the product can be given an additive as has been seen with toothpastes detergents and petrol, or a new recipe or specification. If the product cannot be changed or improved, sales promotion schemes offer one of the most effective ways of competing.

The best way to compete is to offer something better or extra which keeps the product alive. The word 'new' or the expression 'new formula' can work wonders.

Sometimes it is a case of keeping the product firmly before the public. People are fickle and quickly forget. The product must continue to be on the shelf before the customers' very eyes. This is not possible if the shopkeeper decides not to stock the line. What can be done to make sure he does? Yes, he will be impressed by the promise of advertising, but every other manufacturer advertises too. The answer may be good representation by the sales force, good delivery service, but especially good trade terms. The key to re-ordering is the stockists' profitability. There are two ways in which the retailer makes money:

by trade discounts and by sales. Are competitors offering better terms? Can better trade terms be offered?

Another way to assist the trade is to provide point-of-sale material, or the loan of special displays in return for certain quantity orders, or the provision of in-store demonstrations, or devices like video displays. By helping the retailer to sell it is possible to be more competitive.

A popular device with some of the larger firms like Nestlé and General Foods is to mount tailor-made sales promotion schemes with one retailer such as Sainsbury's or Tesco, the offer applying to sales in their shops and running for perhaps a month. The stockist may also benefit from bulk purchase prices of stocks to cover the offer.

3.   Special causes of competition

Competition can arise from causes outside the trade and have nothing to do with rival firms. This sort of competition can apply to all the brands in a particular product group, or to all those in a certain class of trade or business. Economic and political factors - in other words market forces - can produce undesirable and unexpected competition. Some of these factors may be:

(a) Competition for discretionary spending. Over the years, a number of new products or services have arrived which have competed for the spending power known as discretionary income. New competitors have been holidays abroad, central heating, double glazing, video cassette recorders, home computers, freezers, privatisation share offers, various expensive collectibles, window replacements, fitted kitchens, and maybe second cars. Even with hire-purchase, credit cards and bank loans there is a limit to the volume of these expensive purchases, and so each competes with the other for the available money.

(b) New technologies. In particular, these compete with standard or conventional products. The less advanced product has to compete with the more sophisticated one. Can it survive, or can it be modified or replaced with something more modern? Products as mundane as razors and toothbrushes face this sort of competition. It is very evident with business equipment such as car phones, word processors, personal computers, fax machines and copiers.

(c) Foreign imports. Competition here is not only with the 'dumping' of foreign products at prices which undercut home produced ones, but with the import of superior foreign products as has been seen with those from Germany and Japan. The British motor-car industry has been decimated by foreign competition. It may be a question of labour costs, but more often it is one of quality which is often coupled with price.

The British camera and watch have both disappeared. Most electrical and electronic products have foreign-made components although the equipment may bear British names. The question is, does a company continue to manufacture, or does it simply assemble using imported components? Or does it go into partnership with the foreign company as Leyland has done with Daf for the manufacture of trucks?

WHEN COMPETITION GETS TOO HOT

It is possible for competition to become so fierce that a cease-fire is called by the rival companies and it is agreed not to continue a trade or price war which has become unprofitable.

In the late 30s the cigarette coupon war was ended by mutual consent, and cigarette coupons disappeared until the re-emergence in a comparatively small way in post-war years. When commercial television was introduced in the 50s, the whisky distillers agreed not to compete with television commercials.

However, one competitor may decide to drop out of that particular form of competition, as happened with certain newspapers which were attempting *The Sun's* use of bingo to win circulation.

Another method is for companies to amalgamate and so remove the competition. This happened with the Amalgamated Press, Odhams Press and George Newnes, all of whom had too many competing magazines. Amalgamated as IPC, there was a rationalisation of titles.

Competition may also be squashed when the leading company takes-over its smaller rivals as we have seen with a number of brewery companies, hotel groups, department stores and with Thomson Holidays and Horizon.

The reduction of competition may or may not benefit the consumer, but it can reduce the costs of rival companies competing with each other. Thus we have the contradiction of most competition being imperfect while there are tendencies towards a certain amount of perfect competition. At the same time we have governments - and not only in Britain - seeking to break up state monopolies and encouraging greater competition.

There are also the effects of the Financial Services Act 1986 and the Building Societies Act 1987 which have led to a freer market and intense competition over the marketing of financial services. Building Societies, for example, now offer cheque book accounts, pension schemes and own estate agents.

SUMMARY

The chapter began by defining perfect and imperfect competition, but recognised that these are extremes which do not always coincide with the real situation. Moreover, the real situation in which marketing techniques can even reverse supply and demand theory, tends to contradict economic theory. As so often happens, theory and practice often conflict with one another.

This discussion was followed by consideration of Clark's useful sub-division of competition which more closely resembles the market place situation. This was taken from his book, *Competition as a Dynamic Process*, Brookings Institution 1961.

The chapter moved on to even more practical discussion and dealt with three specific areas of competition, namely the competitive effects of a rival; the means of competing; and special causes of competition. Finally, the chapter commented on price wars and ways of averting competition.

PAST EXAMINATION QUESTIONS

Question 8, LCC Series 2 1988

A company manufacturing a popular food product has to face the conflict between creating brand loyalty and encouraging impulse buying. How, by the use of certain sales promotion methods, can it achieve both?

Comment

This is an interesting question concerning competitive marketing tactics which can have one or other effect, or both. The sponsor of the sales promotion scheme has to be sure which effect he aims to achieve. Does he want to build up a solid market of regular or habit buyers, can he do this by attracting first-time buyers, or does he aim to merely divert buyers from their normal purchases for a short-term sales boost? What sales promotion schemes can actually achieve both regular and new purchase?

There are two kinds of sales promotion schemes to consider, and is also depends to some extent on the sort of product.

If the customer seeks an unspecified bar of chocolate he or she may buy the one which has a flashed price cut, or - on impulse - an unintended purchaser may be attracted to buy a certain bar of chocolate because it has a special offer.

However, if the offer requires a number of subsequent purchases to obtain the necessary tokens to eventually obtain the offer, brand loyalty may be achieved. This may have begun with an impulse purchase. For example, many schemes run by petrol companies require buying the same brand, perhaps from the same filling station, for a period. This may have begun with a first-time buy when stopping to buy petrol and perhaps attracted by posters outside a filling station which announced the offer. Brand loyalty can be built up by having to buy the same brand in order to qualify for the offer, liking the brand and deciding to continue buying it regularly.

Question 7, LCC Spring 1981

How does discretionary income and elasticity of demand affect the marketing of expensive products or services?

Comment

This question deals with matters discussed in this chapter, and invites a thoughtful discussion. First, it is best to define the terms 'discretionary income' and 'elasticity of demand'.

Discretionary income means income surplus to that required for covering the basic needs of a person's normal standard of living. This will vary from one person to another. Some may have to first meet the needs of a large family, others will have mortgage payments, and while a bicycle may suffice for one a motor-car or railway fares may take up a lot of another's income. Different social grades may have different basic needs. For instance, a poorer person may spend nothing on education whereas a richer person may have to meet heavy school fees. Again, life-style will mean that discretionary income will be spent on different things: one may gamble money on football pools, another will buy sherry.

Elasticity of demand relates to supply and demand and the relationship between price and quantity demanded. However, as shown in this chapter, practice does not always follow theory. It does in some cases: packaged holidays are a good example, their huge popularity making it possible to provide inexpensive holidays abroad. Economies of scale operate.

So, how do these two elements concern the marketing of expensive products and services?

It is very necessary to define the market response most likely to buy the expensive products or services: e.g. who will buy an executive motor-car, a case of wine or a holiday in Honolulu? What sort of people have the discretionary income necessary for such costly purchases? What media will reach them?

Two factors have to be considered. What competition is there for this surplus income, and how can a particular product or service be shown to be the best buy? To what extent does elasticity of demand mean that if the price can be lowered, or the means of payment can be eased, demand can be increased and more can be sold?

Question 5, LCC Series 2, 1987

Describe five ways in which the marketing strategy of fast moving consumer goods might be planned and executed in order to sell successfully through self-service stores, supermarkets and hypermarkets.

Comment

These 'five ways' means that this a five-part question with four marks for each part. If only four ways can be thought of the candidate still has the opportunity of earning up to 16 marks. Candidates should always try to answer every part, but this sort of evaluation should be appreciated and a candidate should not be deferred from answering a question because not every part can be answered. This applies particularly to questions with many parts.

First, it is advisable to explain what fast moving consumer goods (fmcgs) are. They are popular mass market goods which are usually bought repeatedly, e.g. most of the foodstuffs, drinks, confectionery, toiletries, pet foods and so on found in supermarkets but not forgetting the neighbourhood grocers, chemists and sweet shops.

In the context of the question, the goods have to be pre-sold before the customer enters the store, or is actually in the store where the goods have to sell themselves off the shelf.

Five ways of promoting them through the big stores where there are not counter assistants, are:

1. Media advertising, e.g. popular press including women's magazines and publications such as the *Radio Times* and *TV Times;* commercial television; and outdoor advertising. Types of media should be discussed, and some recent campaigns can be mentioned.

2. Packaging - its shape, colour, design so that it quickly identifies the product at the point-of-sale. Examples could be given of striking packages.

3. Trade terms - to encourage the store to buy. They can range from discounts on volume purchases to delivery to either central depots owned by the supermarket chains or direct to their branches.

4. Sales promotion schemes. A number of these should be described, together with the tailor-made schemes which firms like

Nestlé and General Foods organise for Sainsbury's, Tesco and other stores.

5.   Public relations - ranging from product stories and feature articles in the press, to sponsorship like Mars sponsorship of the London Marathon.

Each of these should be developed so that the answer runs to about 1½ pages, and if current examples can be quoted they will please the examiner.

The above comment is virtually an outline of a model answer.

EXERCISE

Study competitive efforts being made by manufacturers by collecting current press advertisements, observing current television and poster campaigns, and commenting on them. Also, visit a supermarket and note the sales promotion schemes which will be found there for various products.

4. What is the product life cycle?

INTRODUCTION

This chapter shows how marketing ideas can be usefully applied to the real world of marketing. The various models of the PLC help to explain the behaviour of different kinds of product or service. They also emphasise that their life patterns are by no means the same.

Moreover, this chapter brings together a collection of PLCs. Most marketing books refer only to the standard model. However, for many years, LCC candidates have been expected to be able to draw and explain them all, as past examination questions show.

PRODUCT LIFE CYCLE DEFINED

The product life cycle (PLC) is a model of the introduction, growth and development or decline of a product or service.

The PLC should not be confused with the human life cycle which is uncontrollable. The PLC can be forecast, changed or modified. It is a means of understanding either the likely sales performance of a product or service, or how it is behaving at the present time.

STANDARD PLC

The original four-stage and bell-shaped *standard PLC* goes through the stages of introduction, growth, maturity and decline.

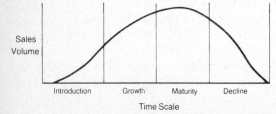

Figure 1 Standard four-stage product life cycle

The base line is the time scale, which may be only a few weeks in the case of a fashion good or a pop record but can be years in the case of something more substantial such as a dinner service which might remain in production for two or three years.

A more practical version of the standard PLC has an extra stage called 'saturation' which allows for a period when sales no longer rise but stay the same until for some reason, such as loss of popularity or the effects of competition, sales fall and the product dies. This could happen with a theatrical production or with a chocolate bar, both of which could enjoy a period of popularity but then suffer a fall in sales and have to be withdrawn. This *second* version can be drawn like this:

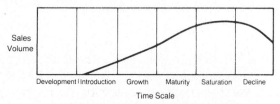

Figure 2 Standard five-stage product life cycle

This *extended standard PLC* also spaces out the earlier stages more realistically because product development occurs before the product is introduced to the market. Development may take many years, as happens with medicines. The product is launched on the market, and if it is successful sales will grow until its popularity will lead to maturity as an established product. But then sales may level out. They may continue at a satisfactory level as happens with many famous products which have become 'household names', although they still have to be promoted otherwise they die.

Some may last for a long time, but eventually disappear like Oxydol detergent, Force breakfast cereal, Gold Flake cigarettes, Rowntrees Motoring chocolate and the Armstrong Siddeley motor-car, all famous names of yesteryear.

PRODUCTS THAT DO NOT DIE

Not all products come and go. They can have very different fates so that other versions of the PLC are possible. The PLC is not just a theory, although it is a quick and easy way to demonstrate a range of events concerning sales volume over time. It can be useful in two ways:

1.   The PLC can be used to *forecast* the likely progress, life and fate of a new product or service. How long will it take to complete the various stages? When will start-up costs be recovered, and profits be made? How long will it survive, or how soon will it have to be modified or replaced?

2.   Year by year, when *planning* the annual marketing strategy, the PLC can be a way of looking at each line in the product range or mix. Companies may have many products, each with its own PLC and each at a different historical stage of its PLC. Some may need new advertising ideas, repackaging, improvements in design or formulation, or even replacement.

Once we start thinking like this we are questioning whether the simple standard PLC is sufficient or relevant. Is it true to real life in the marketing world? We must not be too theoretical. The standard PLC can therefore be too simple, and not really have anything to do with the more erratic or complicated lives of many products or services.

CONTINUOUS PRODUCT LIFE CYCLE

In other words, it is too easy to think that the life of a product is like that of a person who is born, grows up, becomes middle-aged, then old and finally dies. Would you say that about coal or potatoes or leather? For some products, especially raw materials or primary products like timber and stone, and many staples like bread, the PLC is likely to be of continuous life and probably growth, with perhaps some ups and downs. Even products like sugar and oil, which have suffered from change in demand, are unlikely to die. So our *third* kind of PLC can look like this:

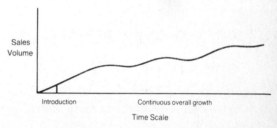

Figure 3 Life cycle of product with continuous growth

Figure 3 demonstrates the course of products which have lasted for thousands of years like coal and copper, and others such as McDougalls flour, Guinness stout, Stork margarine, Ovaltine, Swan Vestas matches and Cadbury's Dairy Milk Chocolate whose PLCs have existed for some generations.

Some of these 'household' names were bought by our grandparents. If you ever see a picture of horse-buses of nearly a hundred years ago you will see these buses carrying advertisements for products that you can still buy at the supermarket such as Colmans mustard and Bovril.

RE-CYCLED PRODUCT LIFE CYCLE

But are some of these long-lasting products quite the same? The Guinness label has been changed, the beer has been packed in cans as well as in bottles, and six-packs have been introduced. There have also been different strengths of Guinness, e.g. Guinness Extra. There have been similar changes with Coca-Cola, such as Diet-Cola with Nusweet sweetener instead of sugar.

So, are well-known products still packaged in the same way? Do they still have the same shape container or label, or the same flavour or colour? In many cases they have been re-vamped or improved over the years. The old favourite HP sauce has been re-labelled. Some have been given additives, like petrols, toothpastes and break-fast cereals, perhaps to meet competition. Such changes have usually aimed to maintain or recover popularity, and to rescue sales and secure profitability.

This activity gives us a *fourth* kind of PLC which shows how decline has been averted.

may also be to meet competition as has been seen with the extra services offered to business air passengers.

LEAPFROG PRODUCT LIFE CYCLE

Here we have a very common situation. The basic product - e.g. a motor-car, lawnmower or sewing machine - continues except that as sales fall of each model it is replaced by a new or modified one. The new one is being designed while the present one is still selling, but when sales of the current model drop to an unprofitable level, the new one is launched. The new model *leapfrogs* the old one.

This happens mainly with mechanical, electrical or electronic products like office equipment, cameras and television sets, more than with mass-market consumer goods which are most likely to enjoy the additives of the recycled PLC or decline absolutely. The motor-car is one of the best examples of the leapfrog PLC which looks like this *fifth* model.

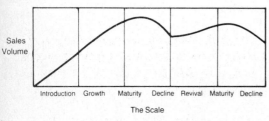

Figure 4 Re-cycled product life cycle

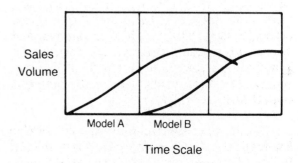

Figure 5 Leapfrog product life cycle

This happens when additives are put into products and they are re-launched with advertisements which say, for example, *now with the new XYZ* or *new improved*. Sometimes this can be a failure as when Shell introduced an additive which harmed motor-car engines and had to be withdrawn. On the other hand, Kelloggs have added nutritional ingredients to cornflakes whose food value had been criticised. The change

STAIRCASE PRODUCT LIFE CYCLE

Finally, there is the *staircase PLC*. This is a particularly interesting variation because it is very true of the ever-changing modern world. It consists of continuous ever-rising series of introduction/growth/maturity curves, usually with no saturation or decline curves. If there is a decline it is simply replaced by a new introduction curve as when a shipping company replaces liners with cruise ships as Cunard and P & O have done.

This is sometimes called the scollaped or scalloped PLC since it resembles the segments of a scallop-shell.

The staircase PLC is drawn like this:

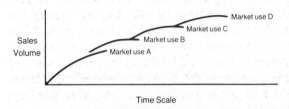

Figure 6 Staircase product life cycle

The classic product with a staircase PLC is nylon which has gone through numerous product uses such as textiles, hosiery, parachutes, fishing nets, carpets and motor-cycle wheels.

The staircase PLC also applies to companies, products or services which, for historical or technological reasons, have seen changes or developments over the years. Shipping lines, for instance, have developed from passenger, cargo and mail ships to container and cruise ships, bulk carriers, car ferries and hydrofoils. Companies which used to make railway wagons now make containers for shipping and central heating systems.

Since the deregulation of the Stock Exchange, the Big Bang of October 1986, and the Building Societies Act of 1987, financial houses have seen a dramatic staircase PLC effect in their greater variety of financial services. This has greatly changed the nature of services offered by banks, insurance companies, friendly societies, building societies and estate agencies. Examples of this are the way in which the Prudential insurance company, General Accident, and the Nationwide-Anglia building society have entered into the estate agency business.

CONCLUSION

From the six versions of the product life cycle described in this chapter it will be seen that there is much more to the PLC than the traditional standard model. They transfer theory into practice and can contribute in a practical way to the planning of the marketing strategy, and to its day to day control since PLCs represent a moving situation.

SUMMARY

In this chapter there was discussion on the two versions of the original *standard product life cycle* which applies to products or services which complete a life span ranging from introduction to decline and withdrawal from the market.

Then, the *continuous product life cycle*, as it applies to long-lived products or produce, was presented.

Next, we considered the *re-cycled product life cycle* in which a product or service on the point of decline is saved by some additive or modification which once more achieves profitable sales.

With the *leapfrog product life cycle* it was shown how one model can be replaced by another so that the company can continue in its particular business.

Finally, the *staircase product life cycle* showed how a company, product or service can survive by introducing new product uses, by changing from old to new activities, or by expanding into new business areas.

These six kinds of PLC demonstrate the versatility of the PLC concept, and its practical application to all kinds of products and services in a changing world.

PAST EXAMINATION QUESTIONS

Question 2, LCC Autumn 1984

Draw charts of the re-cycled, leapfrog and staircase product life cycles and give examples of products to which these special versions of the PLC apply.

Comment

The three charts (as shown as figs. 4, 5 and 6 in this chapter) should be drawn neatly. (Candidates should have a ruler with them.) Examples of products which apply to each version of the PLC could be:

Re-cycled: Toothpaste, detergent, petrol, breakfast cereal

Leapfrog: Motor-car, typewriter, lawn mower, vacuum cleaner

Staircase: Nylon, gold, recorded music (records, tapes, discs) and services could be included such as insurance where different kinds of policy are referred to as 'products'.

Question 2, LCC Autumn 1981

The standard product life cycle model takes a product through the stages of growth, maturity and decline, but how would you chart the life cycle of a product which never declines and even has a life of continuous development? Can you name this type of life cycle? Give an example of a product which has experienced this type of life cycle.

Comment

This question refers to the staircase PLC, which the candidate is expected to know, name and be able to draw. The classic example of a product which corresponds to the staircase PLC is nylon.

Question 2, LCC Autumn 1985

Draw the charts of the four different product life cycles which demonstrate.

(i) A product whose sales reach a peak and then decline.

(ii) A product which reaches peak sales which decline, and is replaced by a new product.

(iii) A product which was saved from decline by the injection of improvements to regain peak sales.

(iv) A product which never declines because new uses or new markets are found for it.

Comment

The examiner is looking for four neatly drawn charts. No wording is required beyond giving each PLC its name, but each must be numbered to correspond with the question. The four different PLCs are:

(i) Standard product life cycle (figs 1 and 2)

(ii) Leapfrog (fig 5)

(iii) Re-cycled (fig 4)

(iv) Staircase (fig 6)

Each correct chart earns 5 marks, provided it is well-drawn and its parts are properly identified.

Question 5, LCC Spring 1986

(i) Draw charts of the leapfrog effect and the staircase product life cycles.

(ii) Give two examples of products or services which apply in each case.

Comment

Correct, well-drawn and properly identified charts will gain half the marks. The remaining 10 marks are awarded for appropriate choice of products or services. Consequently, marks can be lost for drawing the wrong charts, naming them incorrectly, not completing them and offering crude charts. Marks can also be lost for giving the wrong examples in part (ii).

The two required charts are as figs. 5 and 6 in this chapter.

For the *leapfrog*, examples could be taken from motor-car, sewing machine, lawn mower, domestic appliances or typewriter.

For the *staircase*, examples could be taken from nylon, gold, shipping companies, recorded music, banking, insurance and building societies, and in each the sequence of development should be stated. Gold, for example could be given developments such as coins, jewellery, watches, dentistry and computers.

A MODEL ANSWER is unnecessary because in most cases answers require:

(a) neatly drawn charts;

(b) correct names and identification of parts of the charts;

(c) application to products and services.

Part 2: Sales forecasting, price and marketing research

In this part we bring together three aspects of marketing which are rather like insurance, or ways of getting things right if the marketing strategy is to succeed. Marketing is a planning operation, not guesswork. Millions of pounds may be involved. Money is not spent haphazardly. The fortunes and prosperity of thousands of people are involved such as those of employees, shareholders and shopkeepers. Marketing is therefore a big responsibility.

It is essential to forecast sales as accurately as possible, which is not easy if it is an unknown new product, or there is great competition. Upon this careful forecasting depends the correct buying of raw materials, the fitting out of a factory, the employment of staff, the use of salesmen and expenditure on advertising. A company cannot afford to get these things wrong.

From Chapter 5 we move on to price. This is not as simple as it seems. It's not just a matter of buying cheap and selling dear. This chapter explores numerous ways of arriving at a price, and the reasons for doing so. If the wrong price is charged, people may not buy!

Then, in Chapter 7, we look at the fascinating world of marketing research which really is a form of insurance to take any kind of gamble out of marketing. This is a very big subject, but the chapter aims to create an impression of the variety of marketing research methods. Marketing research is a kind of intelligence service, spying out the situation and reporting back valuable information.

5. How are sales forecasts and risk assessed?

INTRODUCTION

This chapter will consider why sales forecasting is necessary, and the ways in which they may be forecast. It will go on to discuss the costs which have to be assessed so that the proposition is a profitable one, and the risks that have to be recognised before it is decided to produce, distribute and sell the product or service.

Also considered will be the nature of consumer demand and of derived demand, and how they differ.

Finally, product pre-testing and test marketing will be referred to again as a form of insurance against possible failure, together with an introduction to advertisement testing as a further form of insurance.

WHY FORECAST?

If a manufacturer has created a new product or improved an old one why is it necessary to engage in sales forecasting? The following are the principle reasons.

1. **To estimate demand.** The nature of demand will be discussed later, but initially it is necessary to gauge the possible size of the market, or the probable share of the market that can be gained. This may concern once-only buys, periodic buys, or repeat buyers, as might apply to a pension scheme, furniture or a can of baked beans.

2. **To calculate production.** What is the output capacity of the plant, is it necessary to increase it and if so does

this mean new machinery, new tooling (e.g. laying down machines to build a new motor-car), or an extra work shift? With servicing companies, it would mean the same sort of consideration regarding office administration. With a retail establishment it would be the capacity to service a certain threshold of customers or to accommodate a certain range and quality of goods.

3. **To estimate the volume of raw materials.** In order to meet the forecast what volume of raw materials will be required, are they available and where can they be found?

4. **To estimate the number of staff and their availability.** In order to produce the volume of goods or services, or supply them, how many staff will be required, can they be recruited and trained?

5. **To estimate the number of outlets.** Will it be possible to distribute the product? Do appropriate outlets exist? Will existing outlets be willing to take up the product?

6. **To determine what sort of sales force will be necessary.** Can the present sales force cope, or will extra salesmen have to be recruited?

There can be other reasons for forecasting. Not to ask such questions is to engage in a hit or miss operation. If there is no forecast it will be impossible to plan production and distribution.

HOW CAN SALES BE FORECAST

A study has to be made of the following factors:

1. **What is the ability of the market to buy the product or service?** Can a cash value be placed on the size of the market? There are government statistics on consumer spending. But is this ability circumscribed in any way by market forces such as the economic health of the country, unemployment, legislation, credit facilities, taxation, interest rates and so on.

Britain has an ageing population which means that there is a market for new products such as retirement homes.

House prices are high which can have an inhibiting effect on young marrieds buying furniture.

There is a prosperous middle class capable of discretionary spending. Sales have to be forecast against the socio-economic climate of the market for the product being sold.

2. **What is the state of competition?** How does this affect the company's likelihood of gaining the desired share of the market? One company successfully launched a new soft drink in spite of there being 400 brands already on the market. Competition is not necessarily a barrier, but it does have to be understood. The new product may have so many advantages that it can surmount its competitors, but if it does not only a small market share can be expected. Is this sufficient? One manufacturer of kitchen units bought every existing product, dismantled and analysed it, and designed superior units and beat the opposition at its own game.

3. **What will it cost?** This aspect will be discussed again for other reasons, but forecasting is possible only if careful budgeting shows that a profit can be made if a certain volume of sales can be obtained. This can be a crucial study, revealing the break-even volume of sales, and the volume necessary to make a profit and, even more important, the volume

necessary to make the desired volume of profit. This goes back to the components of price set out in Chapter 2. This study revolves round the price to be charged, and the likely quantity that can be sold at this or that price.

4. **Will people buy?** The market can be researched to measure the propensity to buy if the product or service was available. What proportion of the sample say they would actually buy? Newspapers and magazines research serials to see whether they will or will not increase circulation. From such studies they decide (a) whether to publish the serial and (b) whether to invest money in advertising it.

5. **How well is the competition doing?** Competitive sales can also be studied to see what others are achieving. Figures on advertising expenditure are published by MEAL and it is possible to calculate what it is costing rivals to achieve the shares of the market declared in dealer audit reports such as the Nielsen Indices.

These and other studies which may be pertinent to a particular product or service can be undertaken. On the basis of this intelligence or information, forecasting becomes feasible.

FINANCIAL CONSIDERATIONS

Risk is bound up in profit and loss. An optimist can forecast any sort of sales target, but is it worth it? A product can be successfully made and sold in large quantities but (recalling the CIM definition) can it be done profitably? Before the revolution took place in Fleet Street and newspapers turned to new typesetting and printing processes which cost much less, great financial losses were suffered. The Mini has been one of the most popular motor-cars ever made, but it has made no money.

On the other hand, Alan Minter Sugar has made a fortune with his Amstrad computers, imported from Korea. Labour costs were the problem in the first two cases, but hardly existed in the third.

Some of the important financial considerations are:

1. **Cost of research and development.** How much has it cost, or will still cost, in product development and testing? Some products take years to develop, as with medicinal drugs, or lengthy testing may be necessary in test houses or by guinea-pig users, and other things may need testing such as brand names, packaging and advertising. Can these costs be covered in a price capable of meeting the sales target?

2. **Production costs.** These include purchases or leasing of machinery, tooling up, and labour. To what extent is production labour intensive, or can it be automated or robotised? Again, these factors influence price and the sales target necessary to recover them and make a profit. A book publisher may, for instance, decide to typeset in India and print in Hong Kong to solve this financial problem. Some newspapers find it economic to use contract printers rather than have their own printing plant, e.g. *The Independent*. Or components may be imported from Taiwan, Hong Kong or other places where labour is cheap. Industrial relations including single union no-strike agreements may be vital, as the Japanese have found in setting up plants in Britain.

3. **World prices of raw materials.** These can greatly affect costs as is seen with chocolate and coffee, and companies buy 'futures' in crops. Or it may be a case of choosing one metal rather than another, tin, copper or steel. Many raw materials such as the numerous ingredients for simple products like soups, sauces and pickles mostly have to be imported. Many canned food products, bearing British brand names, are actually canned where the fruits, fish or meats are produced - pineapple from S.E. Asia, ox tongue from Brazil, salmon from Canada and so on. World prices fluctuate. Sales forecasting may depend partly on the availability, partly on the cost, of imports, in the sense that a certain volume of sales must be gained to justify the costs of raw materials.

4. **Cost of entering the market.** With a new product, and especially with an entirely new enterprise, a company has to buy its way into the market. This may mean making no profit for an initial period (e.g.it took *The Independent* about two years to be in profit), or it may be necessary to charge a high price to recover costs (as when a novel is first published in hardback and then the cheap paperback edition follows later on).

The cost of entering the market may include special offers (such as a cheap rate for founder subscribers of a new magazine as when *Precision Marketing* was offered at only £10 for the first 50 copies) or a sales promotion scheme in the shops such as a 'special introductory offer'. A typical method is to offer retailers especially advantageous trade terms or discounts to get the product into the shops. Launch advertising is also a major cost, and this advertising is likely to be heavier than normal advertising in the future. The extent to which money is invested in these ways will depend on the sales forecast.

It may be that because of either limited production capacity (as happened when St Ivel Gold was launched), or limited funds it is necessary to start with a zoned campaign which may be based on an ITV area. As production capacity or sales are built up other zones or areas of the country can be taken on until the product is eventually sold nationally. Regional television can be very useful for zonal launches.

WHAT RISKS ARE INVOLVED?

Nothing can ever be taken for granted. The most unexpected calamities can occur, and a wise sales forecaster will be a pessimist and try to anticipate what could go wrong. By so doing, he may be able to organise alternative solutions to avert trouble. But his forecast will have to be based on 'all things being equal', which they rarely are. Some of the possible risks may be the following, but while this list may be formidable and frightening it is by no means exhaustive. There may be special risks which afflict particular industries, trades and businesses.

1.   **Industrial action**. This can be the most far-reaching and is unpredictable since it can include:

(a) A company strike which handicaps production and delivery.
(b) A suppliers' strike resulting in withdrawal of raw materials and components.
(c) An energy industry strike affecting gas, electricity, coal or oil.
(d) A transport strike affecting road, rail, ferry or air transport.
(e) A postal strike, dislocating the flow of orders and payments.
(f) A media strike affecting press or television advertising.

2.   **Competition**. This has been covered in Chapter 3 but it is possible that a competitor will react with a price reduction, sales promotion scheme, heavy advertising, or new trade terms. It has been known for two or more competitors to hit the market with identical new products. On one occasion, a new garden insecticide had to contend with a competitor's whisper campaign alleging defects in the new product. Some products, like fashion goods and motorcars, can expect seasonal competition when a number of new models are launched simultaneously.

3.   **Product failure**. It has not been unknown for a new product to suffer product failure and have to be recalled.

4.   **Pricing problems**. Unexpected rises in the costs of raw materials or production may result in an embarrassing need to revise prices, or they could be affected by changes in Value Added Tax (VAT), interest rates, credit limits, or initial payments required for hire purchases.

These are a few of the possible risks short of rejection of the product by the market. With such predictions of woe it may be asked why bother to forecast at all? The pessimistic sales manager has to be an optimist at heart, and never a cynic!

SALES FORECASTS AND SALESMEN'S TARGETS

The total sales forecast can be an amalgam of the sales targets set for individual salesmen in separate territories. This will be based on the forecast sales potential of each area, and territorial targets can be encouraged by bonuses, incentives and sales contests. In this way the sales manager can control the attainment of the overall forecast.

SALES FORECASTS AND INVENTORY CONTROL

Large manufacturing companies, especially producers of industrial goods, operate an ongoing forecast based on the input of orders. This daily figure can be transmitted by computer to the factory to control the manufacture of parts. By this process it is possible to control the inventory or stock of parts so that money is tied up to the minimum extent in warehousing parts. Stockpiling can be expensive, and it can apply to finished goods as well as parts for assembly as orders come in.

CONSUMER DEMAND

This can fluctuate and sales forecasting may have to consider numerous external effects on supply and demand. The weather can affect sales of products as varied as umbrellas and soft drinks. So can a general election or a scare story about an ingredient in a food product such as sugar, salt or starch. Sales forecasting has to anticipate trends, or the effects of changes in buying patterns. This has been seen in the introduction of diet drinks or low or non-alcoholic beer which may be influenced by health fads or 'don't drink and drive' campaigns and prosecutions of drivers who failed to pass breathaliser tests.

Consumer demand is very personal and it can be devastating if a sales forecast ignores what is happening in the market place. It is no use depending on advertising to conquer a bad or changing situation, and sometimes too much reliance is placed on advertising. People are not as brain-washed by advertising as it critics claim.

DERIVED DEMAND

Derived demand consists of demand resulting from the sale of other goods.

This can be very difficult to estimate or control because it is a question of 'back selling' goods to manufacturers or other users who rely on demand, whether consumer or industrial, for their finished product. It is necessary to understand or know the sales potential of *their* product before being able to forecast the demand for *your* product, and this may be subject to competition from rival suppliers. The example of the kitchen unit manufacturer was quoted in the section on the state of competition, and his principal market was the house-builder. His sales depended on the rate at which new private houses were not only built but sold which again depended on the ability of the builder to acquire land, and on buyers to borrow money or sell their houses if they were not first time buyers.

Another form of derived demand is that created by a product which requires additional products to make it work, and which may be made by other manufacturers. Examples are batteries for battery-operated goods, and films for cameras.

PRE-TESTING AND TEST MARKETING

Another influence on sales forecasting is both the pre-testing of the product, and the test marketing of the campaign.

Product pre-testing may be done at consumer level by means of consumer panels or door-to-door recruitment of people willing to test, say, a tea or coffee in their home, or through an independent test house which might be necessary in the case of, say, a fire retardent paint.

These tests may indicate the willingness of people to buy, the size or kind of market available, or any limitations on potential sales.

Test marketing was discussed in Chapter 2. Here, two considerations concern sales forecasting. There is the cost of mounting and conducting such a test which may run for weeks or months, and there is the opportunity to test ability to gain a given percentage market share.

Test marketing can, of course, result in the abandonment of the product and the end to sales forecasting. A brewer attempted to produce a rival to Guinness stout. The response during a test marketing exercise was so poor that it resulted in the product being withdrawn.

ADVERTISEMENT TESTING

This topic will be discussed more fully in Chapter 7, but here it has a place in sales forecasting since the take-up of the product and the volume of sales will depend to some extent on the cost-effectiveness of the advertising. It will be one of the promotional inputs and quite likely the most costly. However, that cost - like many other investments - is relative to results.

Advertisement testing can be adopted in three ways. First, there is the pre-testing of proposed advertisements to measure likely response, detect faults and thus perfect the advertising for its eventual appearance. Second, immediately after its appearance impact or recall tests can be conducted to test whether it was seen and remembered. Third, various kinds of post tests (such as assessing direct response or checking market share via dealer audits) can be undertaken to assess the results of the advertising.

SUMMARY

This chapter began by asking why forecast, and went on to discuss ways of forecasting sales, and the financial considerations involved, together with the risks which may be encountered. It then looked at salesmen's targets and the relationship between sales forecasting and inventory control.

The nature of both consumer demand and derived demand were explained, and finally reference was made to the influence of product pre-testing, test marketing and advertisement research upon sales forecasting.

PAST EXAMINATION QUESTIONS

Question 2, LCC Series 4, 1987

(i) What is derived demand?

(ii) How can an industrial company influence sales of its products if they depend on derived demand?

Comment

(i)   Part one requires a definition such as derived demand results from the demand for other goods. This can take two forms: the supply of materials, components or ingredients for use in the manufacture or supply of another good or service; or the demand for accessories and associated products to support use of the product. In the first case it could be steel for the manufacture of motor-cars, and in the second it could be floor mats bought by the motorist.

(ii)   The second part refers to the 'back-selling' of components or other items used in the manufacture of a finished product which might be an industrial or consumer one. A promotional problem is that the end-user may have no knowledge of the supplied product, and have no influence on whether or not the manufacturer buys from a particular supplier.

This varies. A person buying a new house could specify the make of central heating he prefers, but more often it will be part of the general specification of the house.

Sales can be influenced in a number of ways such as:

1.   **Press advertising.** This will be mainly in trade, technical or professional journals read by possible buyers. The kitchen-unit manufacturer already twice mentioned adopted the ingenious strategy of placing advertisements adjacent to those of the house builder to whom he aimed to sell his units, changing this each month. These advertisements appeared in magazines bought by prospective house buyers.

2.   **Direct mail** shots can be addressed to buyers, and they may include technical data sheets.

3.   **Exhibitions.** Stand space can be booked in the appropriate trade shows.

4. **Technical seminars**. This is a PR method whereby buyers, or individual buyers, are invited to attend a technical presentation at an hotel, building centre or other suitable venue.

5. **External house journal**. Addressed to buyers, a magazine can be distributed which contains technical articles and perhaps case studies on the use of the product by customers.

6. **Videos**. A VHS/Betamax video could be made demonstrating the production and use of the product. This can be loaned to buyers, and used at events such as exhibitions, technical seminars, demonstations by salesmen or at press receptions. It could be offered in trade press advertisements.

7. **Trade press PR**. News stories, photographs and feature articles can be published in journals read by buyers.

These methods are additional to the normal representation by sales staff who will probably be technically qualified to advise buyers, especially their designers, specifers or formulators.

(NB. This is virtually an outline model answer. A problem with introducing past exam questions at the end of chapters is that questions may be omnibus ones, and they will assume that the candidate has completed a course. Some of the above refers to the content of this chapter, but it also draws on topics discussed in later chapters.)

Question 10, LCC (Selling and Sales Management), Series 2, 1987

*Qualitative sales forecasting techniques are sometimes referred to as judgemental or subjective techniques, since they rely more upon opinion and less upon mathematics in the formulation. List **three** such techniques and **briefly** explain their working.*

Comment

A number of qualitative sales forecasting techniques have been described in this chapter. Others are given special names such as the jury method or panel of executive opinion when a group of experts from inside and outside the company are questioned about the feasibility of a project. This is really another name for industrial research. Various forms of consumer research may be used, as mentioned in the chapter. Product pre-testing by consumer panel, test house, or recruited testers (as when calls are made on housewives who are asked to test a new drink in the home). Test marketing is yet another method. Inviting members of the sales force to estimate sales potential is sometimes called a 'grass roots' or salesforce composite method.

From the above array of techniques the candidate should list his chosen three and then proceed to describe their operation.

EXERCISE

As sales manager of a company producing shoes you have to produce a sales forecast for the introduction of sports footwear with soles made of a new material which is restful for the feet. Your company has developed this material so there is no competitor in its use.

Draw up a list of all the production, distribution and customer considerations which need to be studied in order to produce a sales forecast for the next year.

6. What Determines Price?

INTRODUCTION

The importance of price is discussed first in this chapter.

The four basic kinds of price will be discussed next, followed by the strategy of pricing based on delivery. Then certain specific pricing variations will be outlined, together with some special price considerations as they affect marketing. This will supplement the components of price already listed in Chapter 2 when discussing the marketing mix of which price is a prime element.

THE IMPORTANCE OF PRICE

Inevitably, price has featured in earlier chapters, particularly in the analysis of the elements of the marketing mix in Chapter 2. It is an important part of marketing communications as it creates a positive link in the exchange process. Goods and services are exchanged for a price, and it represents an important difference between the barter of goods which mark their value to each partner to the bargain, and the selling of goods where price is the point of agreement.

For the manufacturer or supplier price is the sum of money for which he is prepared to forego ownership of the goods. For the customer price is the sum of money he is prepared to forego to take ownership of the goods. Consequently, the price must be agreeable to both sides. 'Profitably' and 'satisfaction' are the results of this transaction. It becomes a marketing transaction when the manufacturer or supplier has first sought to 'identify' and 'anticipate' what will achieve that satisfaction profitably. We are back to the Chartered Institute of Marketing definition to marketing, only now it is possible to see the relevance of price to it.

The marketing strategy cannot succeed if the price is not right, but different kinds of price apply to various products and services, and in particular circumstances.

While it is all very well to say that price must be mutually agreeable, it also represents a conflict between seller and buyer. There can be a seller's market when goods are scarce and the seller can sell all he has at his prices, and a buyer's market when there is an abundance and the buyer can buy all he wants at his price. There is also the elementary principle of buying cheap and selling dear on the seller's part, and the buyer's anxiety to get the best buy. This can lead to price competition. Price can be something of a tug-of-war.

Price becomes a major factor in the exchange process, and it is significant that although fixed prices and maintained prices are nowadays replaced by recommended or list prices, most advertisements make great play of price in one way or another. This is because customers are extremely price conscious. More than anything else, price sways buying decisions. This psychology was even reflected in the television game show, *The Price is Right*. In some parts of the world, where the bazaar mentality prevails, no-one accepts the given price and expects a discount. However, the 'last price' is actually the real price. This is seen in Britain with list and discount prices: hardly anyone pays the list price and there is always a last price.

FOUR BASIC KINDS OF PRICE

The following four kinds of pricing are generally the basis for most prices, although some variations will be discussed later in this chapter.

1.   Economic price. Not to be confused with the effect of supply and demand on price, the economic price is the lowest

that can be charged if the manufacturer is to recover his *fixed* costs (rent, rates, power etc) and his *variable* costs (labour, materials, transport, trade discounts, advertising etc) and also gain his desired percentage of profit. Similarly, this applies to all distributors whose on-cost, percentage or mark-up will recover their costs and show a profit.

2. **Market price**. This is the price the market is prepared to pay. This may be the same or better than the economic price. However, if it is lower than the economic price the manufacturer has either to take a smaller profit than he desires, or no profit at all, in which case there is no point in entering the market. Critical decisions have to be made about the acceptance of the market price.

It may or may not be sensible to subsidise this price out of the profits made elsewhere. Before the publishing of national newspapers became a more economic and profitable proposition some money-losing nationals were subsidised by the profits from regional newspapers owned by the same company. *The Times* was a great loss-maker, but the same firm also owned Scottish Television which the late Lord Thomson described as 'a licence to print money'.

3. **Psychological price**. There are two kinds of psychological price. First, there is the one which creates the illusion that the price is less than it really is, e.g. 99p or £399. Second, there is the status price, like that of a Rolls-Royce motor-car or a Rolex watch. While it is generally true that you get what you pay for, it also depends on what you are paying for! Is it a bargain to satisfy one's ability to spread money further, or is it to impress someone with a known-to-be-expensive gift? Thrift and snobbery can be represented by price.

This is further expressed in the mark-up or profit margin used by different stores which literally classify customers. Two stores may be selling the same brand of carpet, but one has a $33\frac{1}{3}$ per cent mark-up and attracts middle-class buyers and another - perhaps on the other side of the street - has a 50 per cent mark-up and attracts wealthier buyers. At the other end of the scale there are carpet shops which seem to run perpetual sales.

4. **Opportunity price**. This relates particularly to discretionary income purchases where the choice has to be made between expensive items, and may depend on credit terms, budget schemes or plastic money. The buyer has the opportunity to buy only one of a number of choices because they are big purchases.

PRICING BASED ON DELIVERY

Some products incur delivery charges, or the location of the sale may influence the price. Five such pricing policies are:

1. **Non-discriminatory price**. This is the 'manufacturers recommended retail price' (MRRP) or retail price, sometimes marked on the product or given in the catalogues to which the retailer refers when quoting a price. The retailer may offer to discount to attract trade. Generally, the price of a motor-car is standard, as often seen in television commercials, but it may be subject to deals which the buyer is able to make with the dealer such as the trade-in price for his old car, free credit terms or a discount for cash.

2. **Uniform delivery price**. In this case, the costs of delivering the product to the retailer will be averaged out so that the price is the same everywhere, subject to the retailer increasing or reducing it.

3. **Special price discrimination**. Here, the customer never quite knows what price he will be charged, as with the different mark ups mentioned above under psychological price. This can happen even in a street market where the price of the same product may be higher at the beginning of the market when people enter and cheaper as they penetrate towards the stalls in the middle. High prices occur where there is a monopoly situation such as where a firm has a concession at an exhibition, or a motorway service area, or when in a restaurant a bottle of wine costs twice the normal retail price, which is known as 'corkage'.

4. **Basic point pricing**. This kind of price permits variation according to the distance from the source of supply or the difficulty in making delivery. The classic example is the pit-head price of coal compared with that charged by a coal merchant further away. Petrol usually costs more at a petrol station in the country than in a town.

5. **Multiple basing point pricing**. In this case, the price increases as it passes through different middlemen such as importers, wholesalers, markets and retailers. This is typical of most products not bought direct from the original source.

SPECIFIC PRICING VARIATIONS

There are also some interesting variations which should be considered. Throughout this chapter it will be seen that the manufacturer has great problems in setting prices from his own points of view of recovering cost and making a profit, and he is often at the mercy of outside influences which may affect his desire to achieve customer satisfaction via price. If mark-ups are too high *he* can be blamed for charging too much, if discounts are too generous it may trivialise the quality of the product or suggest that it is unpopular. A bargain may seem to be a good buy, but it can suggest that the product is a poor seller. The following are some variations on the four basic prices.

1. **Skimming or creaming**. This usually applies to an initial or launch price which is high for one of two reasons. It may be intended to recover research and development, tooling or production costs, after which the price may be reduced or cheaper versions may be produced. It may also be used to cream off the market which will buy the product because it is new or has a novelty appeal.

2. **Penetration price**. The penetration price can be the reverse of the skimming price, and it could be an uneconomic price, but it is the price which will secure a share of the market. Later, the price may be increased. It is a 'foot-in-the-door' policy to get a new product established. It could be a privilege low price for new subscribers to a magazine, or a special introductory sales promotion offer, or a price which undercuts already established competitors.

3. **Competitive price**. Here we definitely have a price-cutting policy, trade being achieved by charging less than competitors. It occurs particularly among retailers, some of whom offer refunds if the same goods can be found priced more cheaply elsewhere.

4. **Divisionary price**. This is a deceptive form of pricing where extra costs such as installing or fitting, say, a domestic appliance, are not shown in the price of the product. It can apply to number plates on a motor-car.

5. **Distorted price**. The addition of import duty, VAT or the sales tax or airport tax which holidaymakers encounter abroad, can all increase a price beyond the suppliers' control and the customers' expectations. Are such extras included in the stated price or not?

6.   **Dumping price**. This usually applies to foreign producers anxious to enter an overseas market. To do so they undercut the home producers by selling at a low price which just permits a small profit. Their motive may be to open up an overseas market, or to sell excess production, or to obtain foreign credits in order to buy raw materials.

7.   **Double-pricing/price bashing**. This is a common if criticised tactic by which the manufacturer publishes deliberately high and unrealistic list prices to enable the retailer to sell by discounting them. Thus, the *real* price is the shop price. It is a Western version of bazaar trading with its haggling and 'last price'. But it gives the retailer a considerable margin in which to set his price, and the result very often is that different shops are selling the same product at different prices, and all doing so quite profitably although the illusion is that they are all offering bargains!

8.   **Guaranteed prices**. These are prices guaranteed by governments so that producers such as farmers are encouraged to grow certain crops, or produce certain volumes of meat or dairy products. They are the prices that government agencies or markets will pay for the produce, e.g. the Milk Marketing Board.

9.   **Subsidised prices**. These prices occur when the Government makes a contribution to prices to stabilise them, or to keep them down, as a means of controlling the cost of living. Thus, the customer benefits, but is unaware of the real or economic price, and in any case the benefit is paid for out of taxes. The benefit is mainly for lower-income people who pay no or little income tax.

10. **Controlled prices**. This is not the same as either guaranteed or subsidised prices since the producer does not benefit and may even suffer, although the customer enjoys price protection. The danger is that if the goods are scarce a black market is encouraged. This can apply just as much to, say, foodstuffs as to tickets for Wimbledon tennis tournaments.

11. **Geographic pricing**. This is rather like special price discriminating, the price for the same product varying according to location. A branded toiletry will cost a higher price in a West End of London pharmacy then in the average High Street shop. The cost of cigarettes in a five-star hotel will be higher than from a tobacco kiosk in the street. There can also be price differences between countries, although this depends on the strengths of the currencies. Nevertheless, there is a vast difference in the cost of staying in an hotel of the same group in London and Singapore, a factor which has made long-distance holidays, in spite of air fares, very attractive.

OTHER PRICING CONSIDERATIONS

Three other aspects of price are of marketing interest.

1.   **Price plateau**. Rather similar to market price there can be said to be a price level beyond which people will pay no more. They put a price value on the product or service beyond which they will not go. It could be as simple as the difference between second class and first class postage. The expression is sometimes heard of a product being 'priced out of the market' which can be a manufacturer's fear when there are excessive rises in costs. It happened to Spillers who gave up their plant bakeries when they were caught between the trade union wanting higher wages and the supermarkets wanting cheaper loaves of bread.

2.   **Price stability**. This can be a major factor in marketing, such as when taking

orders for future delivery as occurs with the holiday trade. Can the price at the time of delivery be maintained? This was a great problem when oil prices were escalating, or when contracts are based on a cost plus basis. Stable prices create confidence, both with the trade and with customers or clients.

3.   **Paying for the name**. 'You are only paying for the name' is a common criticism, and one sometimes used by a retailer who is trying to sell an unknown, unadvertised and cheaper product. This can be an unfair and misleading comment. A manufacturer stakes his reputation on a branded and advertised product, and by so doing there should be a guarantee of a standard of quality. This may include a promise of satisfaction, with offer of a refund or replacement if not satisfied, which does not attach to the unknown product. Thus, there may be a distinct advantage in paying extra for the famous name.

SUMMARY

In this chapter the importance of price was discovered, followed by a description of the four basic kinds of price. Then five methods of basing price on delivery or location were described.

Next followed eleven specific price variations. The chapter concluded with three special pricing considerations, the price plateau, price stability and paying for the name.

Throughout was shown the problems the manufacturer faces in formulating prices which will enable him to recover costs, make a profit, satisfy customers and also establish the image of his company, products or services through the price factor.

PAST EXAMINATION QUESTIONS

Question 10, LCC Series 2, 1987

Discuss the significance of price as a vital factor in marketing strategy.

Comment

This chapter provides a range of pricing topics on which this answer can be based, as does the section on price in Chapter 2 on the marketing mix. The answer should bring out the various forms of pricing which the manufacturer or supplier can adopt in order to make his marketing strategy succeed. The psychology of getting the price right from the points of view of recovering costs, making a profit and pitching the price correctly for the particular market, should be stressed. The significance of price should be seen from the points of view of the manufacturer, distributors and customers.

Question 3, LCC Spring 1986

Why is the right price so important in the marketing of a product? Discuss this question with special reference to (i) psychological attitudes to price and (ii) market segmentation.

Comment

The first part has been explained in this chapter in relation to psychological prices of a bargain or a prestige nature, with further comment on the psychology of mark-ups by retail stores, and the psychological effect of stores either charging higher prices than expected or discounting prices. There are also the questions of price plateaus, price stability and paying for the name.

The second part concerns the price brackets which suit different segments of the market, and examples can be given of ranges of products like houses, cameras, motor-cars, hotels and holidays which fulfil the price needs of different groups of buyers or segments of the market.

Question 5, LCC Autumn 1984

Explain the following forms of price:

(i)   *Psychological*
(ii)   *Market price*
(iii) *Opportunity price*
(iv) *Economic price*
(v)   *Skimming and creaming.*

Comment

Each of the five parts requires one or two paragraphs of clear explanation, and it is always a good idea when answering a question like this to give an example to demonstrate that the candidate understands each term. All five are explained in this chapter.

Question 7, LCC Spring 1981

How does discretionary income and elasticity of demand affect the marketing of expensive products or services?

Comment

Here is a short but meaty question which calls for a definition of the terms used in the question, and an essay-type answer.

Model answer

Q.7. Discretionary income consists of surplus income above the basic costs of maintaining a customary standard of living, which may vary between social grades. This money is available to spend on better quality or expensive goods and often once-in-a-lifetime purchases. It is related to opportunity cost and the benefit lost in buying one item rather than the other. Thus, a consumer may have the money to buy either a luxurious holiday or a new motor-car but the opportunity to buy only one or the other. He may, for instance, forego taking a holiday in order to have the outside of his house painted.

Elasticity of demand relates to supply and demand. Demand is elastic when there are fluctuations in price and supply, but inelastic when a product is an essential or staple and price does not effect demand.

Discretionary income and elasticity of demand are linked in the sense that if demand for luxury goods makes it possible to produce and sell them more cheaply they become semi-luxuries and demand becomes more inelastic. This has happened with many high-tech goods like personal computers and office copiers while some of the advantages of expensive cameras have been introduced into less expensive compact cameras.

The marketing of expensive goods is affected by the prosperity of the country, taxation, interest rates and credit and loan facilities. When there is more spending power there is both encouragement to put on the market more expensive goods like executive motor-cars, and increased competition between suppliers to capture the discretionary income.

This also tends to boost the media which carry advertisements for these products, or make it viable for media to be published in which such products can be advertised. It has led to a big increase in the use of direct response marketing aimed at this segment of the market, using both off-the-page press advertisements and direct mail.

The competition for discretionary income can also help to expand the market if economies of scale can be applied to reduce prices so that more of the goods on offer can be obtained because the discretionary income can be spread further.

The presence of discretionary income can also lead to the sale of better quality products, such as more expensive clothes, foods, home fittings and accessories, holidays and so on. Similarly, it can encourage stores to go 'up market' and sell more expensive merchandise as Woolworth have done, or better quality lines and extra lines as Marks and Spencer have done.

This is not limited to retail products but also to services like restaurants, entertainments, travel agents, banks and insurance companies which are all taking their share of discretionary income.

EXERCISE

Plan the pricing policy for a domestic appliance which is to be sold by retailers of electrical goods, including advertising in which recommended price will appear. Retailers can include Electricity Board showrooms, department stores, electrical dealers and discount stores. Consider everything which can influence the retail price from the points of view of the manufacturer, the trade and purchasers.

7. What is marketing research?

INTRODUCTION

Marketing research is a very big subject and this chapter can be no more than an introduction, demonstrating its application to many aspects of the marketing mix, describing research techniques, and explaining some of the more essential jargon.

First there will be a definition, with marketing research distinguished from market research. What can be researched, and how this research can be conducted will then be discussed. Following this there will be a brief introduction to sampling techniques and questionnaires. Social grades and life styles will complete the chapter.

DEFINITION

Marketing research is the systematic study of data, including the use of scientific methods, to obtain information relevant to the marketing of products or services.

It will be noted that *marketing* and not *market* research is defined. The two terms are often loosely used to mean the same thing. Marketing research covers all forms of research to do with marketing, but market research is limited to study of the market. There is also *social* research, as conducted by the Central Statistical Office, which researches social topics and tends to use different methods such as its system of social classifications.

WHAT CAN BE RESEARCHED

The following are the main topics which can be researched in connection with the marketing mix:

1.   **New product concept** - what are the attitudes of potential customers towards a proposed new product or service? Would they buy it if it was on sale?

2.   **Corporate image** - how does the company's image compare with those of its rivals over a range of subjects such as price, delivery, service etc.

3.   **Awareness** -to what extent does the market know the company and what it does, makes or supplies? In one such survey one of our largest insurance companies discovered that 98 per cent of adult males had never heard of it!

4.   **Branding** - which out of maybe a hundred possible brand names is voted the best by a sample of potential buyers?

5.   **Pricing** - alternative prices can be researched to discover which produces the greatest sales response.

6.   **Packaging** - various forms of impact, memory and questionnaire tests can be used to discover the most appealing package, or to test features of pack design.

7.   **Buying patterns** - mainly with consumer panels, research can discover what categories of consumers buy which brands in what quantities how often and where.

8.   **Brand shares** - what shares of the market are held by the brands in a product group, including those of the enquirer if he already had one?

9.   **Product preferences** - what colours, flavours or improvements do people prefer according to the nature of the product?

10. **Product pre-testing** - testing of products by consumer panels, recruited users, independent test houses and research laboratories.

11. **Advertisement pre-testing** - testing press advertisements and television commercials to measure recall and response.

12. **Media** - using the circulation, readership and audience survey reports published by the media research organisations.

13. **Advertising expenditure by competitors** - by studying MEAL reports of estimated expenditure.

14. **Measuring response to advertising** - by keying coupons and calculating cost per reply and cost by conversion to sales, and by tracking studies which investigate advertisement recall more thoroughly.

15. **Exports** - using Government or private facilities foreign markets can be investigated for export possibilities.

From the above list, and omitting test marketing which has been dealt with separately in Chapter 2, it will be seen that every element of the marketing mix can, stage by stage, be researched. Very large companies may well sponsor research for all, or nearly all, of the above purposes when introducing a new national brand. Research can be an investment which can make or save a fortune.

METHODS OF CONDUCTING RESEARCH

The principle of research is to question or investigate a sample in order to assess the whole. This resembles the wine-taster or the tea-taster who needs to try only a little to evaluate the whole bottle, cask or pot. Similarly, a handful of grain from a sack will give a good impression of the whole sackful. In marketing research only a small number of people have to be surveyed to be able to measure the motives, opinions, awareness, knowledge, ignorance or preferences of a very much larger number. The only 100 per cent sample is that used for a population census. Sampling

techniques will be explained later.

There are two kinds of research, *primary*, and *secondary*. Primary research is original research, carried out for a new and specific purpose. Secondary research is existing research, the findings of which may be useful to those who care to buy or read the published reports. This kind of research may consist of government statistics, private surveys carried out for other people's purposes, or survey reports which are available on subscription like readership or dealer audit reports.

Ad hoc research is carried out on a once only basis and is complete in itself. *Continuous surveys* are conducted regularly, and each succeeding report shows the movement of trends over time, as with opinion polls on the popularity of politicians and political parties.

Quantitative research is measured in percentages, showing the percentage of different types of people who gave particular answers. *Qualitative* research seeks information on reasons, perceived images or motives rather than numerical measurement of information.

With these introductory explanations, the following are some of the methods of conducting the above research.

Desk research

It is not always necessary to engage in new or primary research. Valuable information may already exist. This may consist of internal information such as salesmen's reports and sales figures or material that can be gathered from external sources. The Government publishes numerous statistics, such as the Census of Population and various others reports based on, say, motor-car registrations. Thus, if it is known how many vehicles are registered it is possible to assess the market for motor-car accessories. Many research organisations publish reports which can be purchased.

A guide to these sources of information is the excellent annual *Marketing Pocket Book* published by the Advertising Association, Abford House, 15 Wilton Road, London, SW1V 1NJ. The *Pocket Book* contains numerous tables on consumer expenditure, distribution outlets, advertising expenditure, marketing expenditure, media statistics and so on.

Field research

This is a general term for any kind of research which involves teams of researchers who interview samples of respondents, usually in the street or on the doorstep. These may be *ad hoc* or continuous surveys.

Consumer panels

There are two kinds of consumer panels, large national ones of recruited people such as housewives who complete monthly diaries about their purchases, and smaller panels of recruited people who call in at the research office to collect products for pre-testing. There are also variations as when panel members are visited to check the brands held in their larders, refrigerators and bathroom cabinets, or are saved in a plastic bag for recording by a visiting researcher.

There is also the omnibus survey method when a consumer panel is mailed with a regular questionnaire containing sets of questions on behalf of a number of sponsors who 'piggyback' on the omnibus survey. This 'piggyback' method is an inexpensive way of using an existing research system. These are all forms of continuous research.

Dealer audit

A number of firms, such as A.C. Nielsen of Oxford, conduct dealer, shop or retail audit surveys. They are quite different from surveys involving lengthy questionnaires and interviews and do not provide information on dealer's views. There are panels of representative retailers, usually on an ITV region basis, whose invoices and stocks are inspected regularly to check the movement of fmcg brands. This information is collated to show the shares of the market for each brand. Fluctuations in brand share - perhaps because of the response to advertising or a sales promotion scheme - will be revealed. This is a form of continuous research.

Motivation research and discussion groups

In both cases a small sample is used, and it is necessary that this group of people is representative such as when they have a common interest in the subject of the study.

Motivation or motivational research is based on clinical tests, rather like intelligence tests, and was pioneered in the USA by Dr. Ernst Dichter. The people involved are probably unaware of the purpose of the survey, but undergo tests like the famous ink blot tests when they are asked what certain shapes mean to them. These tests reveal the characteristics of the respondents. Examples of this sort of research are described in Vance Packard's famous book *The Hidden Persuaders*.

This research reveals buying motives - or objectives - which are held deep down in the subconscious and would not be voluntarily admitted. There is the classic case of ordinary field research suggesting that businessmen would not fly because they were afraid of flying, but of a motivational study going further and showing that they would not fly because they were afraid of leaving widows and orphans.

Discussion groups are a more simple and fairly inexpensive development from the original motivational method. A group of people is recruited and under the direction of a chairman a number of topics are discussed. The chairman closes each discussion and records a concensus of the views expressed. Because the group is small, say 25 people, it can be an unrepresentative sample unless the members of the group have a common interest in the subject being studied. For instance, if they were all owners of the same make of motor-car, or users of the same airline, the small group could be representative if the subject being studied was customer attitudes to that motor-car or airline.

Opinion polls

The Gallup Poll, set up in the USA in 1935, made this kind of research famous. Conducted by many research firms like Gallup and the National Opinion Poll, it sets out to seek opinions, awareness and shifts of attitude. Questions are usually of the Yes, No, Don't know type, and quantitative results are produced showing the responses, in percentages, of different types of respondent. Although popularly associated with political polls, they are used commercially to discover, say, the perceived image of a company, or - for public relations purposes - how awareness or understanding has changed over a period. The objective of a PR campaign might be to achieve a certain percentage improvement in attitude, knowledge or understanding.

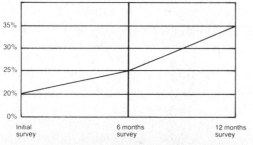

Figure 1 Graphical presentation of the results of an opinion, attitude or shift survey

Assuming that before the advertising, PR or marketing campaign there was a 20 per cent awareness of the company product or service a survey at six months shows that awareness has

improved to 25 per cent. A further survey at twelve months shows that 35 per cent awareness has been achieved. A target final percentage would be set.

Image studies

Often used in industrial research, an image study uses techniques different from opinion polls to produce a graphic representation of opinions held by a number of companies over a range of topics, one of the companies being the sponsor. Respondents are asked to rate each company on a scale from excellent to bad (see *semantic differential* under Questionnaire). The final result shown in graphic form shows how attitudes to each company differ over the range of topics. This is demonstrated by Figure 2.

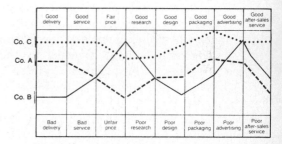

Figure 2 Graphical presentation of the results of an image studying comparing opinions of the performance of three companies

One of the companies shown is the one commissioning the survey; any number of companies and any number of different topics could be compared.

Telephone surveys

A number of surveys, especially where quick results are required as happens during elections, are conducted by telephone and there are research firms who specialise in this kind of work. A problem is that the uninvited call may not be welcomed. In industrial research, where the sample may be small and scattered throughout the country, telephone interviews are conducted by appointment.

Postal surveys

Questionnaires sent by mail are inexpensive compared with employing field research staff, but the results may be biased if only those particularly interested bother to complete and return the questionnaire. However, much depends on how interesting the survey is to the recipient. It may be necessary to include a modest inducement such as a pen, a sample or a cash voucher.

Product pre-testing and packaging research

This can be done by the consumer panel method, but it depends on what is being tested. With a product such as an electrical domestic appliance it may be advisable to have it tested by the Electrical Research Association, while a building product could be tested by the Building Research Laboratory, but a farm implement or machine might be better tested with a farmer who was prepared to make a practical test under working conditions. A domestic product could be tested in people's homes, such as by calling on householders and asking them to try the product for a period and report on their likes and dislikes.

Hall testing is another method when, say, a product is given a variety of colours or casings, and a sample of people is invited off the street and asked to give their first and second choices. This can be done in the hall-way of an office building.

The **blind-product** test is another method when respondents are asked to state their preference between two products in plain packages. The *paired comparison* method goes a stage further and the choice from the first pair is then compared with a third unidentified product. This sort of testing can also be applied to packaging research especially to something like sweet wrappings.

Packaging research is often conducted under laboratory conditions when a group of respondents is asked to comment on the package which stands out most from the rest, or they are observed in a mocked-up shopping situation to see which package they select from shelves.

Research can also be conducted into label design, types of bottle or other container, and kind of cap or lid, usually by means of a field survey conducted in or near a shop, by calling on people at home, as well as by simulated shop situations.

Advertisement research

Press advertisements and TV commercials can be pre-tested to measure recall and response including intention to buy. A number of techniques can be employed, such as the *folder technique* whereby a number of advertisements are inserted in plastic sleeves of a binder that looks like a menu cover. Those interviewed are asked to look at each advertisement in turn, hand back the folder, and say what they remember about each one. In this way, the strength of different elements such as headline, picture, sub-headings, selling points, price, body copy or coupon can be assessed. This may lead to amendments so that the final advertisement contains the best remembered elements or revised ones.

Such research can often hit on an unexpected flaw which was not obvious to the designer or copywriter. This could be a single word which stops the reading flow. There may be certain trade terms which are taken for granted by both client and agency, but which are unfamiliar to the public or have other more frequently used meanings. For example, roof void is a trade term, but loft is the everyday word for a space in the roof. Advertisements may be tested repeatedly until the right formula is found. In their own interest, good advertising agencies insist on pre-tests.

Similarly, television commercials are shown to invited audiences during 'in theatre' tests, where a programme of commercials, cartoons and other short films are shown. There are various formats for these tests, but basically they need to discover which commercial produces the best expressed intention to buy.

Advertisements can also be tested in normal circumstances, that is when printed or broadcast.

One method is the *reading and noting test*. Members of the public are stopped in the street, and asked if they read the previous day's issue of the newspaper (a local or regional edition) in which the advertisement appeared. If the newspaper was read the person is asked if they saw the advertisement. If they did, questions are asked about its content. From the information obtained, percentages for men and women are given to each part of the advertisement, thus revealing its strengths and weaknesses. The advertisement can then be revised for its actual appearance nationally.

Another method is the *split run test* in which alternative advertisements are run in different editions of the same issue of a newspaper or magazine, and the results compared. This is easiest done with a couponed advertisement where returned coupons (identified by a *key* such as a minor change in the address or a number printed in the corner of the coupon) can be counted.

A variation on this which is popular with direct response marketing companies is the *cross-over test*. Different advertisements are run in different journals, and then switched from one journal to the other when the next issue comes out. The pulling power is tested of both the advertisements and the publications.

Recall tests are conducted following the appearance of a new television commercial. Members of the public are again stopped in the street, asked whether they watched television during the previous evening, which programmes they watched, whether they saw the commercial, what they remembered of it and whether they would buy what was advertised.

A split run version of this is possible where an ITV station has two transmitters, and a different commercial can be shown simultaneously on each. Audience reactions in each receiving area can then be tested next day, and the results compared. As a result of such a test a new Brooke Bond PG Tips chimp commercial was abandoned although it had cost several thousand pounds to produce.

Tracking studies can be mounted to obtain information more sophisticated than impact and recall, testing more deeply the responses of consumers to advertisements. The aim of a tracking study is to record what actually happens after an advertisement appears. This is a continuous study unlike a recall or impact test which is an *ad hoc* once-and-for-all investigation. There are various forms of tracking study, but the objectives are usually to measure the quality or strength of the response to advertising in terms of brand buying, brand usage, brand awareness, advertising awareness, brand goodwill and price image.

Media research

Most above-the-line advertising media are researched, both by their owners and independently by bodies representing advertisers, media owners and advertising agencies. This kind of research is among the oldest in Britain and in one form or another has been conducted for the past fifty years. It concerns the circulation and the readership of newspapers and magazines, and audiences for radio, television and outdoor advertising. Attendances at exhibitions are also recorded.

Circulation is the net average sale of a journal over a period (now every month), all free and returned copies being deducted from the print run figure. These figures are certified by the Audit Bureau of Circulations. Member publishers certify audited figures for certification as ABC figures. The ABC itself conducts no research.

Figures for controlled circulation magazines (which are distributed free of charge to selected and request readers) are also given ABC figures. Free newspapers have their circulation figures certified by the ABC's subsidiary, Verified Free Distribution.

Readership is the estimated number of readers per copy of a newspaper or magazine, and is sometimes referred to as secondary readership since it is usual that at least more than one person reads a publication. Some journals have considerable *secondary readership* because they are read by families, or are passed round at workplaces, or are read in various reception and waiting rooms. The *Financial Times*, for example, has a small circulation figure but a large readership figure. A magazine like the *Reader's Digest* could have a readership fifteen times its circulation figure.

In Britain, the National Readership Survey is conducted by the Joint Industry Committee for National Readership Surveys. Not only readership figures are given but also demographic profiles of the types of people who read particular journals. The JICNARS surveys are based on social grades (*not* socio-economic groups) which divide the population (15 years of age and over) into social grades based on employment rather than income.

The percentage breakdown varies slightly from year to year, partly because of an ageing population and an increasing number of pensioners and partly because of other influences such as unemployment. The social grades at the times of writing are:

Social Grade	Social Status	Heads of Household's Occupation	%
A	Upper middle class	Higher managerial, administrative or professional	3
B	Middle class	Intermediate managerial, administrative or professional	15
C1	Lower middle class	Supervisory or clerical, and junior managerial, administrative or professional	23
C2	Skilled working class	Skilled manual workers	28
D	Working class	Semi and unskilled manual workers	18
E	Those at lowest levels of subsistance	State pensioners or widows (no other earner),casual or lowest grade workers	14

Figure 3 Social grades as used on the National Readership Survey organised by JICNARS, and widely used for marketing research purposes

These social grades can be used to demonstrate the main readership of the national daily press:

A   The Times, Financial Times
B   Daily Telegraph, The Guardian,
        The Independent
C¹   Daily Express, Daily Mail, Today
C²   D, E The Sun, Daily Mirror, Daily Star

When comparing the relative costs of buying advertisement space in journals with different rates and circulation/readership figures a common denominator method of achieving comparison is the cost-per-thousand circulation or cost-per-thousand readership.

Television audience research for both BBC and ITV programmes is conducted by the Broadcasters' Audience Research Board. A panel of viewers have meters attached to their sets, and diaries in which they record programmes watched.

Allowance is made for additional receivers and VCRs in a house.

Each week, Top Ten tables are issued which are published in the press. A typical Top Ten report is reproduced in Figure 4.

Television viewing ratings (TVRs) are based on the size of audience recorded. When planning a campaign on commercial television the target may be a certain volume of TVRs, after which the commercial is withdrawn. After an interval, the commercial may be shown again. By this process, a target audience is achieved and the commercial does not suffer from overkill. Some commercials have a life of 18 months to two years because of this careful screening.

In fact, the PG Tips piano shifter commercial has been shown so many times that it is quoted in the *Guinness Book of Records*.

THE NATIONAL TOP TENS

BBC 1	Individuals Viewing (Millions)	ITV	Originating Programme Company	ITV areas	Individuals Viewing (Millions)
1 EASTENDERS (THU/SUN)	18.70	1 CORONATION STREET (WED)	GRANADA	ALL	13.60
2 EASTENDERS (TUE/SUN)	15.95	2 CORONATION STREET (MON)	GRANADA	ALL	13.45
3 NEIGHBOURS (TUE 13:32/17:36)	15.00	3 BLIND DATE	LWT	ALL	12.50
4 NEIGHBOURS (WED 13:31/17:36)	14.45	4 TAGGART	STV	ALL	11.95
5 NEIGHBOURS (FRI 13:32/17:36)	14.40	5 THE BILL (TUE/FRI*)	THAMES	ALL	11.70
6 NEIGHBOURS (MON 13:30/17:36)	14.25	6 EMMERDALE FARM (WED)	YORKSHIRE	ALL	10.95
7 NEIGHBOURS (THU 13:30/17:36)	14.15	7 THE EQUALIZER	ITV	ALL	10.50
8 BREAD	13.95	8 EMMERDALE FARM (THU)	YORKSHIRE	ALL	10.45
9 'ALLO 'ALLO	12.85	9 WHEEL OF FORTUNE	STV	ALL	10.35
10 ALL CREATURES GREAT AND SMALL	12.15	10 KRYPTON FACTOR/OLYMPIC SPECIAL	GRANADA	ALL	10.00

* FRIDAY LONDON ONLY

BBC 2		CHANNEL 4	Individuals Viewing (Millions)
1 THE DUTY MEN	5.95	1 BROOKSIDE (WED/SAT)	5.70
2 1941	4.80	2 BROOKSIDE (MON/SAT)	5.50
3 SUNDAY GRANDSTAND (14:00)	4.50	3 WHITE MAMA	3.75
4 M*A*S*H	4.30	4 THE LAST RESORT	3.60
5 COOL IT	3.55	5 THE GOLDEN GIRLS	3.50
6 RED DWARF	3.10	6 FIFTEEN-TO-ONE (FRI)	3.35
7 SILVER CITY	3.05	7 FIFTEEN-TO-ONE (WED)	3.30
7= RIDE LONESOME	3.05	8 OLYMPICS 1988 (FRI 23:17)	3.15
9 CAR OF THE DECADE	2.85	9 THE GIFTIE	3.05
9= REACH FOR THE SKY	2.85	10 FIFTEEN-TO-ONE (THU)	2.95

Figure 4 A typical weekly Top Ten chart of television viewing produced by AGB for BARB

Radio and outdoor research figures for commercial radio audiences are produced periodically, based on diaries completed by listeners, and published by the Joint Industry Committee for Radio Audience Research (JICRAR). Less regularly, surveys of outdoor advertising have been published by the Joint Industry Committee for Poster Audience Research (JICPAR), showing opportunities to see (OTS) particular sites and by Outdoor Site Classification and Research (OSCAR).

NEIGHBOURHOOD CLASSIFICATIONS

A valuable form of research which has many applications of which the best known is targetting for direct mail shots, is that based on census enumeration districts and postcodes.

ACORN (A Classification of Residential Neighbourhoods) was created by CACI Market Analysis, and identifies 30 neighbourhood types as shown in Fig.5 on the following page. There are other demographic-geographic neighbourhood systems: MOSAIC (CCN Systems Ltd) which identifies 58 types; PIN (Pinpoint Identified Neighbourhoods) run by Pinpoint Systems Ltd which identifies 60 types; and Super Profiles (McIntyre Marketing) which identifies 150 types.

With these systems it is possible to select particular target groups by their residential characteristics. Companies as diverse as mail order catalogue firms and investment services have used neighbourhood classifications systems to identity mailing lists of prospects.

QUESTIONNAIRE

Except for depth surveys, discussion groups and other qualitative research, a questionnaire is necessary. When reading a research report it is sensible to study the questionnaire first because the results will depend on the questions asked, together with the types of people who were questioned. Survey findings from rival firms can vary, not through inaccuracy but because of differences in what was asked of whom.

The early questions in a questionnaire usually establish who is being interviewed and these personal details of name, address, sex, marital status, occupation, age group and so on are called the *face sheet data*.

A structured questionnaire may occupy several sheets. Some questions will apply only if certain ones are answered, and there may be jumps to later questions. For instance, if the questionnaire asks 'do you take holidays in Britain or abroad?' there could follow completely different sets of questions for each kind of holidaymaker. Consequently, a questionnaire may look bulky, but not all the questions will apply to every respondent.

Questions are usually varied in style, which helps to avoid boring the respondent. In a field survey, the interviewer will read the question and record the answers. Four types of question are common, these being:

1. **Dichotomous question.** This is one which requires a Yes or No answer.

2. **Multiple choice questions.** Here, the respondent is asked to choose from a list which make of product they use, or which company they have heard of, which newspaper they last read, or something of that nature.

3. **Semantic differential.** The respondent is invited to rate a subject on a plus or minus scale such as excellent, very good, good, fairly good, fair, poor. This can provide the calculation of plus 3, 2, 1 and minus 1, 2, and 3.

4. **Open-ended.** This is where a comment is invited, and a verbatim reply is noted.

Control questions can also be included which often ask the same question in a different way to see if a reliable answer has been given.

Acorn Groups		1981 population	
A	Agricultural areas	1811485	3.4
B	Modern family housing higher incomes	8667137	16.2
C	Older housing of intermediate status	9420477	17.6
D	Poor quality older terraced housing	2320846	4.3
E	Better-off council estates	6976570	13.0
F	Less well-off council estates	5032657	9.4
G	Poorest council estates	4048658	7.6
H	Multi-racial areas	2086026	3.9
I	High status non-family areas	2248207	4.2
J	Affluent suburban housing	8514878	15.9
K	Better-off retirement areas	2041338	3.8
U	Unclassified	388632	0.7

Acorn types			1981 population	
A	1	Agricultural villages	1376427	2.6
B	2	Areas of farms and smallholdings	435058	0.8
B	3	Cheap modern private housing	2209759	4.1
B	4	Recent private housing, young families	1648534	3.1
B	5	Modern private housing, older children	3121453	5.8
B	6	New detached houses, young families	1404893	2.6
B	7	Military bases	282498	0.5
C	8	Mixed owner-occupied and council estates	1880142	3.5
C	9	Small town centres and flats above shops	2157360	4.0
C	10	Villages with non-farm employment	2463246	4.6
C	11	Older private housing, skilled workers	2919729	5.5
D	12	Unimproved terraces with old people	1351877	2.5
D	13	Pre-1914 terraces, low income families	762266	1.4
D	14	Tenement flats lacking amenities	206703	0.4
E	15	Council estates, well-off older workers	1916242	3.6
E	16	Recent council estates	1392961	2.6
E	17	Council estates, well-off young workers	2615376	4.9
E	18	Small council houses, often Scottish	1051991	2.0
F	19	Low rise estates in industrial towns	2538119	4.7
F	20	Inter-war council estates, older people	1667994	3.1
F	21	Council housing for the elderly	826544	1.5
G	22	New council estates in inner cities	1079351	2.0
G	23	Overspill estates, high unemployment	1729757	3.2
G	24	Council estates with overcrowding	868141	1.6
G	25	Council estates with worst poverty	371409	0.7
H	26	Multi-occupied terraces with Asians	204493	0.4
H	27	Owner-occupied terraces with Asians	577871	1.1
H	28	Multi-let housing with Afro-Caribbeans	387169	0.7
H	29	Better-off multi-ethnic areas	916493	1.7
I	30	High status areas, few children	1129079	2.1
I	31	Multi-let big old houses and flats	822017	1.5
I	32	Furnished flats, mostly single people	297111	0.6
J	33	Inter-war semis, white collar workers	3054032	5.7
J	34	Spacious inter-war semis, big gardens	2676598	5.0
J	35	Villages with wealthy older commuters	1533756	2.9
J	36	Detached houses, exclusive suburbs	1250492	2.3
K	37	Private houses, well-off elderly	1199703	2.2
K	38	Private flats with single pensioners	841635	1.6
U	39	Unclassified	388632	0.7
Area total			53556911	100.0

Figure 5 ACORN profile of Great Britain

INTERVIEWERS

Those employed as interviewers are expected to show no bias when asking questions and to make no comment on replies. It is usually a part-time occupation, but interviewers are trained and spot checks are made to see that respondents did give the answers attributed to them. They usually carry a professional identification card, but unless it is obvious as with pre-testing a branded product, the identity of the sponsor of the survey is not revealed. For instance, the survey will be conducted on behalf of 'a national food company'.

SAMPLING TECHNIQUES

With certain variations, there are two fundamentally different forms of sample, the quota and random. The sample is a proportion of the *universe* or *population* of people relevant to the survey, e.g. a sample of all motorists, doctors, smokers etc. The degree of accuracy will depend on the size of the sample which again will depend on the funds available. The size of the sample can also depend on the number of *characteristics* or different types of people who are to be interviewed.

Quota sample. With this kind of sample the interviewer is responsible for finding percentages of people, the simplest example being men and women according to their percentages of the national census population. But it could be based on age groups or social grades. A quota sample will be smaller and less expensive than a random sample, but its accuracy could be subject to interviewer bias in finding the correct quotas.

Random sample. This is not 'taken at random' and is perhaps a misleading expression, nor are random numbers used in marketing research. It is really an interval or probability sample, and by the law of averages the probability is that it will represent a fair cross-section of the given population. Names and addresses are selected at regular intervals from a list, often referred to as every *nth* name. These names and addresses are given to the interviewer to find, and reserve names are resorted to only after perhaps three or four attempts have been made to locate the original people.

To reduce the number of locations, polling districts throughout the country are usually randomly selected to form a *stratified random sample.* Random samples are best used when large numbers and variations of people are relevant to a survey, or when the highest degree of accuracy is required.

The *sampling frame* is a specification of the type or types of people to be interviewed. *Sampling points* are the places where interviews are to be held.

RESEARCH IN DEVELOPING COUNTRIES

It is not always possible to apply marketing research techniques in some developing countries. Some of the problems which may be encountered are:

1. Lack of statistics such as a census of population, or lists or addresses.

2. Limited urban areas, long distances between towns, large rural populations.

3. Lack of suitable people to conduct interviews.

4. Multi-language problems.

5. Objections to questioning for various ethnic and religious reasons, and suspicion of motives for asking questions, research not being understood by the people being interviewed.

In some countries problems have been overcome by conducting the random walk method, houses being called on at equal intervals down a street. Qualitative research is also possible with lengthy discussion interviews.

LIFE STYLE RESEARCH

In recent years attempts have been made to re-define the groups of people in modern society, doing so more on a basis of their aspirations and behaviour than on their characteristics. Expressions like *yuppie* (young upwardly mobile professional), *empty nester* for those without children, and the *silver market* comprising those over 60 years of age have been common.

The expression yuppie has become so internationally accepted that the Italian state telephone company has branded its most expensive receiver Yuppie.

A more optimistic acronym is *Uppie* which stands for unpretentious, privately individualistic egoist, representing those of any age who seek to control their own destinies and face up to a rapidly changing world. There are also the *Woopies*, the over 55s who are well-off older people. The advertising world pitches its campaigns at *aspirers, reformers, succeeders* and *mainstreamers*.

A number of research organisations have distributed very comprehensive questionnaires covering numerous possessions, activities and purchases, with the reward of cash tokens if completed and returned. This information is fed into databases which are available to those wishing to direct mail people with certain life styles as revealed by the activities and purchasers.

SUMMARY

This has necessarily been a broad introduction to a very large subject but sufficient information has been given to show what can be researched, and how this can be done.

Marketing research was defined and disting-

uished from market research. Fifteen examples were listed on marketing topics which could be studied. After defining some terminology, twelve kinds of research methods were described, including an explanation with tables of social grades, television Top Ten weekly reports, and the ACORN system of neighbourhood classifications.

The make-up of questionnaires, the people who conduct interviews, and quota and random sampling techniques were explained. Research problems in developing countries were also discussed. The new subject of life style research completed the chapter.

PAST EXAMINATION QUESTIONS

Questions 10, LCC Series 2, 1988

Describe the marketing research techniques that can be applied to the testing or measuring of:

    (i)   Brand share
    (ii) Packaging
    (iii) Price
    (iv) Flavour of a food or drink
    (v) Awareness of an advertising campaign.

Comment

As will have been observed while reading this chapter, it is possible to use more than one kind of marketing research for the same enquiry. The following could be applied in each case, and each should be described *and not merely named*.

    (i)   Brand share - *dealer audit*
    (ii)   Packaging - *motivational, discussion groups*
    (iii) Price - *test offers at different prices, field surveys*
    (iv) Flavour - *in-house product tests, consumer panels*
    (v)   Awareness of advertising - *recall or reading and noting tests, tracking studies*

Question 12, LCC Spring 1986

How do consumer panel research and dealer audit research differ in (i) how they are conducted and (ii) the information they provide:

Comment

First the two kinds of research should be defined. Then the operational difference should be explained followed by a description of the type of information each provides.

All these points have been dealt with in this chapter.

Question 5, LCC Autumn 1985

Explain the differences between:

- *(i)* *Qualitative and quantitative research*
- *(ii)* *Continuous and **ad hoc** research*
- *(iii)* *Market and marketing research*
- *(iv)* *Random and quota sample*
- *(v)* *Product pre-testing and test marketing*

Comment

All six terms have been explained in the lesson. Where possible, examples should be given, e.g. a discussion group is qualitative research and an opinion poll is quantitative research; consumer panels and dealer audit are forms of continuous research.

Question 7, LCC Spring 1984

In what circumstances would you use a random sample rather than a quota sample?

Comment

Here is another of those short questions that calls for an essay which demonstrates that the candidate knows what he is talking about. Analysing it, it will be seen that two definitions are required, and as many as possible circumstances should be discussed.

Model answer

Q.7. A random sample in marketing research is not really a random sample but a very strict one, every nth name being selected at regular intervals from a list such as the electoral roll, telephone directory or a membership list. It is a probability sample since the probability is that everyone will have the chance of being selected, thus forming a cross section of the total universe or population. Degree of accuracy can be decided by means of a mathematical formula, unlike a quota sample. The size of the sample will depend on the number of characteristics or different types of people, e.g. people who drive different kinds of cars and for different purposes - together with the plus or minus degree of accuracy required which in turn will be governed by the money available.

This kind of random sample, which is a contradiction in terms, is not to be confused with 'stopping people at random in the street' which is no kind of sample, or with books of random numbers which are sometimes used in academic and social research.

The interviewer is given a list of names and addresses and has to find them and conduct the interviews. These people may be scattered over an area, and they may be absent on the first call. Time is involved which is expensive. A person may have to be visited four times before being abandoned, and replaced from a reserve list.

For a political poll a sample of about 1,500 will suffice, and the respondents need not be scattered nationwide. With the National Readership Survey, which deals with both national and regional publications and a great variety of readers, a big sample of 30,000 is used and it is a stratified random sample which first requires the sampling of polling districts to product a geographically manageable sample.

A quota sample is more simple and less expensive to operate. When a broad cross-section of the public is not required and the characteristics are fewer, it is possible for interviewers to find their own quotas. For example, quotas of housewives in the proportions of the social grades might be required. An experienced interviewer will know in which districts to find each group of people. Less time is spent finding the respondents, many of whom might live in the same street.

However, a quota sample does depend on the skill of the researcher whereas with a random sample he or she is reliant on the responsibility of actually classifying people. The random sample will represent a cross section of all social grades.

A number of circumstances have already been touched on in explaining the two kinds of sample. These circumstances can now be summarised as:

Random sample

1. When maximum accuracy is required.
2. When the characteristics of the sample are numerous.
3. When the characteristics of the subject being surveyed are numerous.
4. When interviewer bias is to be avoided.
5. when the higher cost can be met.

Quota sample

1. When the characteristics of the sample are easily defined and uncomplicated.
2. When an interviewer can be relied on to find the right quotas of people.
3. When a less expensive survey is justified, or that is all the budget will permit.
4. When the degree of accuracy is not critical, or the sample is such that a high degree of inaccuracy is unlikely.

(**NB**. This answer includes one or two points not mentioned in the chapter. An answer should not read as if the candidate has swallowed a textbook or is recalling his lecture notes. Good marks are scored for intelligent application of knowledge, and evidence of independent reading such as of trade magazines like *Campaign*, *Marketing* and *Marketing Week* which can be found in a college or public library.)

EXERCISE

If a new soft drink is to be marketed what research techniques can be applied to test:

(a) The best brand name.
(b) The most popular flavours.
(c) The most popular container, e.g. can, plastic or glass bottle or waxed paper carton.
(d) The most acceptable price.
(e) The most appropriate advertising media.
(f) The advertising theme likely to attract the best response?

Part 3: Distribution

INTRODUCTION

The three chapters in this part deal with how goods and services actually move from the manufacturer or supplier to the final customer. How do goods get into the shops? When one walks round a shop it is easy to take for granted all those attractive products there before our very eyes.

In Chapter 8 the methods of distribution are described, and again it is a planned operation. After all, if shopkeepers will not buy and display and cannot sell goods the manufacturer will go out of business. He has to have an organised way of getting his products to customers, which in turn maintains the regular output of his factory production.

But methods of distribution keep changing, and these innovations are described in Chapter 9. Some of these changes have happened very rapidly in recent years. It is easy to grow up alongside these shopping revolutions without realising what is happening.

One of the big developments is described in Chapter 10. Now called direct response marketing, this is really mail order or selling by post which has a history going back as long as the Post Office and the railways - more than a century. But in recent years it has become the fastest growing area of marketing, boosted by sellers of financial services, with the retail stores joining in.

8. How are goods and services distributed?

INTRODUCTION

In this chapter the importance of distribution as a key element in the marketing mix will be emphasised, with special references to *adequate distribution* and the *distribution cycle*. Distribution will be defined. The various channels of distribution will be charted and analysed.

The many different kinds of middleman and retailers will be defined and explained. To this will be added the geographical location of shops and the reasons for the location of certain outlets.

Direct response marketing or shopping without shops, originally known as mail order trading, will be discussed.

Direct selling and party selling will be explained, together with franchising, pyramid selling, symbol groups and other special forms of selling.

After this, the chapter will consider the distribution systems best suited to certain products.

DEFINITION

Distribution consists of every activity involved in the transfer of goods or services from the producer or supplier to the final user or consumer.

Involved in this transfer are warehousing, delivery, depots, distributors, selling, sales promotion and advertising. These represent 'distribution costs'.

A distributor is a person or organisation which acts as an intermediary between the producer and the buyer, providing services such as storage and display which enable customers to buy goods and services as conveniently as possible.

Convenience is an important factor here because the producer will not sell his goods if it is not easy for customers to find and buy them. Customers will not normally travel all the way to the factory or head office: they will soon lose interest if their convenience is not catered for.

Distributors can include:

Importers and exporters	Factors
Wholesalers	Agents
Markets - trade and public	Direct response marketers
Retailers	Direct sellers
Franchisers	Vending machines

Of these, there are numerous kinds of retailer. All will be described later in the chapter. Meanwhile, the routes or chains of distributors known as the *channels of distribution* will now be discussed. It is important, as part of the marketing strategy, that the best channel is chosen. Not every product of the same kind will follow the same route, and an organisational decision has to be made.

For example, one watchmaker may sell through wholesalers, but another will sell direct to retailers. Again, one watchmaker may be anxious to sell in volume and will supply anyone from incentive merchandisers and gift catalogue promoters to direct response marketers, bazaars and so on, whereas another watchmaker (with a more expensive product) will restrict his distribution to jewellers who give his watch the desired prestige.

Most essential is the provision of *adequate distribution*. Distribution is said to be adequate when the product or service is readily available to meet demand. If it is advertised on television, will viewers be able to buy it next morning at the shop where they would normally expect to find it? Adequate distribution is also tied up with stock control, at retailers, at the wholesalers, and at the factory warehouse.

Coupled with adequate distribution is the *distribution cycle*, which is the time it takes a product to go through all the processes of physical distribution to reach the consumer. When one advertising campaign is being planned it is vital to know the length of the distribution cycle. It has been known for products to be advertised on television but unavailable in the shops, a combination of inadequate distribution and misunderstanding of the distribution cycle. Channels of distribution need to be organised which can cope with demand, which may mean that wholesaler warehouses have to be sufficiently well stocked to meet computerised ordering from big buyers like supermarkets, hypermarkets, discount stores, and direct response firms. Computerised stock re-ordering is linked to bar coding on products, and the electronic reading of bar codes by the cashier at the check out. All this depends on being able to anticipate the lead time between ordering and delivery.

CHANNELS OF DISTRIBUTION

Very broadly, the main channels of distribution are as shown in Figure 1, but as will be seen from the descriptions which follow, there can be some variations on this simple chart. There may be importers and markets (both national and local as with meat, fruit and vegetables), and direct to consumer distribution may include a variety of methods too.

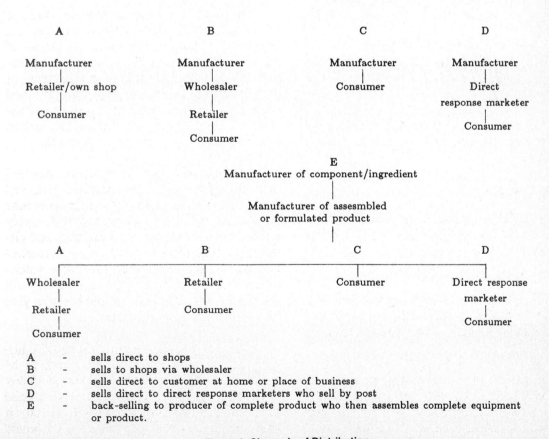

A - sells direct to shops
B - sells to shops via wholesaler
C - sells direct to customer at home or place of business
D - sells direct to direct response marketers who sell by post
E - back-selling to producer of complete product who then assembles complete equipment or product.

Figure 1 Channels of Distribution

TYPES OF DISTRIBUTOR - Special Terms

Importers and exporters are firms which bring goods in or take them out of the country, and they have to be experts in freight handling and documentation, by all means of transportation such as road, rail, sea and air, including knowledge of docks, airports, inland freight terminals and so on. Considerable legal knowledge is also required regarding Value Added Tax, Excise Duties, import quotas, bonded goods (e.g. tobacco) and so on. they are middlemen whose handling charges have to be included in the price.

Wholesalers. The principle of wholesaling is the buying of goods in bulk and the breaking down of quantities to meet orders of varying lesser size. This is valuable when:

1.　The manufacturer has a small sales force, or does not wish to have a large one.

2.　The manufacturer does not know the possible retail outlets.

3.　There are many retail outlets and it would be uneconomic to have a sales force calling on them all.

4.　The product is sold in small quantities per retailer, whereas a wholesaler can sell it together with associated products in mixed orders.

5.　The wholesaler's warehouses serve as local depots which the manufacturer does not have to provide.

6.　The wholesaler has his own sales force, and probably publishes a catalogue, and may advertise to the trade.

From the above list it will be seen that the wholesaler can perform valuable functions and earns his percentage, but since this may save the manufacturer many costs such as field salesmen and a delivery service the wholesaler's percentage may not actually increase the price.

There are however, some disadvantages over using wholesalers which are:

1.　The manufacturer loses control of the selling-in situation with the retailer.

2.　The manufacturer does not know who his retail distributors are.

3.　The manufacturer has no direct communications with retailers. This could be a major PR disadvantage.

4.　Because of this remoteness, the manufacturer is less able to persuade retailers to buy *his* brand. There is a passive selling situation, dependent on whether or not the wholesaler's representative pushes the product, and on orders volunteered by retailers. Moreover, the wholesaler is probably holding a variety of rival brands, and cannot be expected to promote one more than another unless perhaps it is being supported by a new advertising campaign or a sales promotion scheme. All this can be very frustrating to a manufacturer.

These pros and cons have to be understood very carefully. For example, a maker of windows sold through glass merchants or wholesalers who supplied builders according to specifications from architects. The manufacturer never knew in which buildings his windows were being used. His sales contact was the architect. This sort of remoteness between a manufacturer and the final user who, in this case, may not even know the identity of the manufacturer, is an interesting distribution dilemma.

There are certain weaknesses of marketing communications in this channel of distribution which can impair the manufacturer's ability to promote his product. One method that was adopted by the window maker was a market education programme of PR articles in the trade press describing the use of the windows in all kinds of buildings, thus demonstrating their versatility. This involved a tour of buildings under the guidance of a glass merchant who knew where the windows had been installed.

Cash and carry warehouse. These warehouses operate on two principles: the buyer pays cash and takes the goods with him. They are semi-trade wholesalers since a member of the public, usually when issued with a trade card, can buy from a cash and carry warehouse provided they buy in bulk such as by the case or gross. These warehouses enable retailers to top up their stocks while awaiting delivery from their main supplier. Also, smaller buyers like clubs can make occasional purchases. They are not to be confused with out-of-town discount stores like MFI and Comet. They are not generally open to the public.

Symbol groups. Large retailers buy in bulk and are able to offer low prices which the independent or neighbourhood shop is unable to enjoy. However, to overcome this problem and to make small businesses viable, some wholesalers offer better discounts to small traders who buy all or most of their stock from the one wholesaler who in turn helps with advertising. Thus small traders display the logo of the wholesaler. Examples are Spar, Mace and Wavy Line. Symbol groups are thus voluntary chains attached to wholesalers. They are not to be confused with large chain stores like Marks & Spencer which have their own logos and own labels.

Agents. A sales agent or commission representative handles sales and distribution for a manufacturer, usually having an exclusive franchise for a specified area, territory or country, and being paid a commission on sales.

Jobbers. This is another name for middleman or wholesaler, and there is the *rack jobber* who stocks up supermarkets with non-food items such as proprietary medicines and toiletries.

Factors. They operate like wholesalers except that they take over account collection and earn a commission in collecting debts. Book publishers often distribute through factors who virtually buy the suppliers' invoices. Then, a producer does not have to collect accounts.

Retailers. A retailer is any trader, whether or not he has a shop, who buys at one price from the manufacturer or wholesaler and sells at a higher price, thus making a living. In so doing, he provides the customer with a service, making the product easily available. To this he may add other services like technical advice, home delivery, fitting or installation, spare parts and repairs, and his retail premises may also be a pleasant place in which to shop with attractive displays and demonstrations and somewhere where shopping may be enjoyed. This may, as it does with superstores, include car parking, petrol stations, restaurant, toilets, and baby changing facilities. But he can also be something much simpler like the newspaper street vendor, the keeper of a small sweets and cigarette kiosk, or an ice-cream salesman with a mobile van.

The following are different kinds of retailer:

1. **Independent.** According to the Census of Distribution, a retailer with less than ten brands.

2. **Neighbourhood.** A retailer in a residential area, but not necessarily a one-man business or an independent. A number of multiple confectioners, newsagents, butchers, estate agents and so on have branches in local shopping parades.

3. **Multiple.** Chain stores and supermarkets with many branches are also termed multiples. They are defined in the Census of Distribution as a firm other than a co-operative society having ten or more retail establishments. These are the shops which are repeated in High Streets throughout the land or at least in certain

regions. The first multiples were W.H. Smiths' railway bookstalls.

4.　**Self-service.** In this type of shop there are no shop assistants, only a check-out assistants or cashiers who take the money. The shopper takes items from the shelves and fills a supplied basket or trolley. This can be a small shop such as a pharmacy, newsagents or confectioners, but self-service also typifies not only the supermarket but many other types of large store.

5.　**Department store.** As the name implies, this is a large store with many sections or departments selling different kinds of merchandise, mostly household and personal lines.

6.　**Supermarket.** This is a large large self-service store which sells mostly foods, drinks, toiletries and household fmcgs. Many, like Tesco, Gateway, Safeway and Sainsbury's, have large chains of branches, central warehouses and their own delivery transport.

7.　**Superstore.** This is a very large self-service store, which falls mid-way between a supermarket and a hypermarket. It is a single floor store with a great variety of food and non-food merchandise, occupying at least 2,500 sq.m net of floor space and having a car park.

8.　**Hypermarket.** Because of its land area, the hypermarket is usually found out-of-town or perhaps on the perimeter of a town or at re-developed space like a former gas works. It is a large super-store, megastore or mass merchandiser, occupying at least 5,000 sq.m of net floor space with perhaps 15 check-outs. There is usually a large car parking area, with services such as a petrol station and bus stop. *One-stop shopping* is associated with these huge stores.

9.　**Bazaar or variety store.** There are big chain stores which sell a great range of products, originally at low prices although these shops have gone up-market. Typical examples are Woolworth, Marks and Spencer, BHS and Littlewoods. Bazaar trading really refers to the groupings of traders in streets or areas, as found in many Middle East and African countries, but also in groupings of like traders such as stamp dealers, book-sellers and antique dealers, perhaps in one building or area. These colonies of shops may be called *congeries.*

10.　**Own shops.** Some manufacturers maintain their own shops where they may sell only their own brands or also carry national rival brands. These are shops like Wedgwood which sell their own ceramics, or Boots which sell both their own brands and others, or Singer which sells its own sewing machines. Marks and Spencer has its own brands (St Michael and St Margaret) but does no manufacturing itself, its merchandise being made or packed to specifications laid down by M & S. So, Marks and Spencer should not be confused with 'own shops'.

11.　**Mixed retailer.** A retailer is called 'mixed' if more than 20 per cent of his turnover falls outside one of the special-ised trading groups, e.g. grocery; foot-wear; confectionary; textiles; household. It can be any size shop. This fairly new term can apply to many retailers.

12.　**Main dealer.** A common term in the motor-car trade, a main dealer usually sells only one make and so represents the manufacturer in the area. A 'Ford dealer' is a main dealer, maintaining a showroom, parts service and workshop.

13.　**Discount store.** This is the name given to large warehouse-like stores, often with minimal displays and some-times no servicing, which sell mainly expensive goods like electrical and electronic equipment at discounted prices.

14.   **Broker**. A broker usually advises clients as well as sells services, and ideally he should know the market and make the best possible recommendations to clients. The Automobile Association does this with motor-car insurance. Since the advent of the Financial Services Act, such brokers have acquired the illustrious title of 'financial adviser' which is rather like calling a rat catcher a rodent operator. A *sales broker* is a firm which handles advertising, sales and distribution of a number of non-competing brands, often in the food industry.

Seven special types of selling can be added here:

1.   **Direct response marketing**. Otherwise known as 'shopping without shops' this is the increasingly popular method of selling direct to customers. It originated in Chicago with Montgomery Ward and Sears Roebuck in the mid 19th century selling almost anything mail order to the isolated farmers of the mid-west. This trade accelerated with the growth of railways and parcel post.

Meanwhile, in Britain, Antonio Fattorini arrived from Lombardy and became a travelling packman selling domestic and table wares. From those beginnings in the early 19th century developed the Fattorini jewellers' shops in Yorkshire and 'watch clubs' selling watches by instalments to working men. Eventually, in 1890, the origins of Empire Stores, the mail order company, came about with a mail order catalogue of household goods.

Direct response marketing - the modern name for mail order and catalogue selling - is big business. Among the leading exponents today are those selling financial services (e.g. insurance, pensions, unit trusts, credit cards) and large retail stores which find they have to compete with this sort of trade.

This postal trade is obtained by off-the-page advertisements in the press, direct mail and catalogues, door-to-door mail drops and occasionally (as with gramophone records, tapes and compact discs) on television with a computerised ordering system.

2.   **Direct selling**. Like mail order, this is a very old form of distribution. When most people lived in the countryside the travelling itinerant salesman or packman (like Antonio Fattorini above) took their wares by pack mule from village to village. Direct selling still exists, although rapidly becoming uneconomic. The door-to-door baker has virtually disappeared, but the milkman with his electric milk float remains peculiar to Britain. There have been modern adopters of direct selling as with the promotion of double glazing and replacement windows.

Direct selling may also occur with industrial products, and with business-to-business trading such as the selling of office equipment and stationery supplies direct to offices.

3.   **Party selling**. A comparatively modern development, party selling or home selling relies on recruiting people who will organise tea or coffee parties at their homes, during which a company representative demonstrates and sells a product, the hostess receiving a gift or commission on sales.

4.   **Pyramid selling**. This is a racket which re-emerges from time to time, and is subject to the Multi-Selling Marketing Act 1972. One agent sells the product to another who sells it to another in a heirarchy of levels, of which there may be

no end and no actual consumer. The last buyer loses his money.

5. **Telephone selling.** This is really another kind of direct response marketing. It can be a form of 'cold calling' when a telephone salesperson takes the initiative and rings likely prospects, or it can stem from enquiries to media advertisements. It tends to suit certain types of trading of which space-selling by newspapers and magazines, and insurance selling by brokers and salesmen are among the most common.

6. **Franchising.** All kinds of businesses which enable the independent person to virtually run his or her own business are based on franchising. The franchisor usually injects some capital, the franchiser may assist with finding premises if they are necessary (e.g. a hamburger cafe), and the franchiser undertakes to buy the franchiser's product. Examples range from ice cream parlours, instant print copy shops and laundrettes to carpet cleaning and drain cleaning services.

On a much bigger scale, manufacturers of many soft drinks and beers grant franchises to bottling companies throughout the world, e.g. Coca-Cola.

7. **Vending machines.** Another very old method, early examples being chocolate machines on railway platforms, vending now extends to machines that provide stamps, newspapers, contraceptives, hot drinks and cooked meals. Vending machines can be installed at work places and they can supply all manner of goods from food and drink to proprietary medicines and ladies' tights.

GEOGRAPHICAL LOCATION OF SHOPS

The location of shops is often associated with the type of merchandise. There are three types of goods: (i) *shopping* goods, which require careful selection to find the right goods; (ii) *convenience* goods or fmcgs which are bought frequently; and (iii) *speciality* or durable goods which are bought infrequently.

Shop location is often associated with each type of good. Speciality and shopping goods tend to be sold in shopping centres, but convenience goods are more likely to be found on the perimeter of the shopping centre, e.g. in street markets, supermarkets and out-of-town hypermarkets. A butcher's shop or a fishmonger's is not to be found in London's Oxford Street or Bond Street where one would normally buy clothes, furniture or jewellery.

Innovations of recent years have been the *traffic free shopping centre,* the one-level *shopping mall,* and the *high-rise shopping plaza* containing hundreds of small shops, all of which bring together a large number of shops in one place or under one roof. Department stores often contain concessionary shops, sections or counters for manufacturers or specialist suppliers.

A number of retailers such as Sainsbury's have developed stores on the basis of certain threshold or estimated number of possible customers. This had led to the closing of small local branches and concentration on superstores and hypermarkets, and also on combinations such as those of Sainsbury's and BHS called Savacentres.

TYPES OF DISTRIBUTION SYSTEMS FOR CERTAIN PRODUCTS

From the above it may seem that there is an endless choice of possible outlets for goods. This has to be turned the other way round in order to determine which outlets are favoured by the majority of a manufacturer's customers, or at which outlet or kind of outlet will potential customers expect to find the goods? They must not be disappointed, otherwise they will buy something else or nothing at all.

Outlet and customer go together, and there is nothing banal about the advertisement which proclaims that the product is available 'at all grocers' or 'at all good chemists' as the case may be.

The problem is getting that distribution. If it is a fmcg in the food trade it will háve no future if it cannot be sold at the major supermarket chains. In London and the South of England that means Sainsbury's or Tesco. If it is an electrical appliance it needs the accolade of being sold in electricity board show-rooms since it is known that they test every brand they sell. It may be a new polish, but if the shelf space for polishes has been fully allocated a new brand will be unwelcomed. Supermarkets may appear to carry an incredible range of brands but within each product group only so much shelf space and so many different brands can be stocked, both physically and profitably.

The days are long past when the Heinz salesman set forth with his case of samples and was told to seek distribution through every possible outlet. Today, the salesman haggles with the central buyer at the supermarket head office.

At the other extreme is the need to find a distributor who can act as the sole supplier in a given area - an *appointed dealer* - who has a monopoly of local distribution. This can enhance the status of the dealer; it can pin-point the source of supply and the dealer's address can be advertised; and it probably involves technical services such as advice, spares and repairs.

There are products which people will not buy unless they are assured of servicing facil-ities, whether it be a foreign motor-car, a sewing machine, or a lawn mower. Appointed dealers (and selling direct to dealers and not through wholesalers) become imperative.

At a very early stage of planning the marketing strategy it is therefore essential to determine both the channel of distribution and the type of retail outlet, coupled with the availability of a sales force capable of making the distribution system work.

SUMMARY

After defining distribution and distributor this chapter moved on to discuss the various channels of distribution. In addition to the conventional four channels, a fifth was included for products that are sold to firms which use them in the production of finished products.

The roles of wholesalers, and different kinds of wholesaler were next explained. The advantages and disadvantages of using wholesalers was discussed. After this, fourteen kinds of retailer were outlined, followed by a commentary on seven special types of selling.

The chapter ended with sections on the geographical location of shops and types of distribution systems for certain products.

PAST EXAMINATION QUESTIONS

Question 7, LCC Series 4, 1987

Explain:

(i)   How symbol groups help small traders to compete with supermarkets.

(ii)   How cash and carry warehouses offer special services.

(iii)   How factors help manufacturers to distribute their goods.

(iv)   How franchisers satisfy manu-facturers' distribution needs.

Comment

The answers to this question will be found in this chapter. A descriptive paragraph should be written on each.

Question 6, LCC Autumn 1986

Write short notes on four of the following:

(i)   *Discount stores*
(ii)   *Shopping plazas*
(iii)   *Cash-and-carry warehouses*
(iv)   *Symbol groups*
(v)   *Vending machines.*

Comment

Again, each has been explained in this chapter.

Question 2, LCC Series 2, 1987

(i)   *What is meant by 'adequate distribution' and how is this achieved?*

(ii)   *How does adequate distribution affect the success of an advertising campaign and, ultimately, the success of the marketing strategy?*

Comment

Adequate distribution was discussed at the beginning of the chapter but here is an interesting question which invites the candidate to think about this topic and to make some practical observations. The question does, however, draw on some knowledge of advertising which is covered in Chapter 11.

There are two parts worth equal marks. Part (i) requires a definition, and an explanation of how adequate distribution is achieved. Part (ii) seeks a relationship between adequate distribution and advertising, and with the marketing strategy as a whole.

Model answer

Q.2.(i) Adequate distribution occurs when an advertised product is available at retailers to meet the demand produced by the advertising. This means that the company's sales organisation must anticipate likely demand and set sales targets accordingly. The sales force must obtain orders from the trade early enough for them to be serviced and for the goods to be delivered before the advertising breaks. Moreover, the goods must be displayed, shop staff should be aware of them, and any point-of sale material should be in place. All this requires careful training and stock control so that the customer is satisfied.

This also means that salesmen should be able to complete their journey cycles before the delivery date, and since a journey cycle covering all the salesman's regular calls may occupy four to six weeks, this is a good example of the importance of timing. It will be useless if salesmen are still taking orders after the advertising has appeared and before deliveries can be made.

Adequate distribution is thus dependent on a timetable like this:

1.   Manufactured goods in warehouse.
2.   Salesmen make calls and submit orders to head office.
3.   Goods and point-of-sale material delivered.
4.   Advertising breaks.
5.   Customers find goods on display in shops.

Q.2.(ii) Unless there is adequate distribution, the advertising campaign will fail. It aims to persuade consumers to go to the shop as soon as possible, such as next morning after a television commercial, but certainly when next buying that sort of product. If the customer is unable to locate the product, with the retailer making an excuse about delayed delivery, the customer may either buy a substitute - perhaps encouraged by the retailer who does not wish to lose a sale - or leave the shop empty-handed. The situation is even worse in the supermarket when inability to find the product on the shelf may simply destroy interest.

Advertising can provoke interest and willingness to buy, but it will be like a spent rocket if it fails to achieve its objective because of poor planning by the sales organisation. Money invested in advertising will be wasted.

Moreover, it is a false policy to expect advertising to create enquiries which will induce the retailer to order stocks. That is too late and the customer may not return. The goods must be there when the customer, prompted by the advertising makes his enquiry and expects to be supplied. Lack of supplies can also disappoint the customer regarding the retailer's ability to supply, and so send him elsewhere.

Consequently, if the procedures necessary to adequate distribution are inefficient, the whole marketing strategy will either collapse or be enfeebled, impetus will have been lost, the advantage can be surrendered to competitors, and the whole operation will be uneconomic and incapable of achieving the sales forecast.

EXERCISE

A new inexpensive personal computer, suitable for either private or business use, is being imported and a distribution network has to be established. Eventually, the advertising will direct potential buyers to suppliers.

Consider all the available kinds of stockist, and plan a suitable distribution network which can be serviced by your sales force and made known to potential buyers. Consider also how distributors will be made known to customers - by the manufacturer's own advertising, by retailer's advertising (perhaps subsidised by the manufacturer) or by any other means.

9.   How has distribution changed in recent years

INTRODUCTION

Two aspects of change in distribution will be discussed in this chapter. First, there are the *reasons* for these changes, and second there are the *actual* changes. Some of these changes have been occurring over the past forty years as full employment and greater variety and choice of goods followed wartime rationing and controls, and the distribution scene became very different from that of the 20s and 30s. But there have been other changes resulting from entirely new social, political and economic conditions. Some of these are quite recent and concern innovations like bar coding, cash till stock control and computerised stock control, re-ordering and warehousing inventory control.

REASONS FOR CHANGES

In the last chapter a chart was given of the main channels of distribution, and this was followed by descriptions of different kinds of distributor, but they may have been insufficient to demonstrate the revolution that has taken place in distribution. Moreover, it has changed decade by decade since the 50s and is still changing. It is no co-incidence that this co-incides with the arrival and development of commercial television.

The changes during that period can be seen in the development of Sainsbury's. In the 1950s and 60s there were still pre-war style shops with marble counters where they patted up butter from a huge block, sliced bacon to the thickness required, and customers queued up at different counters for tea, bacon, butter and so on. Eggs were packed singly in paper bags. Sainsbury's had hundreds of these shops. Then they started opening large supermarkets and closing down the small shops. Next, they raised money by selling shares, and housewives could buy them in £5 lots over bank counters! By 1988, some of the supermarkets had become too small to cope with the volume of trade, and superstores with car parks were opened on the fringe of town. Sainsbury's now not only has fewer but bigger stores, but the Savacentre joint-ventures with BHS, and operate Homebase DIY with gardening centres.

Why? The reasons for such momentous changes are as follows:

1.   **Economy.** Most fmcgs are small profit lines unless there are volume sales. To solve this problem, costs have to be cut. The most efficient way is to buy in bulk and virtually outdo the wholesaler by buying at wholesale prices, providing the necessary warehousing, and reducing the number of deliveries to larger ones to a smaller number of very large retail outlets. These economies have been achieved by the supermarket multiples which have hundreds of strategically located supermarkets, superstores and out-of-town hypermarkets. They include Sainsbury's, Tesco, Safeway, Co-op, and Lipton.

2.   **Wider ownership of motor-cars.** Shoppers have become more mobile, and the big stores invite them to buy perhaps a week's supply and pack it in the motor-car. If the store has its own car park, or is out-of-town, car-parking or meter charges are unnecessary.

3.   **Accessibility.** With a network of motorways, out-of-town hypermarkets and shopping centres are easily accessible. Garden centres also benefit from this, and they represent another retail development. There are few seedsmen's shops in today's towns.

4. **Plastic money**. Now that charge and credit cards are as well as cheque books, so common, it is both possible and convenient to buy a week's supply at one shop. If cash is needed, the larger stores have bank cash dispensers. A number of stores also issue their own credit cards while others have budget accounts or other credit facilities.

5. **Telephone** buying has also increased with the greater ownership of telephones, and this can also be linked with credit cards. Almost anything can be ordered by telephone, even a theatre seat or an airline ticket. A great deal of direct response business is done by telephone, including that of the mail orders clubs. Off-the-page advertisements give free-phone numbers. Telemarketing has become a thriving form of distribution.

6. **Television advertising** has speeded up the sale of fmcgs, including newly launched brands, and this has helped both volumes of trade and rate of turnover, which has justified the size of the modern stores.

7. **Young people** have greater spending power than in the past, influencing the sales of clothes, pop music recordings, hi-fi equipment such as walkmans, motor-cycles, fast foods and other young people's products.

8. **Television** has broadened people's knowledge and interests, creating demands for goods and services associated with the foods, hobbies, sports, travel and life styles seen on television, and these demands apply to all social grades and age groups.

9. **People go abroad more**, on school trips, on business and for holidays and these experiences have triggered off not only extra travel business but sales of things associated with travel such as cameras, luggage and clothes together with greater interest in wines and foreign foods.

10. **Financial services have grown and changed** with people saving and investing in building societies and unit trusts, buying shares (especially during privatisation share issues), and borrowing money. There is now the rapidly growing personal pension business, again promoted on television.

11. **Convenience foods and freezers**. Buying habits have changed, either because meals have to be prepared on return from work, because more homes have refrigerators, or because of the popularity of freezers. Pre-packed foods of all kinds, prepared meals like Lean Cuisine, frozen foods, and bulk supplies for the freezer, have encouraged many people to give up buying fresh foods and preparing them in favour of time-saving convenience foods. This has led to entirely new kinds of retailer like Bejam and Iceland.

The remarkable thing is that the greatest changes occurred during a period of recession and unemployment. The companies most frequently offering jobs have been supermarkets. People must still eat, whether working or on the dole. Thanks to North Sea oil revenue the Government was able to cushion the monetary effects of unemployment. Meanwhile, new industries in the south, new urban development and modern shopping facilities have represented increasing spending power, even though it was often that of the credit card. It has meant huge imports and its price was the stupendous trade deficit of August 1988. But it revolutionised distribution during the 80s. There were record new car registrations in August 1988 although share prices were falling and mortgage rates were rising.

THE ACTUAL CHANGES

While the rate of change in the 80s certainly accelerated, a number had been growing throughout the post-war decades. In general, they reflect a changing country and the effects of a computer age.

RISE OF THE MULTIPLES AND BIG STORES

There is nothing new about multiples. Most of the multiples to be found in the High Street of most British towns were there sixty years ago. Some have disappeared, or have been absorbed by the leading ones of today. Boots, W.H.Smith, Freeman Hardy & Willis, Dorothy Perkins, and Burtons are among the oldies that remain.

Some have made phenomenal growths. The little untidy Tesco shop lit with 40 watt bulbs has been replaced by the vast emporiums of one of the leading supermarket multiples.

But the Co-ops have either vanished or been replaced by large supermarkets in strategic locations, replacing their numerous branch stores and large department stores of the past.

Multiples, representing chains of several hundred stores, dominate the retail scene. They combine bulk buying with competitive prices.

Similarly, by amalgamation and expansion, department stores in principal shopping centres have become huge stores, made even larger and more attractive by the inclusion of concessionary shops within a shop. For example, a glass and china department will be made up of sections representing the manufacturers and staffed by their sales ladies, not the store's. There may also be an arcade in which all kinds of tradespeople are selling their goods such as wine, bread, cold meats, plus estate agents and people mending shoes or making keys. All these sections, counters, boutiques and shops are concessions which all increase the store traffic of the main store, quite apart from

helping to pay the rent. They all add to the interest and attractiveness of shopping.

Linked with this has been the development of shopping precincts and traffic-free shopping zones which make shopping safer and more convenient. To some extent these moves have helped to counteract the appeal of the out-of-town hypermarkets and shopping centres. People still need to come into town for non-food purchases, principally clothing and furnishings.

GROWTH OF OWN BRANDS

Own labels or own brands have become more popular with the increased size of the retailers selling them so that, with the big multiples, an own brand can have sales approaching those of a nationally advertised brand. The multiples often have as good a reputation as the manufacturer. With products whose brand names are less familiar, such as wines, a Sainsbury's or Marks and Spencer label may be more significant than that of a traditional shipper.

In fact, own labels are such good sellers that it has become a struggle for some national brands to avoid being de-listed. The price difference between own-label products and national brands in shops like Boots and Supadrug is such that the price-conscious shopper does not hesitate to buy the cheaper own label. This is especially so when there is no *apparent* difference in quality and a big difference in price. Paracetamol cures headaches whatever the price.

This represents a small war between the multiples and the manufacturers, with the multiples tending to win and more and more manufacturers agreeing to lose their identity and pack private brands. It becomes a question of pride or profit, and only a few firms are prepared to resist the challenge as Nestlé has done. Elsewhere, comment was made on 'paying for the name' but today there is often genuine competition between the name of the store and that of a manufacturer. Many stores sell their brand rather than their store.

GROWTH OF SELF-SERVICE

Self-service has become a way of shopping which provides convenience and encourages purchase. The customer does not have to enquire of a shop assistant, and perhaps have to wait his or her turn to do so. Prices are displayed and can be compared. Baskets and trolleys are provided to make carrying easy. Impulse buying is also encouraged by displays, wire stands and dump bins. This has also encouraged manufacturers to pack items on cards and bubble packs, or in see-through packs so that they can be suspended on hooks for self-service purposes.

Many bazaars and department stores now have cash desks and check-outs rather than counter assistants. Many customers prefer the freedom of self-service to the constant cry of "can I help you madam?" which can be inhibiting. Another extension of this is the self-service petrol station, which either saves staff or provides security for the cashier at night.

LATE NIGHT AND WEEKEND SHOPPING

The convenience of shoppers, and the opportunity to sell out-of-hours, has become a feature of some retailers. There are the 7-Eleven shops, late night shopping on Thursdays, petrol stations that sell food at all hours and every day, department stores that open on Bank Holidays and DIY stores, garden centres and out-of-town stores that defy Sunday trading bans. Many supermarkets are open in the evening.

These facilities extend shopping to those whose working lives make shopping difficult, or who are mobile and can shop at the weekend. A premium may have to be paid for the convenience

but the facility is there if one runs short of milk, or suddenly decides to paint the bedroom or stock the garden.

To some extent this is a return to pre-war days when shop hours were long, and Saturday evening shopping was the norm, and it also reflects the willingness of immigrants to work long hours, or for shops to offer the services found overseas where most shopping is done in the evening or at the weekend. A more cosmopolitan attitude pervades the British shopping scene.

AUTOMATIC VENDING

This is another form of convenience shopping which is not new but which has grown, not forgetting cash dispensers at banks and building societies which extend their services after they are closed. Vending machines, as mentioned in the previous chapter, have extended sales to many non-retail premises such as work places. There have been problems of vandalism but nevertheless, many items are available from vending machines in public places, including travel insurance at airports.

FRANCHISING

With its appeal to the independent small businessman, and in keeping with the self-help philosophy of the times, numerous trades are open to the person who will run his own business with the support of a supplier. As a result, High Streets are full of fast food restaurants and instant print shops, or people with vehicles are offering domestic services. This has become a means of distribution for manufacturers who are able to enjoy a monopoly situation through their vendors.

DIRECT RESPONSE MARKETING

This subject will be discussed more fully in Chapter 10 but it has become a sophistication of the long established selling of goods and services by mail order. The remarkable thing is that in a largely urbanised country where retail outlets of every kind are in abundance it is possible to sell by post. Direct response marketing is the enigma of modern distribution, a principal reason for the huge expansion of Royal Mail services and increased employment of postmen, and a major victim of the Post Office strike of September 1988.

Some direct response catalogues are Aladdin's caves of merchandise, showing that almost anything can be sold by post. The big catalogue firms like Littlewoods are old masters at this business, but one has only to study the press advertisements, and look at one's mail, magazine inserts and door-to-door mail drops to see that direct response marketing is very big business.

It is aided by the availability of mailing lists, especially through list brokers and databases, and by careful targeting using the ACORN and other neighbourhood location systems described in Chapter 7. The realism of full-colour offset litho printing has taken the shop into the home. Some of it may carry the ignominious nickname of junk mail but the fact is that although people may pretend to resent it they respond to the tune of many millions of pounds a year.

THE CHANGING HIGH STREET

While it is true that throughout the country, every High Street has its familiar facades which have been there for years, there have also been some changes which reflect modern society.

A few years back there were several big plant bakeries and bread was mass produced. Today, there are many baker's shops where bread and cakes are baked on the premises. Similarly, at one time there was a great amalgamation of breweries and a fairly small number of national brews. Today, old brewery names have returned, and there are even pubs where beer is brewed on the premises. There is also competition from foreign beers.

New speciality shops have arrived, especially ones which cater for the clothing styles of different age groups. The men's outfitters has been largely replaced by shops that sell trendy clothes to fashion conscious young men. Another type of speciality shop or recent introduction is that which sells only one type of clothing such as socks or ties or shirts.

Although many building societies have amalgamated so that there are fewer of them there are nevertheless new building society branches in smaller shopping centres, and prime sites have been taken up in city centres. The Stock Exchange crash of October 1987 and the unsettled equity market in 1988 sent money pouring into the building societies, while the Building Societies Act meant that they were able to spread into new business areas such as cheque-book accounts, pension schemes and the acquisition of estate agencies.

The cosy well-equipped betting shop is another development, while afternoon opening has given pubs a new daytime presence.

Partly as a sign of our cosmopolitan society and partly as evidence of greater travel experience, there has been a growth in foreign restaurants such as Chinese, Indian, Thai and Japanese. These are not just in the eating spots of large cities but in smaller towns and villages, the latter catering for the executive types who now live in the country.

Some of these changes are in contradiction to the spread of the supermarket multiples. They are a rebellion against the sameness, lack of personality and overwhelming size of the giant stores with their rows of shelves, overloaded trollies and queues at the check-outs. The new, smaller shops offer individuality and a face behind the counter.

TECHNOLOGICAL CHANGES

A number of electronic and computerised systems have been introduced which make warehouses and stock rooms, stock control and re-ordering more efficient. They include:

Inventory control. The warehouses of wholesalers and multiples have computerised inventory control systems which recognise the lead times required for manufacturers to supply, and so signal re-ordering requirements as stock levels fall on a changing daily forecast of stock requirements.

EPOS (electronic point-of-sale systems) were introduced into UK supermarkets in 1982 and are to be seen at the check-outs in Sainsbury's, Tesco, Boots, Children's World and similar large stores. They provide the means of reading EAN (European Article Number) bar codes on packages, price labels and coupons. There are two principal EPOS methods by which the cashier can read bar coded items. One is a 'pen' which has a rest like a telephone, and the cashier brushes the 'pen' against the bar code. The second is a fixed device which reads the bar code when presented to it. The EPOS reader simultaneously gives the price to the till, and printed on the till receipt are the items bought as well as their price. The system also informs the stock room. Sainsbury's stock 12,000 bar-coded items and by means of EPOS sales of all these items are analysed daily and overnight stock deliveries are ordered electronically.

EFTPOS (electronic funds transfer at point-of-sale) is a method of effecting transfers from bank accounts or charge, and credit card accounts. It is so unobtrusive that customers are probably unaware of what is going on. For instance, when paying for petrol by credit card a paper receipt appears on a till roll machine and the customer signs it. But the card has been 'wiped' on an EFTPOS terminal which reads the logo on the card, contacts the bank or credit card company (e.g. Visa, American Express), checks its authenticity, and records the transaction so that the retailer is paid and the card member is charged. This takes 15 seconds while the customer is waiting to sign the till roll.

SUMMARY

This chapter has dealt with the way distribution has changed, first setting out reasons for change and then detailing how these changes have taken place. Some have been evolutionary over the past forty years, others are more recent. They represent the effects of economic, social, political and technological change. But as with many things, history sometimes repeats itself and there are contradictory revivals as has been seen in the return of small businesses and local names as witnessed with local bakers and local breweries.

PAST EXAMINATION QUESTIONS

Question 3, RSA March 1985

*(a) Naomi Creswell, a talented painter, plans to replace her two high street retail shops with a small, catalogue-based mail order business. Identify **two** types of cost that might be reduced and **two** that might be increased by this change.*

(b) How might change in information technology affect the sale of goods through mail order?

Comment

This question seeks a comparison between the cost of running a retail shop business and what is now called a direct response marketing business. In the second part the candidate is expected to know something about modern technology as it can be applied to direct response marketing.

Two types of cost that might be reduced are:
(1) Renting shop premises; and
(2) Rates on shop premises.

Other possible costs are decorating the exterior and interior; sales staff since she cannot be in attendance at both shops.

Two types of cost that might be increased are:
(1) Printing the catalogue and any accompanying sales literature;
(2) Postage since the catalogues have to be sent out on a mailing list.

Changes in information technology could affect sales in the following ways:

(1) With a small personal computer enquiries, follow ups and orders can be recorded, with print outs of invoices, statements and labels.

(2) Mailing lists can be bought or hired from list brokers and databases which hold computerised mailing lists.

(3) Sales letters can be produced on word processors or by laser printers which can insert personal names in letters, or introduce colours or change type faces.

(4) There are also the various computerised neighbourhood classification systems like ACORN, MOSAIC and Super Profiles.

These and other computer services can help to make mail order trading efficient and effective.

Question 4, RSA June 11 1985

Woods Ltd, has been established for 50 years as builder's merchants supplying local businesses. Three years ago, to take advantage of a developing trend, they set up a large retail DIY self-service store on a trading estate on the outskirts of town. They stock a wide variety of kitchen and bathroom fitments besides gardening goods and general DIY equipment. They are now worried because sales are not as high as expected, as a branch of a national chain of DIY centres has recently opened nearby.

(a) Describe two ways in which the demand for the builders merchants part of the business is likely to differ from the market for the retail side of the business.

(b) Explain three marketing methods which Woods Ltd, could use to compete with the newly opened DIY centre.

(e) Explain one advantage and two disadvantages to Woods Ltd, from the location of their retail store.

(f) Explain one advantage and one disadvantage Woods Ltd is likely to have in competing with the branch of the national chain.

Comment

Here is a question which invites understanding of a number of retail situations.

(a) Demand for the two sides of the business will differ in at least the following two ways:

(i) the builders merchants side will require a large stock of parts or components;
(ii) they may be bought in quantities greater than those bought by DIY enthusiasts.

(b) Three marketing methods which Woods Ltd could use to compete with the newly open DIY centre could be:

(i)   free delivery;
(ii) discount on orders over a certain amount;
(iii) door-to-door delivery of leaflets announcing special offers.

Again, other marketing methods could be offered such as advertising special offers in free newspapers, featuring seasonal special offers week by week, giving special credit terms on large orders, or buying in special competitive lines.

(e)   One advantage of the location of Woods Ltd could be car parking; two disadvantages could be:

(i)   distance from town;
(ii) lack of public transport.

(f)   One advantage the local firm will have is that it is already established and should have built up a regular clientele and considerable customer goodwill. In competing with the new local branch of the national chain the local trader will lack the strength of the national chain's advertising in national rather than local publications. The national chain, for instance, can advertise in a national DIY magazine, listing its branches or at least naming towns where there are branches, but the local trader cannot do this and will not enjoy the national chain's prestige.

EXERCISE

A fashion house wishes to expand its business with the younger fashion-conscious market. Consider the possibilities such as setting up concessionary shops in department stores, opening own shops, or adopting direct response marketing with off-the-page press advertisements and catalogues. Analyse the strengths and weaknesses of these or any other methods of distribution. Make your recommendations, stating your reasons for choosing a particular form of distribution.

10. How is direct response marketing conducted?

INTRODUCTION

First, direct response marketing will be defined. Then there will be a discussion of why it has become so popular, and how it has been adopted by new users of this form of marketing. The special media used will be detailed. Finally, there will be an introduction to the organisations which service the direct response marketing industry.

DEFINITION

Direct response or direct marketing is the selling of goods or services without shops, usually by post or telephone.

It is a form of trading or distribution, formerly known as mail order, and often called 'shopping without shops' or 'retailing without stores'. It should not be confused with direct selling which is doorstep selling. Most of it is conducted postally or by telephone with delivery by post, carrier or private delivery service. Nor should the word 'response' be confused with the general response which ordinary advertising may be expected to provoke. Nor is it limited to the Littlewoods type of mail order club.

WHY IS IT SO POPULAR?

Its popularity can be looked at from the points of view of the trade and of the customer. It is a trade which can be conducted in a big way from an office or warehouse or in a small way from a private house. Provided one has a marketable product or service and the means of handling the business, which may include dealing with accounts and packing and despatching goods, almost anyone can sell almost anything by this method. This can be done locally, nationally or internationally. The opportunities to trade in this way are therefore limitless, but it does call for initiative and imagination plus good business sense.

From the trader's point of view, direct response marketing is popular because:

1. **It is easily controllable.** The trader can select his merchandise or service to satisfy a chosen market and he can target his prospective buyers. He may allow credit, but he can work on a cash-with-order basis and so have no cash flow problem.

2. **Low overheads.** He does not have to spend money on maintaining a shop. In fact, he need not even store goods because there are fulfilment houses which can despatch his orders. This depends on the nature of his business.

3. **Convenience of location**. He can operate from anywhere, thanks to the various postal, telephone and carrier services. Distance from customers is immaterial. This allows him to use economical premises. Unlike shop retailing, he does not need perhaps expensive premises in which to display goods or where customers can find him. He does not need to have any personal contact with customers.

4. **Own resources.** Some direct response marketers have developed business around existing resources such as the names and addresses of customers who are held on computerised data bases. This applies to many companies like banks, insurance companies and other investment houses which have created separate direct marketing departments.

5. **Additional business.** As with the companies mentioned above, a number of retailers have extended their businesses by selling by post. A growth area has been department stores and fashion houses which have met the competition of the mail order firms by adopting this form of trading

themselves.

6.   **Exports.** It is possible to sell on a world basis, using overseas mailing lists and directories. Mainly, this will apply to sales to businesses or professionals whose names and addresses are available. He may use off-the-page advertisements in foreign publications.

From the customer's point of view, buying by post or telephone is popular because:

1.   **Original merchandise or services.** Many direct marketing firms offer goods exclusive to them, or which would be unknown to customers unless offered by these firms.

2.   **Pleasure.** Armchair shopping can be fun, customers indulging themselves in making effortless purchases from an attractive catalogue which is like having a shop brought into their home.

3.   **Convenience.** It is unnecessary to go into a shop, with all the problems of parking the car, or having to carry large items home by public transport. The goods are delivered to the door. Some people may not like shopping. This may seem a contradictory statement, since shopping can be a pleasure, and some people are addicted to shopping. Even so, there are others who dislike being jostled by crowds, or who are self-conscious about asking questions of counter assistants. There is also an ageing population, for whom direct marketing can be a boon. It is so simple to choose goods, make payment, and receive what has been ordered.

4.   **Price.** The goods may be cheaper than in the shops, and even the cost of postage or carriage may be worth paying because of the convenience mentioned above. There are often special price offers. Moreover, the prices are clearly stated whereas prices in the shops may not be known beforehand. For expensive items there are often attractive credit terms, maybe spread over a long time which makes purchase possible. Payment can often be made by charge or credit card.

5.   **Choice.** Catalogues offer an amazing choice, and one which may not be obvious when shopping. This is because of the compact, condensed and comprehensive nature of catalogues, and more than one catalogue can be compared. For instance, if seeds, bulbs or plants are being bought, every seedsman's or nurseryman's catalogue contains hundreds of varieties, often illustrated in colour. At the turn of a page at home on a winter's night the following year's garden can be planned and items ordered with pleasure and in comfort. It is unnecessary to drive miles to a garden centre and tramp around it to buy very expensive plants. Most of them cost little to grow from seed. The same choice applies to products and services as diverse as clothes, books, music tapes, collectibles (e.g. coins, stamps), motor-car accessories, investments and insurance. With some of the big catalogues it is possible to clothe a family and furnish a house.

DISADVANTAGES

While direct response marketing is popular because of the advantages discussed above there are certain disadvantages concerning both the trader and the customer as now outlined:

1.   **Skills.** It does require good organisation to promote, handle, pack and deliver, and this is a combination of skills which can sometimes defeat the inexperienced. For instance, for the smaller operator, it calls for an understanding of advertising on which money can be spent unwisely. It is also necessary to be a good buyer of merchandise, and to have the ability to identify and anticipate the market. Some quite large businesses have collapsed through faulty marketing.

2. **Despatch.** Large or small, the direct marketer depends on the various despatch systems, which also include the facility to return unwanted goods. Significantly, during the comparatively short postal strike of September 1988, many well-known firms had to lay off both packing and returned parcels department staff. A postal, railway or road carrier strike can produce great problems, including ones of cash flow. Traditional retailers are less likely to suffer from such disruptions to trade.

3. **Lack of inspection.** In spite of the attractions of armchair buying, and the realism of explicitly worded and well illustrated catalogues, sales resistance can result from inability to actually see and inspect the goods. An immense degree of trust is required. Can a customer be convinced that a pair of shoes will actually fit or that the knock-down do-it-yourself kit is easy to assemble? Some goods can be returned if not satisfactory, but that means re-packing them and taking the parcel to the Post Office, which may be a nuisance.

4. **Export problems.** If overseas sales are sought, this will require more complicated despatches and understanding of customs documentation, insurance and special postage rates. Cash-with-order will usually be necessary as it is difficult to offer credit and collect accounts from abroad. Payment may have to be specified in a particular currency, e.g. sterling. Some countries are best avoided because of foreign exchange problems, and advice should be sought from the Department of Trade or other sources of export information. It can be useless and costly to encourage enquiries from people in countries from which sterling cannot be exported, e.g. some African countries.

METHODS OF CONDUCTING DIRECT MARKETING

1. **Off-the-page selling.** This can operate in three ways. First, advertisements can be inserted in the press, illustrating and describing the goods (often in colour), with an order coupon. Second, catalogues can be offered or club organisers invited, as can be seen every week in advertisements in women's magazines and journals such as *TV Times*. Third, often with quite small advertisements, an item can be offered and response can produce a mailing list for direct mail offers in the future.

2. **Inserts.** Loose inserts can be tipped into magazines. There are conflicting schools of thought about inserts. They are resented by some readers who tip them out and discard them so that they can more conveniently read the journal. Yet, it has become an increasingly popular medium with advertisers, an insert usually enabling more to be said than in an advertisement on the page and costing less. The proof lies in the response and its cost effectiveness.

3. **Direct mail.** A great deal of direct response marketing is conducted postally. Direct mail has become the third largest medium in Britain. Because most of it is unsolicited and commercial it has earned the unfortunate name of junk mail. This is not helped when items are duplicated and triplicated because computerised mailing lists, containing variations in the same name and address, make de-duplication difficult. Direct mail shots can consist of:

(a) **Sales letters.** A common fault is that they are too long. Laser printing has, however, created some ingenious presentations such as the use of colours, different type faces, and the insertion of recipient's names in the body of the letter.

(b) **Catalogues.** These are usually well written, illustrated, designed and printed, and can resemble a printed shop.

(c) **Inserts.** Additional sales leaflets can be inserted, but too many separate items in the same envelope can be untidy and confusing. Which item is to be read first?

(d) **Order forms, cards.** While these can be included in catalogues it may be necessary to supply a separate means of ordering.

(e) **Gimmicks.** All kinds of novelties can be included with a mail shot to attract attention, create interest and stimulate response. Scratch cards, pop ups, miniature samples (e.g. of a newspaper or magazine) and use can be made of coins, keys and postage stamps.

(f) **Samples.** If the product lends itself to sampling, it can be a good idea to provide a sample which can be examined or tried.

(g) **Cash vouchers.** A money-off voucher - virtually a discount - can be used to encourage responses.

(h) **Special envelopes.** Choice of envelope, and the printing on it, may help to achieve a higher response. It depends on who opens the envelope. Is it a secretary, or a householder who picks it up off the mat? It is possible to sell 'off the envelope'. This works best if the mailing is expected or welcomed, but can be a turn-off if the mailing is regarded as junk mail. A number of envelope makers offer very attractive and ingenious envelopes, including see-through plastic envelopes which reveal, say, the cover of a catalogue.

(i) **One piece mailers.** These are mailing shots which are complete in themselves and may be in sheet or booklet form. A large sheet of paper can consist of panels of copy and fold down like a map to fit in a DL envelope. The advantage here is simplicity and compactness. There is a saving in printing costs, and one item can be more convenient for the recipient than a lot of loose items.

4. **Catalogues.** While these may be a part of the whole mailing shot, catalogues are a major direct response medium. They range from the big catalogues of the mail order club firms to the specialised ones from horticultural suppliers, book and record clubs, stamp and coin dealers, plus the catalogue of novelty merchandise from firms like Innovations and Kaleidoscope. There are also the gift catalogues, especially at Christmas, issued by charities and voluntary societies in order to raise funds.

Catalogues represent one of the most highly skilled areas of copywriting, illustration, design and printing. They have to overcome every possible demand or objection from the customer's standpoint, so that the customer can order correctly and with confidence and the trader can likewise supply promptly and correctly. It is a model of selling and distribution, and one of the best examples of the need for good marketing communications.

5. **Television.** There are two ways of using television for direct response marketing. One is to give a telephone number for orders, and that can be taken a stage further with a system of phoning the television company, making an order, and giving a credit card number. This information is computerised and fed to the supplier within 24 hours. The second method is to link the commercial with a press advertisement, nationally in, say, *TV Times* or regionally in an evening paper. The press advertisement gives fuller information and contains an order coupon. The first method has been used by record companies, the second by holiday and travel firms.

6.   **Mail-drops.** Another method, popular with local firms such as department stores, photo processors and building societies, is the door-to-door delivery of direct response offers. This is a low-cost method, and areas can be targeted (e.g. using ACORN), but can produce litter on the mat to which householders object. Nevertheless, as with loose inserts in magazines, it all depends on how interesting it is to the recipient.

7.   **Telemarketing.** Direct response trading can also be achieved by telephone, either through telephone ordering or telephone selling. The latter can be subject to abuse as when encyclopaedia salesmen pretend they are conducting research surveys, or the telephone is used to arrange appointments for home improvement services. Telephone selling probably works best with business-to-business propositions: people at home tend to resent out-of-hours commercial calls which invade their privacy. In the media world, a great deal of advertisement space and airtime is sold to advertisers and advertising agencies by telephone. The telephone is also used to follow up coupon enquiries where the enquirer is asked to give a number.

SPECIALISED SERVICES

The following services are available to direct response marketers:

1.   **Agencies.** There are advertising agencies which specialise in planning and handling direct response campaigns. They will conceive complete schemes, design catalogues and produce the advertising whatever the chosen medium. Some are principally specialised advertising agencies, especially where off-the-page selling is concerned, while others are direct mail houses which produce complete postal campaigns.

2.   **List brokers.** The mailing list is a vital element in direct mail. The trader may produce his own lists from sources like past customers and enquirers and directories and membership lists. He may buy or rent lists to other users. This is big business for organisations which have valuable lists. Such lists are actually advertised in *Direct Response* magazine. He can also rent lists from list brokers who deal in making lists.

3.   **Databases.** Some of the lists owned by organisations are on databases, and other traders can buy or rent these lists. For example, it is possible to buy the addresses of those who are on share registers, and with the big privatisation issues like British Gas and British Telecom, many thousands of shareholders are listed.

4.   **Fulfilment house.** This is a company which provides coupon handling, warehousing and despatch services for both sales promotion offers and direct response marketers. It may be noticed that the address on coupon offers or order forms is not that of the manufacturer or supplier. A direct response marketer can thus take advantage of a service that is mechanically equipped to handle the despatch of large numbers of orders.

5.   **Door-to-door distributors.** There are three kinds of door-to-door distributors. There are companies operating regionally or nationally which employ teams of people to deliver mail-drops to houses in specified areas. The Royal Mail has a similar service, using postmen. One of the best methods, and one of the quickest, is to use the services of free newspaper distributors.

SUMMARY

In this chapter direct response marketing was defined, followed by an explanation of the popularity of this form of trading and distribution from the points of view of both traders and customers. Some disadvantages were also commented on. Then the method of and the media for conducting sales by post or telephone were discussed. Finally, specialised services applicable to direct response marketing were explained.

PAST EXAMINATION QUESTIONS

Question 6, LCC Series 2, 1988

(i) Explain why direct response marketing has been so successful in spite of an abundance of retail shops.

(ii) Describe the advertising methods used to provide direct response marketing.

Comment

Here is a question which is very thoroughly answered within the content of this chapter.

Question 4, LCC Series 2, 1987

"Shopping without shops" or "direct response marketing" has become a major area of marketing. Describe four methods by which this kind of marketing are conducted.

Comment

Although there are four parts with equal marks it is wise to commence the answer with a definition. Four methods could be taken from off-the-page selling; catalogues; direct mail; television; mail drops and telemarketing as described in this chapter.

Question 9, LCC Spring 1986

Explain how direct response marketing uses:

(i) the press
(ii) direct mail
(iii) television

(iv) print
(v) the telephone.

Comment

The five parts require information similar to that in the previous question. 'Print' refers to all the printed promotional material or sales literature (referred to in the chapter under 3c, Methods of Conducting Direct Marketing).

Question 12, LCC Spring 1985

(i) What is 'direct response marketing'?
(ii) How are computers used in this form of marketing?
(iii) What advertising methods are used to achieve direct response sales?
(iv) Outline an actual or imaginary direct marketing campaign.

Comment

There are four parts with equal marks. The first part requires a definition. The second part draws on information about computers in this and other chapters, including inventory control. The third part is well covered by this chapter. For the fourth part, a mini-case study is required of a campaign with which the candidate is familiar, or one can be invented on the basis of the candidate's understanding of the subject.

Model answer

(i) Direct response marketing is the selling of goods or services without shops, usually by post or telephone. It has been called 'shopping without shops' or 'retailing without stores' and is the modern name for mail order trading.

(ii) Computers are used in the following ways in direct response marketing:

(a) To handle receipt of orders and to record details of customers, their purchases, payment and delivery, and to process instructions to warehouse for despatch (despatch notes) and invoices or receipted invoices or statements of account.

(b) To effect stock control, recording stock levels, signalling re-ordering requirements, and maintaining inventory control.

(c) To maintain mailing lists on data-bases, and for print out of addresses for direct mail campaigns.

(d) By television companies for receiving and forwarding orders to advertisers.

(iii) The following advertising methods can be used:

(a) Off-the-page press advertisements, containing coupon order forms.

(b) Inserts tipped into magazines.

(c) Direct mail, using sales letters, catalogues, order forms, sales literature, gimmicks, and sometimes with special shape or printed envelopes.

(d) Catalogues - from huge club catalogues to pocket size ones.

(e) Sales literature for inclusion in mailings.

(f) Television commercials, with computerised ordering or tie-up with press advertisements.

(g) Door-to-door mail drops.

(iv) A typical direct response campaign could be one of those run by the Automobile Association to promote books of maps, or an insurance scheme, or a catalogue of goods of interest to motorists.

The mailing list would consist of either all or a selection of the thousands of members of the AA, all of whom would be held on a database. They could be selected according to the type of offer, e.g. all those who had bought a 5-star holiday insurance package could be offered a book of maps of Europe.

The offer would come with the reputation of an organisation familiar to members and respected by them. A member would expect the service or merchandise to be of good quality, thus encouraging confidence and response.

The campaign would consist of an envelope bearing the name of the AA, which would attract attention and interest. The mail shot would contain a sales letter, catalogue or sales literature, and an order form (which could be printed in the catalogue or literature).

Payment could be by cheque or credit card.

(NB. This question does not require a long essay-style answer, and if points are set out neatly in list form it will be easy for the examiner to see that the candidate is well-informed.)

Part 4: Promotion and public relations

This important section brings together what is sometimes loosely called 'promotion'. They are not all quite the same thing, but they contribute to the final success of the marketing strategy. The finest product, the cleverest packaging, the right price, the efficient distribution and so on will all fail if the customer does not know that the product or service exists and has faith in its performance or value for money or the reputation of its maker or supplier.

Chapter 11 shows how advertising carries the sales message to millions of strangers, and justifies the expenditure of vast sums of money on advertising. The world simply will not beat a path to the better mousetrap, to quote an old saying. On the whole, the world doesn't want to know.

Chapter 12 deals with public relations which should not be confused with advertising and has a role of its own. However, advertising can be a waste of money if public relations is lacking.

Sales promotion, like direct response marketing, is a modern growth area of marketing, but there have been interesting changes which are discussed in this Chapter.

Sponsorship is very big business today, and several companies owe their trading success to the skilful use of sponsorship. Chapter 14 shows how sponsorship can help marketing.

Finally, in Chapter 15, we look at some of the special techniques used to market industrial goods. Here we have to consider smaller more specialised markets where mass promotional methods do not apply.

11.   What is the role of advertising?

INTRODUCTION

Advertising will be defined first. Next, there will be a description of the value of advertising. Then the subject will be divided into its three facets, the advertiser, the advertising agency and the media. The activities of each, and their interrelation, will be explained. Advertising will be seen to be the life-blood of the marketing strategy, many aspects of which such as branding, pricing and distribution being associated.

DEFINITION

Two definitions are given with explanatory notes. The first is that of the Advertising Association which is a federation of advertising organisations, and the second comes from the Institute of Practitioners in Advertising which is the professional body of the advertising agencies.

Advertising is the means of making known in order to sell goods or services.

This is a simple omnibus definition which is useful because it shows an extension beyond 'making known' (e.g. the name of a street) in order to achieve the purpose of 'selling'. Advertising is therefore a part of marketing but, as will be explained in the next chapter, it is different from public relations with which it should not be confused. Public relations also makes known, but for a different purpose as will be explained later.

Advertising presents the most persuasive possible selling message to the right prospects for the product or service at the lowest possible cost.

This is a more positive definition, but it is more closely related to the role of the advertising agency as will be seen if the parts are analysed.

Advertising is very much to do with *persuading* people to act as the advertiser wishes. This may be to fill in a coupon or to visit a shop and buy the product or service, to telephone for more information, or to send cash and make a purchase, but it could be just to remember the name when next making a purchase. The *most persuasive selling message* means creating persuasive advertisements through words and pictures.

The *right prospects* refers to a combination of marketing research to find out who they are, or the choice of the correct segment of likely buyers, coupled with the careful selection of media which will reach them.

At the lowest possible cost requires not only the right media but the most economical media which will then reach the largest number of potential buyers at the lowest possible cost. To do this, circulation and readership figures together with advertisement rates will be compared on a cost per thousand circulation or readership basis, and with avoidance of duplication.

Creativity, marketing research and media planning and buying go hand in hand.

THE VALUE OF ADVERTISING

A stall-holder in a street-market can shout his wares to passers-by, and he has direct contact with his customers. A manufacturer is selling to thousands of customers scattered throughout the country and perhaps the world. Advertising is his means of shouting his wares to all these people who cannot be seen and who are unknown. The same applies to service industries, and even to retailers who do have personal contact when customers are in the shop - but they have to be attracted to the shop, whether it be by media advertising, window bills or window displays. Inside the shop, customers have to be attracted by point-of-sale displays, while in a super-market the package has to be the on-the-spot advertisement.

The Advertising Association publishes reports and forecasts of advertising expendi-ture. For 1989, advertising expenditure was estimated to be nearly £ 7 billion, or about 1.8 per cent of the gross domestic product, that is the total value of the net domestic output of national production units. This expenditure has been rising annually. To give some idea of the expenditure on advertising, News International (which publishes *The Sun* and the *News of the World*) spent £ 40.9m on television advertising alone in the year to July 1988.

Advertising is obviously very big business. Is this expenditure justified, bearing in mind that it has to be paid for by the customer in the price he pays for advertised goods or ser-vices? Is advertising necessary? Could not prices be reduced if there was less or no advertising?

It comes back to 'making known'. Without advertising, consumers would not know of the existence of the goods and services they buy. They would not know of the choices that exist. They would also quickly forget even 'household names' if advertising was discontinued.

For instance, a Labour government insisted that certain brands of detergent should not be advertised and that their prices should be reduced. Those brands have disappeared because they were not bought. Such products - the fmcg kind - are priced as low as they are (however expensive they *seem* to be!) because sales depend on volume production and economies of scale. Advertising maintains both demand in the shop and output at the factory. Factories have to be closed down when sales fall off. Actually, the cost of advertising per unit - litre of petrol

or a can of beans - is tiny. The huge expendi-tures on advertising are related to huge sales (e.g. *The Sun* sells over four million copies, and circulation has to be maintained as well as increased if advertisement space is to be sold at a certain rate).

Advertising is thus bound up in the econo-mics of production, selling and profitability. It makes the business world go round and bene-fits the consumer who is able not only to enjoy what is advertised but to have a very wide choice of things to buy.

Evidence of this will be seen in poorer or less developed countries where there is little advertising compared with industrialised count-ries. For example, advertising is gradually increasing in both Russia and China as more consumer goods become available. The people have to be told that they exist and where they can be bought. The same happened in Britain a hundred years ago when factories were develop-ing, towns were growing, more shops were opening and popular newspapers like the *Daily Mail* were appearing.

This is not to say that all advertising is perfect and that there are no abuses of it. But advertising is a tool. There is nothing wrong with the tool. However, if the tool is misused that is the fault of the user. Advertisers, not advertising, are to blame for imperfections in its use.

There are more than 100 laws concerning advertising. The *British Code of Advertising Practice* is administered by the Advertising Standards Authority. The ASA invites members of the public to report offences against the British Code of Advertising Practice. Investi-gations are held and reports are published monthly for all to see free of charge in the ASA *Reports*. It does not pay to be investigated by the ASA and to have this published, whether or not the complaint was upheld. These self-regulating controls can either prevent mis-leading advertising, or quickly control it. This can be more effective than legal controls since it may take years before a case comes to court, by which time the advertisement has become irrelevant.

In Chapter 8, reference was made to *adequate distribution* and it is worth repeating here than an advertising campaign will fail to sell if there is not adequate distribution *in advance* to match the demand created by the advertising. Conversely, it is not surprising that distributors are most likely to take stock if there is promise of advertising to support it. Thus, advertising enters into the total planning of production, selling and distribution, and campaigns have to be planned, created and media booked many months in advance. This somewhat contradicts the 4Ps concept.

THE ADVERTISER

Companies which advertise frequently, and with differently worded advertisements often placed at short notice, such as big tour operators, department stores and large supermarket chains, will be justified in having a fully staffed advertising department resembling an advertising agency.

However, the majority of companies, when their expenditure is high enough to require both outside creative and media buying talents and facilities and is an economic proposition to an advertising agency, will engage the services of an advertising agency. This will be dealt with again in the section on the agency.

Advertising will be the responsibility of the advertising manager, who may operate under various titles such as product or brand manager and sometimes marketing services manager. In an industrial company which may use little advertising but much public relations, advertising may be handled by the public relations, communications or marketing communications manager. There is, unfortunately, a confusing array of job titles. Possibly, there may be no separate executive, and the marketing manager alone will be responsible for advertising.

Advertising will usually be divided into *above-the-line* advertising which includes press, radio, television, cinema and outdoor media, and *below-the-line* advertising which includes other media and activities such as exhibitions, sales literature, point-of-sale displays, direct mail and sponsorships. Sales promotion may also be included in the latter, although it can be a separate operation and the tendency is to regard it as a marketing rather than an advertising activity, and there may be a separate sales promotion executive.

Generally, the advertising agency will handle the above-the-line media of press, radio, television, cinema and outdoor, and the rest will be conducted in-house. However, as will be shown in the agency section, there are specialised agencies which handle certain below-the-line services. There are also the newer agencies which offer *through-the-line* services and cover everything as a complete service.

THE PRODUCT MANAGER

The in-house executive, who for the sake of simplicity will now be called the product manager, is responsible for:

1. **Conveying company policy to the advertising manager.** This may concern sales targets, market segments - nowadays often called 'niche marketing' - and perhaps the style of the advertising. Should it be aggressive or subtle; contribute to the corporate image; compete with particular rivals; and are there areas of the country where advertising should be strongest and so on?

2. **Controlling the budget.** This is not easy because costs can change. A campaign may be planned six months in advance and run for six months and with inflation constant it may be hard to keep within a contingency fund. Nevertheless, the product manager is the paymaster to his superiors, and he has to be vigilant in approving

agency bills. Again, this is not easy because, for cash flow reasons, an agency cannot wait until the campaign is completed before billing the client. Bills will therefore be rendered as costs are incurred, with the final cost out of sight.

The media usually expect payment within 30 days. Production charges can, for instance, be higher than expected, and this can happen when changes are made at the proof stage instead of when copy and visuals were submitted. Budgetary control is therefore a critical part of the product manager's job. He may have to curtail some advertising to stay within budget.

3.   **Approving creative work.** He will be responsible for approving all artwork, copy and proofs from the advertising agency or any other suppliers.

4.   **Liaison with account executive.** He will represent his company in all negotiations with the advertising agency account executive, from the initial planning stage to the appearance of advertisements.

5.   **Checking appearance of advertisements.** He will check that advertisements and commercials have appeared correctly as booked including dates, positions and quality of reproduction. This is important because advertisements can appear wrongly, and it may be necessary to negotiate a refund or re-appearance.

6.   **Buying materials, services.** He has to be a knowledgeable and expert buyer of numerous materials and services such as artwork, photography, print, exhibition spaces and stands, video productions, premium merchandise for sales promotion schemes, and the services of various suppliers and consultants. He may use other consultants for, say, new product development, packaging design, marketing research, sales promotion or sponsorships.

7.   **Public relations.** Ideally, there will be a separate public relations manager, but the advertising manager may also be responsible for public relations.

All this calls for considerable knowledge of technicalities and sources of supply, plus ability to manage, buy and control. The success of the advertising agency's work for the company will depend very much on the excellence of his working relationship with the account executive, and of his understanding of how an advertising agency works.

THE ADVERTISING AGENCY

Advertising agencies have existed for nearly 200 years, but originally they were commission brokers for the early newspapers, earning commission on the space they sold the advertisers. Legally, they remain agents of the media and *not* of their clients, and it is the legally accepted 'custom of the trade' that the 'agent acts as principal'. This means that the agent is legally responsible for the payment of bills, even if the client goes bankrupt.

Agency 'recognition' does not mean that an agency is approved by any trade or professional body, nor does it express approval of its competence. It refers to the 'commission system', an agency being recognised for commission purposes by the various organisations representing newspaper, magazine, radio and television media owners (e.g. the Newspaper Publishers Association, Newspaper Society, Periodical Publishers Association, Association of Independent Radio Contractors and the Independent Television Association).

After the monopoly ruling of the Office of Fair Trading in 1979 (under the Restrictive Trade Practices Act 1976) the recognising bodies were no longer permitted to guarantee a standard rate of commission, and this is now negotiable between agencies and media. Recognition now consists of two requirements only: (i) *creditworthiness*, i.e. ability to pay promptly; and

(ii) *acceptance of the British Code of Advertising Practice.*

The effect of the commission system is that the media bills the agency, say, £ 850 for £ 1,000 of space (representing 15% commission) and the agency bills the client for £ 1,000, thus earning the commission. The client does not pay the agency 15% since it would have to pay the media £ 1,000 if the space was bought direct. Out of the commission the agency provides the time of account executive, services such as buying media and print, and very often copywriting, and takes its profit. The client gets all these services free of charge (or is virtually subsidised by the media) but pays for the media, artwork, photography, typesetting, production of commercials, and other physical costs.

However, there are variations on this. The commission is usually inadequate, and a surcharge is added, bringing the income up to 17½%, or commission is rebated and net charges are made and service fees are charged. A service fee is more professional since it represents the time spent on the account and the quality of the expertise, as with public relations consultancy fees. The commission system is not very relevant to modern business conditions.

Some 265 agencies and member companies (media independents) belong to the Institute of Practitioners in Advertising, representing about 80 per cent of agency business, although some 500 agencies are listed in *Advertisers Annual.*

Agencies developed from being merely space brokers by providing creative services as printing became more sophisticated and it became possible to use various sizes of type and to reproduce pictures. The early press advertisements were simply lines and lines of type of the same size. Now the agencies were able to compete for business by actually writing, laying out and illustrating advertisements, and so the service agency developed. A full service agency can be demonstrated by the chart below.

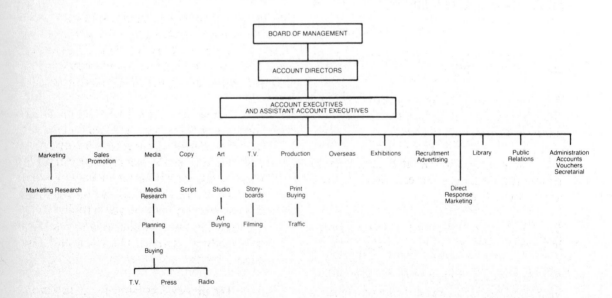

Figure 1 Departments of a full service advertising agency. Structures and services may vary between one agency and another. For instance, public relations may be conducted by a separate subsidiary company, probably with a different business name. Again, a separate subsidiary may handle marketing research, recruitment advertising or direct response marketing. Alternatively, a "through-the-line" agency will also deal with below-the-line advertising.

THE ACCOUNT EXECUTIVE

A client is called an 'account', and the agency representative who works in liaison with the client (e.g. the product manager) is generally called the *account executive*. His job amounts to:

1. Obtaining the client brief and presenting it to the agency department heads.

   Some agencies operate a plans board system of meetings between department heads under the chairmanship of the account executives. Others use a review board system where a proposed scheme is reviewed by agency executives not connected with it. Some agencies operate a group system for big accounts, the group consisting of the account executive and a visualiser, copywriter, media buyer and perhaps a television producer. Such a group might spend many months preparing an advertising campaign for a new product with a multi-million pound advertising budget such as for a new motor-car.

2. Making a presentation to the client of the agency proposals.

3. Supervising the agency production of the campaign in accordance with the client's policy and wishes.

4. Presenting the client from time to time with media schedules, copy, artwork and proofs for approval.

5. Dealing with payment of account problems if the client is a slow payer.

6. Producing a report at the end of the year, and seeking renewal of the account.

All meetings are reported in *progress reports* which are very brief minutes, setting out decisions. On the right hand side of the report is a narrow column separated from the report by a vertical line. In this column will be written personal responsibilities (on the client or agency side) relevant to each item in the minutes). Thus, if the minute read "The client approved the copy and layout for the new catalogue", the instruction in the right-hand column might read "AG to supply proofs", AG being the initials of the account executive. These progress reports are filed in the *facts book,* and provide the basis for writing a report on the year's work for the client. The account executive is responsible for writing progress reports.

The account executive needs to be a good all-rounder who can work with both the client and the agency departments to produce an harmonious and satisfactory agency-client relationship. With large accounts it can be a day-to-day liaison. He is not just a go between. He has to understand both how his agency works and how his client's business works.

AGENCY SPECIALISTS

One of the advantages of using an agency is that it is a team of skilled specialists whose services can be shared by a client for whom it would be uneconomical to employ them full time. The following are some of these specialists:

1. **Visualiser.** He may be called the art director and his task is to produce rough sketches of proposed advertisements. These are called visuals, scamps or scribbles, and a design can be approved at this rough stage before final artwork is produced. The *lay-out man* lays out the advertisement with typesetting instructions as an exact plan of the advertisement. The wording is produced by the *copywriter*.

2. **The production manager** or **traffic controller** acts as a progress chaser to see that the sequence of creative work, proofing, proof correction and final despatch of the advertisement to the media occurs so that the advertisement actually appears on time and as planned.

3. **The media planner** plots proposed media schedules with dates, times, sizes and rates to fit the campaign and the budget. The **media buyer** (or space buyer and airtime buyer) actually books the press space or radio/television airtime, negotiating for the best dates, spaces, times and rates.

4. **Television producer.** When the agency is responsible for television commercials there is an agency *producer* who prepares the idea for the commercial, and then employs an outside *director* and film or video production company to make it. The producer will also commission musicians to write *jingles* and be involved in the casting of actors and actresses to make *presentations* or provide *voice overs*.

Two special terms should be understood. A *storyboard* is a cartoon version (in television screen shapes) of the sequence of action or scenes in a proposed television commercial. A *voucher* is a free copy of a publication supplied by the publisher to show proof of the appearance of the advertisement.

DIFFERENT KINDS OF AGENCY

In recent years the agency world has changed considerably, and many new or specialised types of agency now operate. They are:

1. **Full-service agency.** This has been described already. A number are of American origin and operate internationally, e.g. J Walter Thompson which ranks as number three agency in the UK, number one (in billings) being the British agency group Saatchi and Saatchi. Rankings and billings vary as accounts come and go. On a world basis Saatchi and Saatchi were, in 1988, fifth-ranking with a combined $63.7 million billings total. The latest figures and rankings appear from time to time in the weekly trade journal, *Campaign*. Current campaigns

are detailed and illustrated every week in *Campaign* and students are recommended to study them in their college or public library.

2. **A la carte agency.** Evolving from the 'hot shop' creative agency there is the à la carte agency which concentrates on creating advertising campaigns, and also special short-term assignments such as creating a corporate identity (e.g. logo, typography, house colour, livery, uniforms etc).

This kind of agency does not require 'recognition' because it does no media buying. Moreover, removal of the 'recognition' requirement has enabled small units to be set up with less capital than was required by agencies needing considerable cash flow in order to buy space and airtime and to qualify for 'creditworthiness'. Under the old agency recognition system, an agency had to have a certain volume of business spread over at least three accounts before it could apply to the media bodies for recognition. This requirement is not necessary to set up an a la carte agency.

3. **Media independent.** Since the 70s, agencies devoted to media planning and buying have become known as media independents. They have their own organisation, the Association of Media Independents, although some belong to the IPA. Some advertisers prefer to use a separate à la carte agency for creative work and a media independent for media buying. This may seem a clumsy arrangement when both services can be provided by a traditional agency, but the tendency is for the media independents to prosper. It is argued that they and the à la carte agencies give better service. There are a few big advertisers which buy their own media direct and use only à la carte agencies.

4. **Through-the-line agencies.** There has

been a development of agencies which offer every kind of media and creative service, not distinguishing between above and below-the-line. This is an old idea which has been revived.

5.   **Third Wave agencies.** As the original à la carte agencies have grown in size, almost resembling full service agencies, a new breed of smaller à la carte agencies has emerged. They claim to be able to give a more intimate service and work more closely with clients.

6.   **Specialised agencies.** A number of agencies exist which handle particular classes of work such as new product development, marketing, direct response marketing, recruitment advertising, sales promotion, corporate identity schemes and sponsorship. There are also direct mail houses which create and conduct direct mail campaigns.

All these changes reflect the varied needs of advertisers and the opportunities that exist for those with special knowledge and skills to sell their expertise. The day when the big agency could pretend to do everything is clearly challenged by the emergence of new teams of specialists, while many of the big agencies themselves have set up subsidiary companies capable of providing extra services.

On the fringe of all this are numerous suppliers of particular services such as business incentives, video production, merchandise for sales promotion, list broking and databases for direct mail, specialist printers of promotional items, and organisers of conferences and exhibitions.

ADVERTISING MEDIA

Advertising media are going through great changes, partly because of technological developments and partly because the market has become more and more fragmented as the expression 'niche marketing' suggests. Newspapers and magazines exist which appeal to all kinds of new interests and market segments, or which provide vehicles for the promotion of new products and services.

There are more than 200 computer magazines, and several journals which appeal to investors, while the womens magazines have become more varied than ever before. Television faces tremendous competition from satellite and other alternatives like VCRs and home computers. To some extent the so-called mass market has become less mass, and there are trends towards the de-massification of the media.

One of the technological influences has been the desertion of Fleet Street and its old letterpress printed newspapers to printing plants in the East End, or the use of contract printers in the regions, using offset-litho presses which produce better quality newspapers more economically. All this has ranged over the success of *The Independent*, colour in a number of newspapers such as *Today* and the *Daily Mirror* and the introduction by the *Daily Mail* of an even better printing process, flexography. In the past flexography was used for printing on delicate materials like foil for confectionery wrappings, but it has been developed for good quality newspaper production. It uses photo-polymer plates and fast drying or water-based inks brighter than offset-litho inks.

This section is preceded by the above remarks because the ever-changing media scene is a challenge to any student of advertising. It is necessary to watch what is going on because in many respects it is concerned with those parts of the IPA definition which speak of *presenting the most persuasive selling message* and doing so *to the right prospects* and *at the lowest possible cost*. Modern media makes all three more and more feasible.

Advertising media can be divided into two classes, *above-the-line* and *below-the-line*. These are artificial divisions, and the implication is not that one is superior to the other. They are becoming out-dated but the distinction was really between those media which paid agencies commission and were a major source of agency income, and those which did not. With agencies moving over to fee income, the distinction becomes transparent. However, we shall begin by describing the characteristics of the five so-called above-the-line media, and continue with descriptions of others.

PRESS

The press consists of all publications which are produced periodically whether it be daily, weekly, monthly, quarterly or annually, and they extend from newspapers and magazines to directories and year books. In the UK there are, according to *Benn's Media Directory* for 1988, the following publications:

Daily & Sunday newspapers	133
Weekly newspapers	784
Local free newspapers	931
Periodicals	
Trade, Technical, Professional	5,408
Consumer and specialist consumer	2,323
Free consumer magazines	469
Directories etc	2,128
Total	12,176

Some of the trade, technical and professional magazines are *controlled circulation* and are distributed to selected readers, with some requested circulation, free of charge. From an advertiser's point of view, cc journals can offer greater penetration of a market than that gained by journals which have a paid for circulation. When a journal is purchased it is said to have a *cover price*. Local free newspapers are delivered door-to-door and have saturation coverage of certain areas unlike paid-for local weeklies. Free consumer magazines may be posted, delivered door-to-door or given out in the street.

Daily morning and evening and Sunday newspapers may be national or regional, and there are about 100 regional titles.

One of the most interesting changes of recent years has been the enhanced status of the Saturday morning newspaper which used to have a smaller circulation because those not working on a Saturday did not buy a morning paper on the way to work. Gradually, the Saturday paper gained circulation as it contained more home interest news.

In 1988, some newspapers produced Saturday magazines or moved colour magazines from Sunday to Saturday. Meanwhile, popular as well as the more serious Sundays produced magazine supplements at the weekend of which *Mail on Sunday's You* magazine was particularly successful. This trend was not limited to London nationals but included Scottish newspapers. These magazines offer advertisers well-produced full-colour advertising, and they are popular for direct response marketing campaigns.

Social Grade	Newspapers
A (3%)	The Times, Financial Times
B (15%)	Daily Telegraph, The Guardian, The Independent
C¹ (23%)	Daily Mail, Daily Express, Today
C², D, E (60%)	The Sun, Daily Mirror, Daily Star

Figure 2 Social Grade readership of British national dailies, a breakdown peculiar to the British press and found nowhere else in the world. A similar breakdown can be applied to Sunday newspapers.

In other countries newspapers are read by different political, religious, language or ethnic groups. There will be Communist and Conservative, Catholic and Protestant and, say, Indian, Chinese and Malaysian readers. In the USA, newspapers are regarded constitutionally as the fourth estate, that is, as part of the democratic process. A very different situation occurs in Britain. In the 19th century, newspapers tended to be Liberal or Conservative. Today, they mostly belong to the commercial empires of Murdoch, Maxwell and Stevens, and as Fig 2 indicates British national dailies represent certain social classes.

The press remains the premier medium, and throughout the world the number of publications and the size of circulations increase. There have been fluctuations in Western societies, with famous publications disappearing but others have been launched. The use of satellites has made it possible for some newspapers to have continental and international circulations, e.g. the *International Herald Tribune, Wall Street Journal* and *USA Today*. Some parts of the world, such as the Gulf states, have seen a rapid growth in newspaper production in recent years. Why are newspapers so popular and successful, and especially valuable as advertising media? The following are some of the main reasons:

(i)   **In depth coverage** of topics which is not always possible on radio and television.

(ii) **Portability.** A journal can be carried about and read anywhere.

(iii) **Special readerships.** There are publications on every reader interest.

(iv) **Permanency.** Copies can be retained for future reference. Back numbers can be seen on library files, including issues dating back for decades on microfilm.

(v)   **Databases** hold extracts from publications.

(vi) **Price.** Most people can afford them, and if they cannot there are many libraries with reading rooms where the public can read newspapers and magazines. Many journals also enjoy pass-on readership or are seen in reception and reading rooms.

TELEVISION

Television enjoys the advantages of movement,

sound, colour and realism and it takes advertising into the home where it is seen in an entertainment situation. However, television advertising has certain disadvantages in that, unlike the press, it is ephemeral, and it disrupts the entertainment. Nevertheless, the quality of many commercials is highly professional, and commercials can become popular in their own right. Audiences can run into millions so that television advertising can be a powerful way of advertising fmcgs to the mass market.

Even so, there have been changes in recent years in the products or services advertised. No longer is it the medium reserved for detergents, magarines, beers, toothpastes and pet foods. The newer advertisers include motor-car manufacturers, insurance and pension schemes, share offers during privatisation flotations, home computers, airlines and cruises.

In Britain, commercials can be shown on *one* of the 15 regional channels, or on Channel Four, on a *selection* of regions, or *networked* nationally. Advertisements tend to be short (because of both cost and limited availability of time), and they are restricted to two-minute commercial breaks or to about six minutes in any one hour.

The television day is broken down into segments, and rates vary according to the popularity of the segments. The TV companies sell packages covering all segments, otherwise there would be excessive demand for the prime times.

Commercials appear only on ITV stations, the BBC being non-commercial. Sponsored television, when the advertiser sponsors the programme, is not permitted in Britain, but sponsored television is common in some countries, especially in the Third World.

SATELLITE TELEVISION

Satellite television offers competition with that of commercial television stations, and this may be received by cable television or direct by personal earth station dishes. An interesting aspect of satellite television is that advertisements can be broadcast beyond national frontiers, a prospect for Eurobrands and the single market envisaged for Europe after 1992.

RADIO

In many countries of the world, commercial radio has been the only kind of radio, and it has operated there since the earliest days of broadcasting, perhaps for sixty or seventy years as in the USA and Canada. In Britain, commercial radio from British stations did not arrive until 1972. Previously, the only commercial radio received in Britain was from continental stations like Radio Luxembourg, or illegal private radio stations operating off-shore.

Local radio stations cover smaller areas than regional television and its advertising tends to be more local. It appeals to different audiences at different times of the day such as commuting motorists, housewives at home, workers in factories and young people.

Commercials are inexpensive to produce, and by comparison with television advertisement rates are modest. Commercials depend on impactive voices, music and sound effects, but lack the vision, movement and colour of television.

OUTDOOR

Outdoor advertising consists chiefly of posters, painted and illuminated signs, and advertisements at bus shelters and on litter bins and parking meters. Aerial advertising with tethered balloons, airships, and banners trailed behind aircraft can also be included.

Transportation advertising is usually separated from general outdoor advertising, and includes advertising in and on public transport vehicles and premises including buses, taxis, trains, airliners, ships and on underground railway systems.

The special characteristics of outdoor advertising are size, colour, brief copy and repetition since the same advertisement appears on many sites and is displayed for at least a week and often for up to three months. Transportation advertising (which can be more wordy inside vehicles or premises) reaches not only the travelling public but, when on vehicles, travels among audiences. A feature of this is the bus painted on behalf of a single advertiser.

CINEMA

With the passing of the big three-thousand seater cinemas, and frequent attendance, this medium has diminished but has not entirely disappeared. The makers of television commercials will often make longer versions for the cinema. Commercials are also shown in Forces cinemas, on ships and in airliners. Cinema advertising does enjoy a captive audience, even more so than television. Audiences tend to be young whereas television audiences are generally older.

EXHIBITION

There are indoor and outdoor, public and trade exhibitions and this is a very old medium which has a certain entertainment appeal. People enjoy attending exhibitions. This medium has the advantage of being able to physically present products and services which can be seen, examined and often tested. There is also the personal touch with demonstrators and representatives to talk to. Moreover, new products can be seen, and comparisons can be made on the spot between rival products. Big exhibitions like the *Daily Mail* Ideal Home Exhibition are held annually.

DIRECT MAIL

The principal advantage of direct mail is that unlike most media where the advertising is broadcast to whoever may read, see or hear it, direct mail can be directed to specific, named recipients. It can therefore be a very economical medium with control over quantities and timing, and ability to measure response. It depends on two things: a good mailing shot such as a sales letter and enclosures, and an up-to-date reliable mailing list. This medium has already been discussed in Chapter 10 as one of the media of direct response marketing.

However, it is not limited to direct response marketing: it can be an important means of conducting trade advertising with retailers. It is frequently used in the selling of press advertisement space, airtime, exhibition space, and the services of suppliers to the advertising industry such as printers and photographers.

POINT-OF-SALE

Point-of-sale or point-of-purchase display material varies in value according to how well and how long it can be displayed. In supermarkets space does not permit the window, counter, floor and shelf displays that are possible in, say, a wine merchants, chemists, newsagents or travel agency. Used well, POS material can be very effective, but its distribution and usage has to be controlled otherwise expensive material will be wasted.

A problem can be short seasonal use. A showcard for a garden product might be displayed for only a month whereas a model of an airliner could remain on permanent display at a travel agency.

This is a medium which has to be costed, planned and controlled carefully. Part of that control can be in the way material is *offered* (e.g. in a descriptive mail shot with a request form) and is *placed* (e.g. by the visiting sales representative putting it in position or encouraging the retailer to use it).

Some typical forms of POS material are:

(i)   **Showcards.** These can be strutted or suspended and made of card or metal.

(ii)   **Posters.** They may be called bills and are usually crown or double crown size (381 x 508 mm and 508 x 762 mm). Famous posters like those of Coca-Cola and KLM are often found displayed in public places quite apart from places of sale while Guinness posters have become collectors' pieces.

(iii) **Mobiles.** These do lend themselves to displays in supermarkets as they are suspended from the ceiling. Attention is attracted by the movement of the suspended items.

(iv)   **Display outers.** These are the cartons in which small units such as confectionery arrive, and they can be opened up and the lid folded back to make a dispenser and display piece for placing on the counter or shelf.

(v)   **Shelf edging.** This is a simple way of exploiting the edges of shelves which face the customer standing at the counter or bar.

(vi)   **Dummy packs.** These save using real packs for display purposes, and also prevent deterioration of products if placed in the window. They are particularly useful for displays in the shop windows of smaller retailers, since the actual products will be displayed on the shelves in supermarkets.

(vii) **Display stands.** There are many forms of display stands - wire, metal, wood and plastic stands, glass-doored cabinets, velvet padded display units, dumpers and dump bins and so on which may be particularly suitable for displaying paperback books and newspapers, confectionery, clocks and watches, or packets and cans as the case may be.

They draw attention, isolate a product, invite purchase and monopolise display space when the product might otherwise be buried in the general merchandise of the shop. Some units have special utility value like the refrigerator supplied by the ice-cream manufacturer, or the metal rack which holds bottles of liquid.

(viii) **Models** of all kinds can be permanent display pieces. They may be trade figures like the Black and White whisky dogs or the White Horse whisky horse, or replicas of aircraft, ships, coaches and motor-cars, or working models which demonstrate the product. The latter could be something amusing like a life-size model of a baby elephant bouncing up and down in an armchair to show how well it is sprung.

A product manager's ingenuity will no doubt produce other forms of POS material.

Below-the-line media can extend into almost anything that can carry an advertisement and could be useful in a particular campaign. Carrier bags, wrapping paper, price tags, clothing such as caps and T-shirts, and numerous give-aways from key rings to diaries and calendars, may be included.

SELLING MEDIA

The advertising agency does not just ring up and order space and airtime. Nor do publishing and broadcasting companies, poster contractors and exhibition organisers sit waiting for the phone to ring. Media may be empty space, future time, blank poster sites or empty stand space - a seemingly nebulous 'product' - but it has sales value. This value is a mixture of how many people are likely to have the opportunity of seeing, hearing, passing or in some way being aware of it, and how much it is worth to an advertiser to address his sales message to these people.

Whether it be a space in a national newspaper with a multi-million circulation, or whether it is the back of a deckchair on Blackpool beach or a postcard in the local shop window, it has a value on which a price or an *advertisement rate* can be placed. Like the price of anything else, that price will follow the whims of supply and demand. Television airtime rates have become grossly inflated because there is very limited time available, especially during peak viewing times, worsened by a system of virtually selling airtime to the highest bidder in a gazumping fashion known as pre-empting. There is not this sort of scramble to buy space on the backs of deckchairs on Blackpool beach.

On the whole, media are not 'expensive' when they represent value for money. If a newspaper has a circulation of four million it may be expected that space in it will cost much more than in another newspaper which sells only 400,000 copies. Costs are relative.

The media will, of course, seek to exploit the greatest value by charging the highest rates for it. Quite apart from the statistics of circulation and readership, a premium will be charged for certain 'special positions' which attract more or particular readers. Likewise, a discount will be given for booking a series.

Media owners set out their charges in a *rate-card* which gives the cost of spaces or time segments, together with technical details of production, and dates for supply of advertisements. These rate cards are reproduced monthly in *British Rate and Data*.

There is great competition between the sellers of space, air time, sites and other media.

Selling is organised like that for any other product, with a sales manager (perhaps termed *Advertisement Manager*), and a team of sales representatives who call on agencies and advertisers.

Great use is made of direct mail, with the aid of dummy and specimen copies of the journal, or announcements about future broadcasting plans. There are always special issues and programmes which can be used to sell space or air-time. Many of the statistics published by the ABC, JICNARS and BARB can be exploited in favour of a medium.

Advertisements are also placed in trade journals such as *Campaign, Marketing* and *Marketing Week.*

The media *selling* side is therefore just as important an aspect of advertising as the media *buying,* and the media are themselves involved in a marketing operation on their own behalf.

SUMMARY

Advertising was defined and it was seen that the objective of advertising was to persuade in order to sell. The ability of advertising to take the sales message to distant markets of unknown buyers was explained. Having discussed the value and importance of advertising as a vital element in the marketing mix, and reiterating the need for adequate distribution if advertising was to succeed, the chapter dealt with the three facets of advertising.

These were the advertiser, the advertising agency and the media. Each was analysed with particular reference to the roles of the advertising manager or product manager, the account executive and the advertisement manager. It was finally pointed out that the media are selling a product like any other.

PAST EXAMINATION QUESTIONS

Question 8, LCC Autumn 1986

(i)   Why is the advertising agency such an important means of conducting an effective advertising campaign?

(ii) Describe the agency's contribution to the marketing strategy.

Comment

The question has two parts with equal marks. The IPA definition would make an excellent opening to the first part, and with this the candidate could proceed to an analysis similar to that at the beginning of this chapter. The agency offers the means of conducting marketing research, planning a campaign, creating the advertising and planning it correctly in the best media.

The agency's contribution opens up possibilities for an interesting discussion. An agency can make a contribution to the entire marketing strategy. It should not be brought in just at the advertising stage. An agency can help with product development, branding, pricing, packaging, test marketing and with aids for salesmen plus trade advertising. This is perhaps a far cry from the 4Ps style of marketing mix, but it is what modern advertising agencies, especially the à la carte and specialist ones are all about.

Question 8, LCC Autumn 1985

(i)   How has the system of 'recognising' advertising agencies by the media owners for commission purposes been changed in the United Kingdom to comply with the Restrictive Trade Practices Act 1976, and the requirements of the Office of Fair Trading?

(ii) How do the à la carte agencies and media independents now compare with traditional service advertising agencies?

Comment

This question has been very fully discussed in this chapter.

Question 5, LCC Autumn 1982

If you were appointing an advertising agency, what would you understand by the expressions 'recognised' (or 'accredited') agency, and the 'commission system'? If a prospective agency was not 'recognised' and operated on a fee basis, what would be your reaction?

Comment

In some countries, the term 'accredited' is used instead of 'recognised' and there may be grades of accredited agency. Overseas candidates could explain these differences but basically the question refers to the traditional meaning of the commission system together with an understanding of what recognition means under British law. The final sentence poses an interesting challenge to those candidates who may read too much into recognition, and be sceptical of fees.

Model answer

Qu.5. The commission system evolved from space broking whereby the newspapers gave salesmen commission on their sales of advertisement space. Until 1979, the media owners' organisations such as the Newspaper Association, Newspaper Society and the Periodical Proprietors Association had an extensive form of recognition agreement which, among other things, demanded that the agency had to have a certain volume of business spread over at least three accounts. This made it prohibitive for a new agency to set up because it could not earn its principal income - commission - unless it had sufficient business to qualify for commission. Very little income came from clients in the form of charges for artwork and production. Recognition by the NPA guaranteed a standard 15% from the nationals, while recognition by the NS meant 10% from the regionals and recognition by the PPA meant 10% from magazines. This was seldom satisfactory, and most agencies added a surcharge so that $17\frac{1}{2}\%$ was earned.

However, this was held by the Office of Fair Trading to be a monopoly situation which offended against the Restrictive Trade Practices Act 1976. Recognition was reduced to ability to pay bills (known as 'creditworthiness') and acceptance of the British Code of Advertising Practice. This opened the door to the setting up of creative à la carte agencies which, if they bought no media, did not need 'recognition'. In the past such small units would have been impossible because of all the restrictions on volume of business and capital involvement.

Consequently, recognition is of no consequence to a prospective client, and it does not even apply if he is using an à la carte agency. Recognition does not imply that the agency is competent. It is merely a safeguard which ensures that the media get paid promptly.

The commission system is an anomalous one. Out of the commission the agency performs services for the client, such as providing an account executive and conducting buying and clerical services, which cost the client nothing. The client is virtually subsidised by the media.

However, if the commission is rebated in the sense that the agency charges the client what it pays for the media, and then charges a fee for its time and expertise, this is a more genuine way of obtaining remuneration. Many agencies today work on a fee basis. This is a more professional approach, and if an agency is to be regarded as a professional service a fee is more appropriate than the system with its old 'ten per center' image of the commission agent.

12.   How can public relations help marketing?

INTRODUCTION

This chapter will first of all define public relations and then go on to explain its purpose in creating understanding, effecting change and building goodwill and reputation. Public relations will be seen not only as an integral part of marketing, but of the total communications of any organisation. But specifically, it will be shown why public relations is not limited to 'publicity' and how it can help the whole marketing strategy.

How it differs from advertising and why it is neither a form of advertising nor free advertising will be explained. The merits and demerits of in-house and consultancy public relations will be analysed. The chapter will conclude with a review of some of the created private media used for public relations purposes, and some examples of how public relations can help marketing.

DEFINITIONS

The first is the definition of the Institute of Public Relations, the British professional body, as slightly revised in 1987. The second is called the Mexican Statement because it was issued following an international conference of public relations organisations which met in Mexico City in 1978. Rather like the two definitions of advertising quoted in the previous chapter, one is general and the other is more specific.

Public relations practice is the planned and sustained effort to establish and maintain goodwill and mutual understanding between an organisation and its publics.

This definition contains some very significant words which distinguish public relations and make clear its positive nature. It is a *planned and sustained effort*, not something

haphazard or casual. It goes on all the time, and that applies to marketing as much as anything else. It is not an add-on optional extra, as in the 4Ps reference to 'publicity'. It is concerned with *goodwill*, not with persuading people to buy. *Mutual understanding* means two-way communication, understanding others as well as being understood by them. The essence of public relations and its primary purpose is creating *understanding*. Public relations is also to do with *publics* who are numerous groups of people, large and small, and not just the large target audiences or market segments of advertising.

Public relations practice is the art and social science of analysing trends, predicting their consequences, counselling organisation leaders, and implementing planned programmes of action which will serve both the organisation's and the public interest.

This is a more comprehensive definition. The Mexican Statement begins earlier and finishes later in its span of public relations activity.

First, it refers to *analysing trends* which means conducting research (whether primary or secondary - see Chapter 7) to discover the current situation. This is known as *appreciation of the situation* or the *communications audit*. Where are we now? What is the perceived image? What is right or wrong? Much of public relations work is concerned with converting bad situations into better ones, either by putting right things which are creating a poor reputation or by correcting misunderstandings.

This can be demonstrated by the chart on the following page of the Public Relations Transfer Process, the relevance of which to marketing should be self-evident.

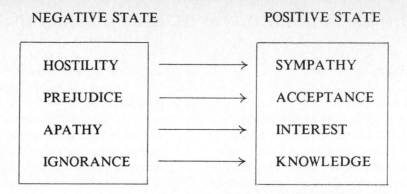

Figure 1 The Public Relations Transfer Process. In the left-hand box are typical negative states whose trends need to be discovered and analysed. The public relations programme will aim to convert these negative states into positive ones – the public relations role of effecting change in order to produce understanding. An advertising campaign can fail if understanding of the company, product or service has not been achieved. New products have failed for lack of this market education or pre-selling public relations input.

Second, these trends, the extent of understanding or misunderstanding, the strength of hostility, prejudice, apathy or ignorance towards the company, product or service, now has to be analysed so that they can be understood and their *consequences predicted*. What will happen if these negative states are permitted to continue? For instance, there was a time when scarcely anyone in Britain had heard of cranberries: now it is possible to sell cranberry sauce and juice.

Third, is the major public relations activity of giving professional advice or *counselling organisation leaders*. Much of this depends on the positioning of the public relations manager who should operate independently, servicing all departments of a company and being answerable to the chief executive. Giving advice is a main function of a consultant. A great deal of public relations work, whether in-house or external, consists of giving advice to management on any number of communications topics from changing the name of the company to assimilating the employees of a taken-over rival company. All this is a long way from the 4Ps concept of public relations as 'publicity'.

Fourth, as with the IPR definition, an essential part of public relations is objective planning, and the Mexican Statement goes on to speak of *implementing planned programmes of action*. These programmes could be in parallel with the recruitment, staff relations, production, marketing, corporate and financial plans of the organisation. In the case of marketing, public relations activities can coincide with and contribute to every stage of the marketing mix. If the public relations manager sits in at marketing meetings from start to finish he can advise on the communications aspects of naming a product, educating the trade, or providing after-sales services and many other things in between.

Fifth, the programmes will not only serve the organisation's interest but the *public interest*. The social responsibility of public relations relates to its professionalism in dealing with plain facts and reliable information. Like advertising, public relations has its voluntary controls, and both the Institute of Public Relations and the Public Relations Consultants Association (representing consultancies are corporate members whereas IPR members are individuals) have their Codes of Professional Conduct.

SIX POINT PLANNING MODEL

The Mexican Statement closely resembles the six-point planning model which can be applied to the planning of, say, a year's public relations programme:

1.   **Appreciation of the situation.**

2.   **Definition of objectives.** The objectives for a marketing-related programme might be selected from the following:

(i)   Informing the trade press of a new product, package, price or advertising campaign.

(ii) Organising a programme of dealer education including works visits and a dealer magazine.

(iii) Educating the market (trade and consumer) about a new product or service so that the advertising will be more effective when the campaign breaks. The market will have been developed to anticipate the product launch. This is likely to apply more to a technical product than to a fmcg.

(iv) Keeping the sales force informed about advertising support.

(v)   Creating awareness of the company or a brand among members of the target audience by organising the sponsorship of something of interest to that target audience.

(The above are just a few examples of possible marketing-related public relations activities.)

3.   **Definitions of publics** who must be reached to achieve the objectives.

4.   **Choice of media and techniques** to reach the publics in order to achieve the objectives.

5.   **Budgeting funds and resources.** Either the cost of achieving a particular objective or objectives will be budgeted, or it will be calculated what can be done for a certain sum. The primary cost is *time* or working hours - public relations is labour intensive - followed by the costs of materials (e.g. stationery, photography, printing, video production) and expenses (travelling, hospitality).

A budget consists mainly of what can be done with a given volume of time which is represented by either the salaries of in-house staff or by consultancy fees.

The budget will impose certain constraints, possibly reducing the number of objectives that can be entertained and limiting expenditure on media and methods such as publishing an external house journal, producing a video of the annual report and accounts for shareholders or opening an information centre. Money, and its careful apportionment, controls the public relations programme to the point that it is more sensible to undertake a limited number of projects properly than to attempt to do so many things so that none is done satisfactorily.

6.   **Assessment of results.** This is more than just counting column inches or centimetres of media coverage, but consists of the measurement by observation, experience or research methods of the extent to which objectives were or were not achieved.

For instance, suppose the initial research showed that only five per cent of executives under 36 years of age were aware of the tax benefits of contributing to a personal pension scheme. If a public relations programme was planned and executed to remedy this state of apathy and ignorance by raising the percentage to 25 per cent, and at the end of a year further research showed that 26 per cent were now aware of the benefits, that could be considered a successful campaign.

From the above it will be seen that public relations, like any other business activity, can succeed only if it follows the normal planning procedures. It has little to do with wining and dining and the old 'gin and tonic' image of public relations: it is to do with purposeful hard work. Nor is it concerned with pretending things are better than they are, of creating favourable images and favourable climates of opinion. It has to deal with the good and the bad, explain each with equal impartiality. In fact, a major area of public relations activity has become crisis management. Crises can hit any company and may take the form of accidents, strikes, product failures, take-over bids, financial loss or some other disaster.

IN-HOUSE OR CONSULTANCY?

The choice between having an in-house public relations department and appointing a public relations consultancy is not the same as deciding whether to have a fully-staffed advertising department or to engage an advertising agency. This needs to be understood very clearly.

While it may be best to appoint an advertising agency when advertising expenditure warrants this and there is need for outside expertise, the opposite is true of public relations. A consultancy may be engaged when a full-time PRO is not justified, but as soon as the volume of work justifies it an in-house public relations manager should be appointed. This is because of the more intimate, internal nature of public relations which is to do with communications at all levels and in all departments on a day-to-day basis throughout a company. Very truly it has been said that the company public relations manager should know more about the company than anybody else in it. The product manager does not need this sort of internal intimacy: most of his activities are directed externally.

To establish this situation in greater detail we will now outline the strengths and weaknesses of the in-house public relations department and the external public relations consultancy. In doing so, it is not suggested that one is necessarily better than the other, but that each is different. Large companies will employ both. As will be explained later, there are also public relations consultancies which offer specialist services which may be used from time to time to augment the in-house department.

THE IN-HOUSE PR DEPARTMENT

Advantages:

(i) A full-time unit. If positioned independently and answerable to top management, it can service the whole organisation, *including* marketing.

(ii) The public relations manager may be technically trained and experienced in the industry.

(iii) The public relations manager can have good lines of communication throughout the organisation so that he has ready access to information and knows what is going on at every level.

(iv) Because he is close to events and people he can work very economically, one job often serving many purposes. For example, when setting up a photographic session he may be able to see several opportunities for using pictures that can be taken at the same time, e.g. to illustrate a feature article, for the house journal, as blow-ups on an exhibition stand, and for the annual report and accounts.

Disadvantages:

(i) If placed in the marketing department, he is less able - if at all - to service the rest of the company.

(ii) He may lack impartiality, and be too biased in favour of the company. While this would be accepted in marketing, advertising and selling personnel it can be a handicap in a public relations manager. In public relations credibility depends on being trusted, especially by the media, for supplying accurate, factual and impartial information.

This is very different from advertising where it would be strange if information given was not selective and highly favourable. Public relations has to deal with the facts, good, bad or indifferent. It cannot pretend that something has not gone wrong, as in crisis situations. Incidentally, partiality is almost bound to happen if a public relations manager is positioned in the marketing department, or marketing personnel are responsible for public relations.

(iii) Because he is an expert in his industry his experience of public relations may be so limited to that field that he lacks a broad knowledge of general public relations practice.

(iv) It is possible that the company is located at some distance from a city so that it is difficult for the PRO to gain training at a college, or he may have been transferred from a totally different job, and has no experience of public relations. Management seldom understand the attributes of a public relations manager, and make some strange appointments. Public relations is also seen in some big companies as a career stage towards higher management, resulting in inexperienced people occupying public relations management positions for a short time.

THE EXTERNAL PR CONSULTANCY

Advantages:

(i) Because many clients have been serviced over a period, the public relations consultancy enjoys long and varied experience.

(ii) As a professional outsider, the consultancy may have advantages of nearness to media and suppliers, venues for press receptions, to City institutions or to Parliament.

(iii) If full-time services are not required, the part-time services of a consultancy team may be shared as with an advertising agency.

(iv) Experience of all kinds of media may be important, and normally a consultancy will be familiar with more media than any one client is likely to be.

Disadvantages:

(i) Usually, only a part-time service is provided, whereas the in-house public relations manager can, if necessary be on call 24 hours a day seven days a week. A consultancy can give only the time for which fees are paid.

(ii) There is an inevitable remoteness when using an outside service. There may be only a one-to-one relationship between the account executive and the client's representative, and there will be a lack of intimate knowledge of what is happening within the client's organisation.

(iii) A consultancy has to divide its time and loyalties between a number of clients in proportion to the fees they are paying. This can be a handicap when a client wants instant service and consultancy staff are otherwise engaged on behalf of other clients.

(iv) The consultancy may lack technical knowledge of the client's industry. Of course, consultancy staff can always learn, and the principles of public relations practice should be applicable to any circumstances, but this can be an area where the in-house PRO scores over the outsider.

These pros and cons have to be balanced to arrive at a decision whether to use one or the other, or maybe both. Many large companies do have considerable in-house departments but use consultancies to augment internal services when exceptionally busy, or when specialised services are required on an *ad hoc* basis.

There are consultancies which specialise in house journal production; corporate and financial public relations; sponsorships; corporate identity; Parliamentary liaison (advising clients on political matters); or which specialise in certain interests such as pharmaceuticals, food, travel, motor-cars, fashion or high-technology.

CREATED PRIVATE MEDIA

Public relations media are not limited to the mass media. There are times when media have to be created to reach specific and sometimes small publics. There can even be face-to-face communications between individuals. Some of the special public relations media and methods include:

(i) **House journals.** These may be company newspapers, magazines, newsletters and wall newspapers which resemble small posters displayed within premises. The video magazine is used by larger companies. There can be either employee publications, or external ones addressed to shareholders, dealers, users, specifiers and other customers.

(ii) **Documentary films or videos** can be made telling the company's story or explaining how a product or service works, or for recruitment and the induction of new recruits.

(iii) **Visual aids.** In addition to videos, slide presentations, mobile displays and portable exhibits may be produced for showrooms, exhibition stands, press receptions, talks to societies, and for showing at seminars and conferences.

(iv) **Educational literature.** Books, pamphlets, leaflets and posters may be produced to educate the market. Material can be produced for schools, and kits can be made up for student projects.

(v) **Technical seminars,** with speakers, videos, slide presentations and exhibits may be set up on company premises or in public places such as hotels, public rooms, libraries or Building Centres. These could range from meetings for clients organised by a bank manager to the introduction of a building component to architects, and similar events with invited guests. The presentation would be informative and educational, and not a sales pitch.

All these and other forms of public relations media can be quite different from those used in advertising.

HOW PUBLIC RELATIONS CAN HELP MARKETING

The on-going activities of public relations can help marketing in the following ways:

(i) Supply of news releases and pictures to press rooms at exhibitions, which may be supplemented by a press reception on the stand.

(ii) Holding press receptions to announce new products, services or policies.

(iii) Organising dealer conferences say, regionally, to introduce a new product or a new advertising campaign. If it is to be a new television campaign, the event could be held at regional television stations.

(iv) Sending media schedules and replicas of advertisements to dealers.

(v) Publishing an external house journal for dealers, users, specifiers or customers. This would be aimed at specific readers, helping them to understand the company, explaining products (e.g. with case studies), or helping dealers with ideas for shop displays or shop management.

(vi) Organising dealer contests such as window display competitions.

(vii) Organising visits (according to trade) to, say, the factory, the holiday resort, the vineyard or whatever is appropriate.

(viii) Publishing news about products, packages, prices and so on in the trade and the consumer press.

(ix) Publishing commissioned feature articles in appropriate magazines, e.g. describing how a customer has benefited from using the company's equipment, or telling housewives how they can use an ingredient in their cooking.

(x) Distributing videos to clubs and societies to show to their members.

(xi) Supporting exports by supplying news releases, pictures and videos to the Central Office of Information for overseas distribution, including use of videos by foreign television stations. Similarly, the External Services of the BBC broadcast news about British products.

(xii) Corporate public relations on behalf of the company which can improve knowledge and understanding of the company among dealers and customers. It can be important that the perceived image is a correct one, but it can only be based on knowledge and experience. The corporate identity, which the public relations department may have initiated, can contribute to the corporate image since it establishes and distinguishes the physical representation of the company.

The above short list will give a hint of the breadth of public relations activity which can help marketing. There is clearly a lot more to public relations than mere 'publicity' and marketing is only one function of a business to which it applies.

It even enters into the thoughtfulness with which various aspects of marketing communications are carried out. How well do brands and packages communicate? Are instructions easy to follow, or do they cause misgivings so that the product is either mis-used or discarded? Does the price seem value for money, or does it make people critical of the company? Are after-sales services well provided so that goodwill is maintained? All these aspects of the marketing mix have good or bad public relations implications. Do they create good or ill will? Reputation hangs on how a company is seen to behave towards customers, and this is a marketing responsibility. It is also elementary public relations or relations with the public.

SUMMARY

In this chapter a very large subject which is not wholly to do with marketing is defined and discussed, using the two most popular and explicit definitions of public relations. Emphasis has been placed on the role of public relations in combating negative states which can undermine successful marketing, and in creating understanding without which marketing cannot flourish. This led into the Six Point Planning Model to further emphasise the businesslike nature of objective public relations.

From this introduction to an often misunderstood subject, the advantages and disadvantages of the in-house public relations department and the outside consultancy were discussed. It was shown that neither was better than the other, that they were different and both could be used. Then followed a description of some of the created private media used in public relations. Finally, twelve examples were given of how public relations can help marketing.

PAST EXAMINATION QUESTIONS

Question 7, LCC Autumn 1985

Describe the public relations implications of the following elements of the marketing mix:

> *(i) Naming of companies or brands*
> *(ii) Pricing*
> *(iii) Packaging*
> *(iv) Sales promotion*
> *(v) After-sales service.*

Comment

Here is a question which clearly flies away from the 4Ps concept of public relations and invites candidates to recognise its broader implications. The question draws on much that has been said, not only in this chapter but in earlier chapters. Company and brand names can communicate easily and favourably and in tune with the corporate image. A name that is difficult to say or remember is poor public relations. Pricing can reflect well or badly on a company and create for it a good or bad reputation. Packaging can please or annoy. Sales promotion can be pleasing or disappointing, satisfying or irritating. The quality of the after-sales service can create goodwill and lead to recommendations, or it can have the opposite effect. All these things can create goodwill or ill will, good or bad relations between the manufacturer or supplier and the customer.

Question 8, LCC Series 2, 1987

The manufacturer of industrial products has a choice of methods by which he can promote his goods. Discuss the strengths and weaknesses of **four** *of the following methods:*

> *(i) Trade exhibitions*
>
> *(ii) Advertising in trade and technical magazines*
>
> *(iii) Technical seminars, attended by buyers and using various audio-visuals and visual aids*
>
> *(iv) External house journals*
>
> *(v) Documentary films or videos*
>
> *(vi) Technical PR articles in suitable journals*
>
> *(vii) Direct mail, using sales letters and sales literature.*

Note: *Your answer may be based on the situation in your own country.*

Comment

This is an omnibus question which draws on media or methods discussed in this and the previous chapter. In relation to this chapter attention will be paid to the four public relations methods which are (iii), (iv), (v) and (vi). These have been discussed in this chapter.

Model answer

Qu.8 (iii) Technical seminars can be organised to explain a product or service to groups of buyers. They could be from one large company, or from a number of companies. They could be, in the case of a building product, separate groups of (a) architects; (b) builders; (c) property owners; and (d) building societies. They represent specific publics.

Guests would be invited to a suitable and convenient venue to hear technical speakers supported by demonstrations, videos, exhibits or photographic displays. Hospitality would be provided according to the time of day such as lunch if it was an all-day event, or drinks and refreshments if it was in the evening. The emphasis would be on information, with opportunities for discussion and questions and to meet people from the company. The event would not be dressed up with advertising banners, but presented as a serious technical occasion.

A weakness could be that it is a time-consuming exercise which requires PR staff capable of setting up and running seminars. Another weakness could be poor speakers, and lack of adequate rehearsal. If it is seen to be merely a sales exercise it may deter people from attending, or send people away feeling it has been too biased and promotional. If hospitality is too lavish it could invite scepticism.

Qu. 8. (iv) External house journals differ from internal employee publications. They should be produced to the same standards as commercial journals, and should not look like sales literature. They should be addressed to particular readers, and not be general prestige journals.

According to the type of company and readership, the contents should be interesting and useful to the readers. Features might demonstrate how a product is made and the uses for which it is intended, or be installation or case study accounts showing how the product is being used by customers. For example, if the product was a computer articles could describe how it is being used in a warehouse, a bank or by a manufacturer. The contents would be factual and instructive. If the readers were retailers, articles could help shop assistants to explain the product, or there could be pictorial examples of how to display the product in a shop.

A weakness can be high cost if there is too large a readership, or scepticism on the part of readers if the tone and presentation is too promotional. If the journal does not resemble the kind the reader would normally buy it will lack credibility. Another weakness could be infrequent publication, and it should appear regularly so that readers come to expect it as a proper periodical.

Qu. 8. (v) Documentary films or videos can be made to demonstrate how the product is made or how it can be used, or the story can be told of how a project was undertaken. The documentary should be made to serve a definite purpose with defined audiences in mind. It should then be used as widely as possible on occasions such as trade exhibitions, works visits, press conferences, technical seminars, conferences, presentations to prospective clients and possibly for overseas showings through the Central Office of Information.

Weaknesses of this medium could be the production cost and how quickly the documentary would date. Effort does have to be made to effect good distribution, and a weakness could be to make a video and then fail to exploit possible showings. This failure could be because the company does not have a public relations manager skilled in such exploitation, and so the video remains largely unused and a waste of money.

Qu. 8. (vi) Technical PR articles should be published on their merits. An idea should be presented to an editor who is asked whether and when he will publish it, and how many words he requires. The article can then be written as a normal commissioned contribution although no fee will be paid to the author. Its strengths lie in being one of the editorial features, bearing an author's name, unlike a news release which may or may not be published and could be altered by the editor. Such articles are often announced or indexed and shown to be part of the issue. They are more authoritative than news items, and may be kept or referred to for public reference. It is also possible to have reprints which can be used for various give-away purposes such as in a showroom or on an exhibition stand.

A minor weakness is that unlike a news release which could be printed in several journals there is only one appearance, and only one press cutting. An article also takes time to research and write, and this cost has to be reckoned against the value of its publication. An article occupies a lot of space, and although publication will be promised it may not be for some weeks or months. Timing may have to be planned very carefully. If more urgent publication is required, a news release may achieve quicker publication. A major weakness can be the inclusion of too much puffery or advertising which will either lead to the editor making cuts, or to readers disliking it as a piece of free advertising. Commercial references should be kept to the minimum and repetition of company or brand names should be avoided.

13. What is the role of sales promotion?

INTRODUCTION

This chapter will discuss sales promotion as a marketing activity which can be used as an alternative to advertising. First, it will be defined within the British meaning of the term, followed by an introductory historical background. Then its advantages and disadvantages will be discussed, and the reasons for using sales promotion will be given. The changing nature of sales promotion schemes will be considered together with the use of tailor-made and third party promotions. A variety of sales promotion schemes will be described. Competitions will be dealt with separately. Finally, problems of misredemption and malredemption, together with redemption services, will be explained.

DEFINITION

A specific definition is:

Special short-term promotional schemes to introduce a new product, boost sales or challenge competition, or as an alternative to traditional media advertising.

The official definition of the Institute of Sales Promotion is:

Sales promotion is the function of marketing which seeks to achieve given objectives by the adding of intrinsic, tangible value to a product or service.

The ISP definition puts sales promotion clearly in the marketing camp, and does not regard it as a form of below-the-line advertising. By *the adding of intrinsic, tangible value* is meant that the customer gains an additional benefit such as a gift, prize, cash or price reduction.

Sales promotion used to be called merchandising which was misleading since merchandising has the retailer's meaning of promoting merchandise.

HISTORY OF SALES PROMOTION

While modern sales promotion schemes are very sophisticated and many new ideas have been introduced, sales promotion has a history going back for more than a century. It was used by big firms like Beechams and Liptons in the 19th century, and by the corner grocer who, for instance, gave a tea caddy with his own label tea.

During the 20s and 30s there were many gift coupon schemes run to promote cigarettes like Ardath, BDV and Black Cat and with Bourneville cocoa. Colman's mustard had its Mustard Club and there were 'flickers' which were books of pictures which had a movie effect when the pages were flicked through rapidly. Pairs of three-dimensional cards were given with De Reske cigarettes, and a stereoscopic viewer could be bought in order to view the cards. Turf cigarettes gave away little silk mats with each packet.

Very popular were sets of 50 cards (with free albums supplied) found in packets of Wills Gold Flake and Players Navy Cut cigarettes, which are today collectors' items. Wills also gave cigarette cards which could be collected to form a picture, and a set could be exchanged for a print which could be framed. This was an old idea from the 19th century. Wills also gave miniature playing cards which could be exchanged for a full-size pack.

ADVANTAGES OF SALES PROMOTION

The following are some of the chief advantages of sales promotion:

(i) It brings the manufacturer closer to the ultimate customer, being less remote than media advertising.

(ii) It can encourage the dealer to stock because there is an incentive to the customer to buy.

(iii) It creates new interest in a product which may have lost favour.

(iv) It can draw attention to a new or modified product.

(v) It can induce impulse buying.

(vi) It can encourage customers to switch brands.

(vii) Conversely, where the collection of tokens is involved, it can create habit buying.

(viii) Similarly, if the customer is encouraged to buy several units, perhaps at the same time, the customer will be deterred from buying a rival brand, at least until the promoted units have been consumed.

(ix) The promotion can be timed for a particular period, and limited to a certain period.

(x) Its effect on sales can be measured by sales figures and dealer audit market share reports, and by the number of acceptances or redemptions.

(xi) The attractiveness, benefits and originality of the scheme can create goodwill and have a good public relations effect.

(xii) It can appeal to the bargain hunting, price conscious customer.

(xiii) It is an effective way of competing with a rival, such as regaining market share which had been lost to a rival.

That is quite an impressive list of merits, and they co-incide very well with the situation where a large volume of production is distributed through supermarkets, and the need is to achieve stock movement off the shelves.

DISADVANTAGES OF SALES PROMOTION

However, there are some imperfections, and the following are possible disadvantages:

(i) Retailers may be unco-operative if the scheme puts them to too much trouble, or prohibits them from selling old stock. There are also problems that they may not yet have received (or put on display) stock bearing promotional packaging, which has been advertised; or the scheme has gone so well that they are out-of-stock when customers want to buy further units with the promotional packaging. These customers go elsewhere.

(ii) A similar problem occurs when there is a closing date to a scheme requiring the collection of tokens, and customers who have not collected the required number by the closing date will be annoyed. This is bad public relations.

(iii) Delays in delivery of premium offers - perhaps because the product manager underestimated demand - can be irritating. Again, this is bad public relations.

(iv) Disappointment may be caused by the poor quality or triviality of an offer which fails to come up to customer expectations. More bad public relations.

(v) Some large supermarket chains quite blatantly accept cash vouchers as price cuts on any product they stock, thus negating the whole point of a manufacturer's promotion. He may state on the package that the voucher can be redeemed only against the purchase of that product, but this is openly ignored.

(vi) Offers may encourage only temporary brand

switching, after which customers revert to their normally favourite brand.

(vii) The frequency of offers by different manufacturers, and even within the same product group, can encourage shoppers to become *cherry pickers* who buy only products with offers. This can easily happen with small unit goods like chocolate bars and toilet soaps.

These demerits point to the possibility of sales promotion schemes inviting the risk of upsetting either the trade or the customer. Sales promotion schemes do have to be planned and operated with great care, otherwise they can have an unfortunate boomerang effect.

REASONS FOR USING SALES PROMOTION

Most of the reasons for using sales promotion have already been stated in the section on ADVANTAGES. There are two predominate reasons. The first is an alternative to media advertising, and some companies find it more successful to devote their advertising spend to, say, a 5p or 10p cut than to spend a similar or even greater sum on press or television advertising. A cash voucher or flashed price cut does not mean that the manufacturer is giving away money. It is buying sales just as much as if it used advertising. Occasionally, there will be a cash token in a press advertisement but there will probably be only one press advertisement in, say, *The Sun* or *TV Times*, not a series of advertisements over a period.

The second reason is that a short campaign is required to either launch a new product or to lift sales of an existing one. Sales promotion lends itself to short impactive campaigns which run only as long as stocks last, which might be only a few days with a fmcg in supermarkets.

CHANGING NATURE OF SALES PROMOTION

There is sometimes a mistaken idea that sales promotion is a new form of marketing. This may be because so many new forms have been created in recent years, and their newness is noticeable. A number of new firms have emerged, either supplying goods that can be offered as premiums or printed materials such as scratch cards, while consultancies exist which can plan and organise a whole sales promotion campaign.

One change that will have to be faced even before the Single European Economy comes about in 1992, and which can apply to Euro marketing and Euro advertising on satellite television, is that Britain has long enjoyed freedom to run sales promotion schemes which would be illegal in many European countries. Free gifts and premium offers are not permitted, especially in Denmark and Germany.

In Britain, there have been two important changes. First, self liquidating premium offers where the customer is offered, say, a tea towel or a set of saucepans at a special price, the promoter making no profit on the deal but merely recovering his costs (thus *liquidating* the costs), are less attractive since such products are often sold cheaply in the high street. Nowadays, a premium offer has to have exclusivity if it is to attract response.

The second change had been to move away from mail-ins, although there are still mail-ins. To send away for an offer, whether free or for tokens or cash, requires an effort which could be a deterrent. Of course, it depends on how attractive the mail-in is. From the promoter's point-of-view, the physical distribution of an offer may be done more economically through one distributor such as a fulfilment house than through stores.

However, it is believed that a greater response will result from a scheme which requires no effort of mailing-in, and where the token or coupon can be redeemed at the point-of-sale. For example, tokens are collected on purchases of petrol and when a sufficient number have been collected they can be exchanged for a gift at any petrol station selling that brand of petrol. This is convenient for the customer, but the customer has to stock up retailers with the gifts, and retailers have to store and dispense them.

With a cross-coupon offer, the customer can buy another brand for less than the usual price. Again, with a High Street redemption offer, a cash token on a product bought in a supermarket can be taken down the road and used against a purchase made at another named shop. Similar schemes have provided rebates on holidays and rail fares. One of the newer schemes has been the catalogue from which quite expensive items like dinner sets and midi-systems have been obtainable for a combination of tokens given with the purchase and cash. This has led to promoters advertising the quality of their offers!

Two other developments have occurred. The *tailor-made scheme* is associated with one retail chain, e.g. Sainsbury's, Tesco, and special offer leaflets are distributed at the stores or perhaps by door-to-door delivery, naming the stores at which the offer is being made. Coffee firms use this method. The other method is the *third party scheme* in which there is a joint venture between the two companies who share the benefits of the offer. This is rather like cross couponing except that it is a mutual promotion. An example in 1988 was the round-Britain cycle race sponsored jointly by Kelloggs and Channel 4 television who gave great publicity to the event in *TV Times* and televised the race day by day. But with most third party schemes there is a mutuality of interest, the two products being displayed together in the same outlets and appealing to the same customers.

The reader is advised to visit places of purchase such as supermarkets and petrol stations, or to look at products in the larder at home, and to become familiar with the great variety of sales promotion schemes in operation. Some offers will be seen advertised in popular newspapers and magazines. There are new ones every week. Features on sales promotion also appear in trade journals, e.g. *Campaign,* *Marketing Week* and *Marketing.*

SALES PROMOTION SCHEMES DESCRIBED

There are so many different kinds of sales promotion scheme that although long the following list cannot be exhaustive. This variety does indicate that at any one time, with products selling in the same kind of store, many firms can be running quite different promotions.

(i) **Gift coupons and trading stamps.** Coupons, redeemable for goods in a gift catalogue, help to achieve habit-buying and brand loyalty, because it will probably take months to collect enough coupons to claim a gift. A variation on this is a token which has to be stuck on a card. Green Shield and other trading stamps are given by retailers on purchases, with gifts redeemable from special showrooms or by post.

(ii) **Picture cards.** Sets of cards, reminiscent of the old cigarette cards, again have repeat-purchase value. They may be tipped into packs but are often printed on cartons and have to be cut out.

(iii) **Matching halves.** Half pictures or coupons can be given with purchases, prizes being given to customers who present matching pairs.

(iv) **Cash premium coupons** or vouchers. Printed in press advertisements, or delivered or printed on packs as a discount against a future purchase, these are virtually free money from the consumer's point of view, and the offer is hard to resist. However, there is the risk of *malredemption,* which is explained later.

(v) **Free samples.** Sampling can take many forms from those given away by a demonstrator in a store to miniature packs and sachets. They may be delivered door-to-door, and a modern version (e.g. hand cream) has been to attach a sachet to an advertisement in a magazine. Free trial offers can also be announced in press advertisements (e.g. a trial run in a motor-car).

(vi) **Self-liquidating premium offer.** This is an oldie. In the 30s the *Daily Herald* used the method to promote circulation, offering dinner services and sets of Dickens' novels. Self-liquidating does not mean liquidating old stock but running a scheme which pays for itself. This was explained in the section on the Changing Nature of Sales Promotion.

(viii) **Free gifts and mail-ins.** The gift may be attached to the pack, or given out by the retailer with the purchase. Alternatively, the gift may be offered in an advertisement and readers are invited to write in for it, usually by means of a coupon. Advertised offers should contain a closing date and better still a limiting number, otherwise demand may exceed supply. This has happened with free 'how-to-do-it' books, calling for either an embarrassing and disappointing apology or a costly and unbudgeted reprint.

(ix) **Cash awards for use of the product.** Again, this is an oldie which is revived from time to time, e.g. a representative calls and gives cash awards if certain brands are in the house, the possibility of a call being advertised. Two of the original versions were cash awards to people carrying a box of Blue Cross matches – which encouraged thousands of people to always keep a box in their pocket! – and Lobby Lud who visited holiday resorts and gave cash awards to people carrying the *News Chronicle* who recognised and challenged him, which caused a lot of fun with mistaken identities! Other newspapers have revived the idea.

(x)   **Banded, multiple and jumbo packs.**

There may be a two-for-the-price-of-one offer, or a price advantage for buying in bulk as with Christmas packs of different chocolate bars. Very attractive for children is the variety pack of eight different Kellogg's breakfast cereals in individual cartons. One form of banded pack is that on which a standard pack has attached to it a smaller gift pack of the same product, as happens with toothpastes, hair sprays and other toiletries.

(xi) **Bonus packs.** These are larger than usual packs which offer so much per cent extra for the same price, or ejector packs of razor blades which contain extra blades. This is another oldie and an ingenious one was the single cigarette in its own packet attached to a packet of Kensitas cigarettes with the message 'one for your friend'.

(xii) **Flash packs.** One of the most common forms of sales promotion is to print an offer on the package, label or wrapping. It may be a simple '5p off' type of flash, or an *on-pack* offer which will be referred to again.

(xiii) **High Street redemption schemes.** On-pack offers, these offer discounts on purchases made at another named shop. The other shop thus gets extra trade and is therefore willing to participate in a joint scheme.

(xiv) **Charity promotions.** These have become very popular, the manufacturer promising to pay a contribution to a named charity. Usually, tokens have to be collected. One firm offered schools free equipment and children bought the tokens to school where bulk collections were made. Another brought together a number of brands which bore tokens on their labels, and these could be collected and sent to the Save the Children Fund.

(xv) **Tokens and cash catalogue.** In order to offer more substantial 'gifts', and to exploit the growth of direct response marketing catalogues, some firms such as Shell have given adhesive tokens with purchases of petrol, together with collecting cards, and goods were claimable for tokens only or tokens and the balance in cash.

(xvi) **In-store demonstrations.** These may include the giving away of free samples, but they may be product demonstrations with subsequent sales and demonstrated products could range from cosmetics to ironing boards.

(xvii) **Games.** These have the advantage of provoking curiosity and providing entertainment. There are bingo games, and scratch cards with lucky numbers or fruit machine symbols. Prizes are awarded for completing cards or getting the right numbers or a combination of symbols.

(xviii) **Lotteries.** These promotions have grown rapidly in recent years, the offer being of a free entry in a prize draw, ostensibly without obligation to make a purchase. While purchase is not absolutely essential, and the scheme evades the gambling laws and the requirement for 'an element of skill' for a contest not to be a lottery, the objective must be to sell the product and purchase may be necessary to get the entry form.

(ixx) **Prize competitions.** These have been left to last because they need more detailed explanation. Prizes are offered for solving a puzzle, the means of entry is some proof of purchase such as an entry token from a wrapper, and to avoid a larger prize having to be divided among a lot of equal winners there is a tie-breaker such as 'why I prefer so-and-so'. Several points have to be considered.

(a)   **Prizes.** They must be substantial and attractive since they have to compete with big football pools, state lottery and other prizes. Sometimes they are glamorised with a new model car, exotic holiday or kitchen equipment for which there may be a large cash alternative. There is usually a good number of consolation prizes so that many prize winners are possible. Choice of prize is important, both as an attraction and as something worth winning. The latter point is very important because some prizes can be an embarrassment if they involve additional personal expenditure. If the prize includes an airline ticket or hotel accommodation a cash alternative may not be possible. Cash prizes usually have universal appeal.

(b)   **Rules.** These should be absolutely clear, and to conform with gaming and lottery laws it is generally required that the contest should require an element of skill. Solutions should not be decided in advance.

(c)   **Judging.** A panel of well-known judges gives a competition added interest and certainly credibility. They do not have to judge every entry, and a preliminary screening usually takes place to eliminate repetitive or poor entries. For example, if the contest seeks a slogan it is surprising how many entrants will offer slogans which are either inappropriate or have been used before.

(d)   **Entry requirements.** There should be an adequate supply of entry forms, either as give-away leaflets, or printed in press advertisements or on packs.

(e)   **Timing.** There should be sufficient time for competitors to obtain the necessary proof of purchase, submit entries, and for proper scrutiny and judging.

(f)   **Results.** These should be announced as publicly as possible, or there should be some means of obtaining the results from the promoters. A fault with some contests is that there is great publicity to announce the contest, resulting in increased sales, but obscure announcement of the prize winners.

A competition is therefore an elaborate undertaking, and it requires painstaking administration.

MALREDEMPTION AND MISREDEMPTION

The meanings of these two terms are different but they often cause confusion. **Malredemption** occurs when retailers accept premium coupons for products other than intended. Thus, a housewife may present the cashier with a clutch of cash vouchers and receive a discount on her shopping, provided the store stocks the goods named on the vouchers. This negates the intention of the promoter who may try to prevent this by stating on the voucher that it may be redeemed only for the specified product. However, this is openly flouted by the biggest supermarket chains.

Both these appeals appeared on a 5p voucher for Fairy Toilet Soap:

Procter & Gamble reserve the right to withhold payment if they have cause to believe that this coupon was redeemed against any item other than Fairy Toilet Soap.

Imagine that threat being carried out against the mighty Sainsbury's and Tesco! The following was addressed to the customer:

Please don't embarrass your retailer by asking him to accept this coupon against any item other than Fairy Toilet Soap.

Housewives don't embarrass retailers by patronising their shops. Proctor & Gamble's naive threat and silly plea could not stop malredemption. The more likely effect is to encourage supermarket chains to de-list branded products in favour of own labels. Sainsbury's sell their brand, not their shop.

Misredemption occurs when there is fraudulent use of premium vouchers as when they are stolen from printers or pilfered from stores. It has been known for a shopkeeper to acquire unsold copies of newspapers in which cash premiums are printed, and to claim their value from a manufacturer, although he has sold none of the product.

A **redemption service** is conducted by the Nielsen Clearing House at Corby to which retailers send premium coupons in order to collect payment, and it handles a million redemptions daily. Manufacturers receive reports giving a breakdown of the sources of redemption. The reports enable manufacturers to define the main sources; permitting a comparison to be made between products sold into outlets and coupons redeemed; and also to produce a comparison between individual retailers and their support for premium promotions. These analyses reveal, for example, to which retailers consumers take coupons cut from press advertisements or delivered door-to-door; the extent of malredemption; and even evidence of misredemption.

SUMMARY

After defining sales promotion, a short history was given and other historical references occurred in descriptions of individual sales promotion schemes. The advantages and disadvantages of sales promotion were analysed, followed by an explanation of the reasons for using it. The changing nature of sales promotion and the reasons for changes were discussed, with descriptions of some of the newer methods. After this, nineteen old and new schemes were described. Prize competitions, and some special considerations, followed. Finally, malredemption and misredemption were explained, and there was a description of the redemption service provided by the Nielsen Clearing House.

PAST EXAMINATION QUESTIONS

Question 4, LCC Series 4, 1987

Many sales promotion schemes used to depend on customers mailing in coupons, tokens and pay-

ments, but the trend is now towards offers and schemes which do not require the effort of mailing in. Describe five of these newer sales promotion schemes and discuss their likely effectiveness.

Comment

The changing nature of sales promotion, and new schemes, are discussed in this chapter. Equal marks are given for each of the five examples where likely effectiveness should be evaluated, comments and opinions being invited. Five suitable schemes could be taken from (i) cross couponing; (ii) third party promotions; (iii) High Street redemption schemes; (iv) charity schemes; (v) gift and cash catalogues; (vi) games; (vii) tailor-made schemes and (viii) free draws.

Question 4, LCC Spring 1986

When a sales promotion scheme involving a special offer is being operated there is a risk of demand exceeding supply. Discuss:

(i)   The consequences of being unable to supply.

(ii) How to control offers so that the situation does not occur.

Comment

For the first part candidates should discuss the ill-will that can be provoked with both retailers and consumers if demand exceeds supply, with all its bad effects on the company's reputation. Other consequences may be that the offer may have to be re-ordered, the cost of this upsetting the budget and perhaps being excessively expensive. It is also possible that the offer cannot be repeated if the quantity of a premium was final. Apologies may have to be sent to disappointed customers, and it may be necessary to either supply a cash voucher in lieu of the offer, or make an alternative offer,

and both incur extra administration costs. There are thus two sides to this: the reaction of customers and the extra costs in dealing with the problem.

For the second part, methods of control can include: careful forecasting of likely demand and ordering of the necessary supply; making sure that the supplier can deliver promptly to meet the anticipated demand; applying a time limit to the offer; limiting the number of applications, e.g.'the first 5,000 applications'; and limiting the number of packages bearing an offer and tokens.

Question 6, LCC Spring 1984

You are planning a sales promotion scheme for a fast moving consumer product. Discuss the merits and demerits of the following schemes which are under consideration:

(i)   A big prize contest
(ii)   A self-liquidating premium offer
(iii) A price reduction with flash packs
(iv)   In-store demonstration in supermarkets and department stores.

Comment

All four forms of sales promotion are explained in this chapter. However, it is not enough to just write a description of each, and the pros and cons need to be debated. This will depend on the ability of the candidate to understand the strengths and weaknesses of each scheme, and to do this it is necessary to be familiar with actual schemes, quoting examples to illustrate arguments. The answers depend on a blend of theoretical textbook learning and classroom instruction plus observation of actual sales promotion schemes in practice in the shops and the home.

Model answer

Qu.6.(i)   A big prize contest has the advantages of drama, excitement and bold presentation which could use media advertising such as the press and television, retail point-of-sale displays, and on-pack announcements. It is essential that the prizes appeal to possible contestants, and it may be necessary to glamorise them with pictures of an exotic holiday resort in a far-off part of the world, or with a new car which is currently being talked about.

A contest requires a lot of organisation in planning the prizes, arranging for the handling of entries, setting up of screening panels and well-known judges, and arranging ceremonies for and announcements of the prize-winners.

Media advertising and displays have to be prepared, together with special packs, and the entry forms. This will be a costly exercise requiring extra calls on staff time who handle the organisation of contests. Is all this extra effort and expense likely to be justified by a satisfactory forecast of increased sales? It would suit a big company like Cadbury or Heinz.

Qu.6.(ii) A self-liquidating premium offer is less popular today because typical premium merchandise can now be bought cheaply in many High Street shops. It also requires the effort of posting in an application with cash. Postal orders are expensive.

To be successful, the goods offered at a premium must be very attractive and preferably unobtainable in the shops. It could be a new product which has novelty value. Or something seasonal and topical. On the other hand, direct response marketing has become very popular, and people will write away for goods that are not particularly exclusive.

Sufficient quantities must be bought or ordered to meet anticipated demand, and the response to the offer must therefore be forecast very carefully, which is not always easy. It would suit a product bought regularly like a breakfast cereal.

From the promoter's point of view, a premium offer requiring, say, so many labels or tokens as well as cash, does encourage bulk buying or repeat purchases which can lead to habit buying and brand loyalty. Having bought so many units, rivals are deprived of sales.

Qu.6.(iii) A price reduction with a flash pack is the least expensive form of sales promotion. A package, wrapper or label has to be printed anyway, and all that is necessary is to change the artwork for a limited print run. The cost is minimal yet the new pack for a fmcg can attract interest to itself on the shelf and so produce extra sales including impulse purchases. Customers are price conscious and will tend to accept a saving on a well-known brand. This happens with many products such as biscuits, toothpaste, confectionery and detergents. People will buy and store some of these products, simply because of the advantageous price.

A possible weakness is that sales will be temporary, and once the flashed pack is no longer available customers will revert to their former brand, or be attracted by the special offer made by another manufacturer. Flash packs can appeal to a fickle market and have only a short-term effect. It would best suit a small unit good such as a chocolate bar.

Qu.6.(iv) In-store demonstrations have the advantage of dramatic and personalised presentations compared with the static role of the package on the shelf. The product can be sampled, and this is particularly useful for something which can be tasted such as a food or a drink.

It has an entertainment value and people enjoy tasting something, especially free of charge. The demonstrator can be persuasive in a way no other sales promotion scheme can be. Seeing someone giving a performance in a shop which usually has just rows and rows of dull shelves is a novelty of immediate interest, and the demonstration stands out in isolation and contrast to the rest of the surroundings.

Disadvantages may be that the busy shopper wants to get on with the shopping and does not wish to be hindered and pestered. Some demonstrators have a patter which sounds insincere, and shoppers dislike being browbeaten by excessive salesmanship. They prefer to choose what they want to buy of their own free will.

EXERCISE

Devise a third party sales promotion scheme, choosing your own product and giving your reasons for inviting another company to join in the scheme as a partner. There should be mutual benefits such as the same type of distribution, similar customer, and opportunities for each to contribute to the success of the other.

14. How can sponsorship help marketing?

INTRODUCTION

Sponsorship will be seen in this chapter as an activity which links marketing, advertising and public relations and is therefore dealt with separately and in its own right. After defining sponsorship there will be consideration of the reasons for undertaking it. Subjects for sponsorship will be discussed, followed by an outline of the costs involved. In conclusion, how and by whom sponsorships are organised will be explained.

DEFINITION

> *Sponsorship is financial patronage given to individuals, participants, events and other activities by commercial organisations.*

This is a broad definition and for the purposes of this book, 'by commercial organisations' is specified. Historically, sponsorship stems from the patronage of the arts when artists and composers relied on sponsorship by wealthy patrons such as kings and members of the aristocracy. While such private, altruistic sponsorship still exists, sponsorship in the context of marketing is conducted by commercial organisations. Some companies may give financial support without seeking to profit by it in the sense of putting something back into society, but here we shall consider sponsorship which has a positive marketing objective and profit is certainly sought.

Sponsorship is of an individual such as a tennis player; of a racing car or show-jumper; of an event such as a golf tournament; of a place such as a theatre, art gallery or museum; or of a prize or award. It does not mean the sponsorship of a whole programme on television, which is illegal in Britain but common in other parts of the world. The distinction between *sponsorship* and *sponsored advertising* should be clearly understood. When a brewer or cigarette company in Nigeria or Singapore buys the airtime in order to broadcast a whole football match, this is sponsored advertising, but if each team had a commercial sponsor and the players wore shirts bearing the sponsor's name, this would be sponsorship. In the course of a sponsored programme the advertiser would insert commercial spots.

WHY SPONSOR?

The objectives of sponsorship can be marketing, advertising or public relations or a blend of two or more of these. At the outset it is necessary to define these objectives precisely, to consider which is the most appropriate recipient of financial support, and to forecast whether or not the cost will produce worthwhile results. These results may not always be measurable in terms of profits: it is difficult to put a monetary value on corporate image, approval by dealers, better staff morale or acceptance by society although all of these could contribute handsomely to the success of a business. They are almost all the reasons why so many Japanese companies sponsor British sports.

Some definite reasons why companies put money into sponsorship are:

(i) **To position a product** in the market by sponsoring something of interest to members of that market segment. This would be useful when a company which is familiar in one market aims a new product at another (e.g. a perfumer produces men's toiletries).

(ii) **To familiarise the market** with the company or product name, or a new corporate identity scheme by which it wishes to be recognised. The first might be a foreign or a new product, and the second could be airline which has adopted a new logo, livery, colour scheme and so on.

(iii) **To increase awareness of a company** as Cornhill Assurance has done with Test Cricket and Canon did for three years with the Football League.

(iv) **To overcome a ban on advertising** as cigarette firms like Players and Marlboro have done in sponsoring motor-racing.

(v) **To provide an opportunity to extend hospitality** to business friends and clients as guests at events which the company is sponsoring, e.g. a horse race or show jumping events.

(vi) **To get media coverage** as when a major sporting event is televised and credit is given to the sponsor, with additional coverage in the press and on radio, e.g. the Ever Ready Derby.

(vii) **To create goodwill among customers who can enjoy the event** as when banks sponsor concerts, operas and ballets.

(viii) **To prove the qualities of a product** under severe trial, and to gain credit for successes, as with motor-car racing, safari and other motor-car rallies, and various feats of endurance which test a product such as expeditions.

(x) **To associate the company with a worthy cause,** e.g. various oil companies and Allied Lyons with the raising, preservation and public exhibition of the *Mary Rose* at Portsmouth Dockyard.

From the above examples it will be seen that sponsorship is not a matter of rich companies giving away money for charitable reasons. Hard-headed financial decisions are involved.

Moreover, there is yet another pertinent reason for sponsorship in Britain. Television air-time rates have been hyped far beyond inflation rates and there is a point when commercial television is no longer cost-effective. At this point a number of companies have decided to divert their promotional budget into sponsorship especially when there is promise of legitimate television coverage.

WHAT CAN BE SPONSORED?

A simple answer would be *anything*, because there is always someone or some organisation which would like to receive financial support. The following are the best examples:

(i) **Sports.** This is the largest area of sponsorship and it can range from a grand prix motor-racing team which travels the world's motor racing circuits to a humble local cycle racing team. Almost every sport one can think of has its sponsors. Some, like darts, bowls and snooker have proved to be very entertaining on television. A number have continued regularly for decades, for example the Whitbread Gold Cup horse race. Others change sponsors from time to time as has been seen with first Gillette and then Mars sponsoring the London Marathon. The young people's sports of swimming and gymnastics are sponsored by Coca-Cola. The chosen sport should be appropriate to the product.

(ii) **Arts and culture.** Artists, performers, pop groups, orchestras, art shows and so on receive commercial support. So do theatres, art galleries and museums.

(iii) **Education.** A number of university 'chairs', college bursaries and research scholarships are financed by industry.

(iv) **Expeditions and feats of endurance** such as explorations and mountain climbs are often supplied by business interests with equipment or funds. A product may be tested under extreme conditions.

(v) **Awards and prizes.** A number of prizes

like the Booker Prize for literature, and numerous PR awards to journalists and photographers, form another field of sponsorship.

WHAT DOES SPONSORSHIP COST?

The budget must be calculated carefully because the cost does not usually rest with, say, awarding a trophy, and there may also be opportunities for advertising by means of arena boards, or of perpetuating the occasion by making a video. Typical costs are:

(i)   The prize, or a sum of money as the basic financial support.

(ii)   The upkeep of, say, racing cars or horses, and their transportation.

(iii) Provision of clothing, equipment and and other necessary gear.

(iv)   Hospitality. This could be of invited guests, or of journalists in the commentary box.

(v)   Souvenirs such as programmes and give-aways like T-shirts or hats.

(vi)   Photography for record and PR purposes.

(vii) News releases, and other press relations activities such as press receptions.

(viii) Shooting of a video, making and supply of copies.

(ix) The salary and resources of an in-house PRO, or the fees and expenses of a specialist consultant.

Like all budgets this is probably only a summary of principal costs. Sponsorship does not come cheap, but then if the aim is to reach millions (maybe abroad as well as at home!) who will see the sponsorship on television the cost may be minimal. Moreover, when one considers the hours devoted to some events (before, during and after) the coverage can be huge. International companies like Coca-Cola, Fuji and Benson and Hedges score from events which enjoy world-wide television coverage. That is why there is such a huge premium on the sponsorship of events like world cup football and the Olympic Games.

THE ORGANISATION OF SPONSORSHIPS

There are two sides to sponsorship - those who want to be financed and those who want to benefit from giving financial support. The sports, arts and other interests have representative bodies such as the various Sports Councils, the associations representing individual sports, and bodies like the Association of Business Sponsorship of the Arts. All these organisations are prepared to negotiate terms with would-be sponsors.

On the other hand there are several well-known consultancies which will conduct these negotiations on behalf of clients. When agreement has been reached they will undertake the entire sponsorship which can be a very complicated operation. Afterwards, they will provide statistical data on the media coverage achieved, having monitored this very thoroughly. If necessary, research can be conducted to measure, say, the increase in awareness or changes in attitude as a result of the sponsorship.

SUMMARY

Although a short chapter, it is necessary both to show how sponsorship can serve marketing, advertising and public relations needs, and because questions are set on this topic. After defining sponsorship it was distinguished from broadcast programmes which are sponsored by advertisers. When the BBC and ITV companies televise a sponsored event they do so independently and with no payment from the sponsors as, for example, with cricket and football matches or teams which generally receive financial support from companies. Reasons for sponsoring were set out, followed by details of the sort of things and people that can be sponsored. The costs of sponsorship were discussed, and then there was a description of the organisation or sponsorships by both sides, those who want to be sponsored and those who want to be sponsors.

PAST EXAMINATION QUESTIONS

Question 9, LCC Series 2, 1987

Sponsorship has two main meanings: (a) the sponsorship of things, events or people, providing financial support and gaining publicity; (b) the sponsorship of radio and TV programmes as a form of advertising.

Discuss:

(i) The marketing advantages of sponsoring a major sporting event.

(ii) The marketing advantages of sponsoring radio and TV programmes with commercial spots.

Comment

This question has been well covered by the chapter, but two points may be added regarding the second part. But for sponsors the viewers in many foreign countries, especially in the Third World, would not see many events except 'by courtesy' of an advertiser. While it is clearly a powerful form of advertising it also has a big public relations input because viewers are grateful to the company for making it possible for them to see the event. Second, audiences in these countries are much smaller than in Britain, and the cost of airtime is much less.

When one considers that it costs thousands of pounds for 30 seconds airtime on British television it would be prohibitive to buy the time for, say, a whole match or tournament even if it were permissible.

Question 13, LCC Autumn 1986

Write an account of a well-known sponsorship, and analyse it to show how it contributes to the marketing of the sponsor's product or service.

Comment

This calls for a case-study answer based on the candidate's reading or observation of a sponsorship. It is typical of the practical question which expects the candidate to have read books, or watched what is going on around him. The question is about a sponsorship and not about a sponsored television programme.

Question 14, LCC Autumn 1981

Describe some of the ways in which sponsorship has been used as a marketing tactic, explaining why you think particular sponsorships have been undertaken.

Comment

The answer to this question will be found in the chapter, especially in the section headed 'Why sponsor'. Two reasons why sponsorships were undertaken occurred when Cornhill Assurance recognised that there was a large market for domestic insurance for television sets, VCRs, cameras and other expensive possessions which were portable and easily stolen. However, because the company's business was mostly conducted through brokers, and the market was unfamiliar with the Cornhill name, it was decided to sponsor test cricket to familiarise a wider public with the Cornhill name. This proved so successful that the sponsorship was renewed. In the case of Canon the managing director of the UK company was dismayed to discover that Olympus cameras were better-known than Canon. The company was also about to launch office equipment including typewriters, copiers and facsimile machines. The managing director aimed to make Canon number one in Britain within three years. Canon sponsored the Football League with its 92 clubs. At the end of the three-year sponsorship he claimed that hardly an office in Britain was without a Canon machine.

EXERCISE

Assume that a company of your choice has entered the domestic market with a product which was previously sold only for industrial purposes. consequently, the company and the product will be unknown to the mass consumer market. Choose a subject to sponsor, plan how this sponsorship would be exploited to the fullest possible extent, and forecast what results may be expected.

15. How are industrial goods and services marketed?

INTRODUCTION

The special nature of capital and technical goods and services sold to industry as distinct from consumer goods sold to the public, and their markets and marketing methods, will be discussed in this chapter, beginning with a definition. Business-to-business marketing will be explained, together with back-selling and its marketing problems. There will also be consideration of the buyers of industrial goods, and how they differ from those who buy consumer goods. The various media employed, and the use of public relations techniques will be described. Export marketing will also be considered.

DEFINITION

Industrial goods and services are those which are sold to industry, either to assist with production or as raw materials, components or ingredients which contribute to the end product.

It will be seen from the above definition that eventual buyers of the finished product may be unaware of these products and services, unless there is a list of specifications or the contents are stated on the label, as may be required by law in the case of a food or drug.

NATURE OF INDUSTRIAL PRODUCTS AND SERVICES

Usually, the market is fairly small (by comparison with a retail consumer product) and the unit cost in the case of equipment, or the volume cost in the case of materials or components, will be high. Specialist technical salesmen may be employed. Technical advice may have to be given to buyers. The range of goods or services may include:

(i) **Capital goods**. These are 'fixtures and fittings' like machinery, and they may be sold or leased to businesses such as offices, banks and shops as well as to manufacturers. They could be very big undertakings like airports, docks, business premises, schools or hospitals. They can include items such as transport or computers.

(ii) **Raw materials**. These are the essential materials such as metals, plastics, timber, building materials, chemicals, food ingredients and so on with which finished products are made.

(iii) **Components.** Products such as motorcars are assembled from numerous parts and accessories supplied by separate manufacturers, to mention only wheels, tyres, batteries, instruments, lights and upholstery. Even small finished products like Swiss watches are assembled from parts made by several specialist manufacturers.

(iv) **Services**. Various professional services including those of accountants, advertising agencies, public relations consultancies, architects, lawyers, insurance brokers, exhibition contractors, packaging designers, recruitment agencies, marketing research firms and many others are sold to industry.

BUSINESS-TO-BUSINESS MARKETING

In recent years business-to-business trading and services have developed as a speciality. There is now business-to-business advertising - the marketing of products and services to business - and there is an Association of Business Advertising Agencies. In this case, the products are mostly those used in conducting a business rather than in manufacturing goods, and they represent the growth in electronic office equipment such as typewriters, word processors, copiers, personal computers and facsimile machines. This extra field of non-consumer marketing can therefore be added to the marketing of industrial goods and services.

BACK-SELLING

Many products sold to industry are unknown, or at least their suppliers are unknown, to the final customer. While the average motorist seldom knows the names of the makers of the components under the bonnet of his car, it is impossible for him to know the sources of the contents of a packet of soup or a bottle of sauce or the paper on which this book is printed. Where did the colour of the soup or the sauce or the whiteness of the paper come from?

The selling of these obscure products to industry is called *back-selling*. Rarely does the final customer have any influence on their purchase by the manufacturer, unless by way of complaint or congratulations. An exception might be when the buyer of a new house is permitted to select certain fittings and equipment.

The supplier of industrial goods is therefore at the mercy of a manufacturer's specifications and costings, and it is less easy for him to identify and anticipate customer's requirements when they are bound up with highly secret new product development, secret formulae and competitive designs. This can, however, lead to a very different marketing situation where the supplier to industry may have to work very closely with industry buyers in order to produce what they want. This is an intimate relationship which is not enjoyed by the manufacturer who sells to the mass market.

Thus, industrial marketing may combine remoteness from the final customer and yet close relations with the intermediate producer. While the person opening a bottle in the home will not know why it has such a top or cap the maker of that opening device had to meet the exact specifications of the bottling firm.

WHO BUYS INDUSTRIAL GOODS AND SERVICES?

The consumer buys for personal satisfaction or on behalf of individuals such as members of the family or friends. If he buys wrongly he wastes his own money. If he doesn't like what he has bought he can throw it or give it away. Only a small financial outlay may be risked.

The industrial buyer buys differently, for defined motives, and with greater responsibility often incurring high financial involvement. He does not buy for himself, and seldom for his own satisfaction. The supplier thus faces some severe and testing challenges. Will his material stand up to certain stresses, contribute to a paint that will be more enduring, help to make a motor-car safer, or make paper whiter? Will it come within the producer's budget so that the finished product will sell to a particular market segment? Will it help to make a product cheaper, better quality, distinctive or in some way more competitive than another? These are the sort of buying reasons which confront the supplier to industry.

What sort of people make these challenges, take decisions and sign the orders and the cheques? They may not be one and the same person. There could be a chain of decision makers such as the specifier, production manager, purchasing officer and managing director. Selling may have to be done at a number of levels, unlike selling the average fmcg to housewives.

Kinds of industrial buyers may therefore comprise:

(i) **Gatekeepers.** These can be all sorts of people who collect and disseminate information, and they could be as diverse as secretaries and librarians, internal information officers and data processors.

(ii) **Specifiers.** Here we have people who actually recommend. They may be quantity surveyors, architects, designers, engineers, formulators of foods and medicines, and various outside consultants.

(iii) **Purchasing officers.** They are responsible for buying, knowing sources of supply, negotiating prices and issuing orders (even if these orders have to be authorised and signed by someone higher up).

(iv) **Final decision makers.** The process of information, specification and ordering may require the approval of a final decision maker. Decisions may be made for reasons of policy, budget, final choice between alternatives, delivery dates, discounts or other conditions of the deal.

Customers themselves could have special characteristics:

(i)   They may be limited in number, e.g. paper mills.

(ii) They may be scattered throughout the country, again paper mills.

(iii) Conversely, they could be concentrated in a particular place like the jewellery trade.

(iv) They are likely to be very knowledgeable about what they are buying.

(v)   If senior people, they will have great buying power.

(vi) Capital goods are bought infrequently so that it is unlikely that a customer relationship can be developed. It could be a once-only buy.

(vii) They could be foreigners. (Export marketing will be returned to later in this chapter.) They may be visiting customers, or have to be visited in their country, or dealt with through buying agencies.

The above characteristics suggest that different *selling skills* will be required from those when selling consumer goods to wholesalers and retailers. On the whole, sales representatives will need to be capable of giving technical advice. The sales force will tend to be small because there are fewer customers than with consumer products, and orders taken may not only be big in value but slow in achieving. There may be no regular journey cycles but irregular or once-in-a-lifetime calls, dependent on the frequency with which the product is bought. The industrial supplier may be asked to quote or tender.

Marketing research will tend to be different too. If customers are few and scattered geographically, *telephone surveys* by appointment will be practical and inexpensive.

Prototypes may be tested *in situ,* e.g. a new dishwasher could be installed in a works, school or hospital kitchen for a trial period.

The *innovator* or *dispersion theory* could be applied, a willing 'guinea pig' customer adopting the equipment and permitting potential clients to visit and see it in practical use. This method is an old one which has been adapted to modern use. From its original use by McCormick to promote ploughs and seed drills in America's Mid-West in the mid 19th century it has been applied in modern times not only to farm equipment but to industrial equipment as varied as computers, printing machines and ware

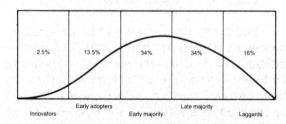

Figure 1 The innovator theory, showing the progress from the original innovator via adopters of the idea to final and very conservative laggards.

house systems. The innovator theory is demonstrated by Fig 1.

Another use of the innovator theory is in the Third World where a new product or a new concept is more likely to be adopted when it is first accepted by a social leader such as the oba, emir, king, local chief or village headman. With his say so others will follow and under his direction or instruction the new product or idea may be taken up. It may even be protocol to adopt this procedure and not go direct to the people.

MEDIA AND METHODS FOR PROMOTING INDUSTRIAL GOODS AND SERVICES

Industrial press advertising media differs from consumer press advertising media in two particular respects:

(i) **Circulation figures** tend to be fairly small because trade, technical and professional journals appeal to a specialised readership, as do business newspapers like *The Times* and the *Financial Times*.

(ii) **Method of circulation** will tend to be either by postal subscription or by controlled circulation. The latter tends to be the larger, readers being chosen or having requested copies, and cc journals tend to enjoy greater penetration of the market than those which depend on postal subscriptions or bookstall sales.

Similarly, with trade exhibitions, attendances are usually smaller than at public exhibitions, and the promoters will seek attendances by likely buyers who are admitted on showing their business cards, or with tickets published or inserted in a trade journal. Control of the quality of attendance is important to exhibitors.

Trade exhibitions offer opportunities for public relations activities from the moment the contract is signed for stand space to after the show. This is an area where public relations work can excel and perhaps serve an industrial product better than a consumer one. It pays to work with the exhibition press officer right from the start. Good publishable news releases about the new exhibit, supported by photographs, can be placed in the press room but lavish press kits should be avoided. Many journals will report the show, and the Central Office of Information may film stands for its overseas television programmes. It is also possible that new products shown at trade exhibitions will provide topics for future television programmes such as *Tomorrow's World*.

Catalogues, data sheets and sales literature will be produced for distribution by salesmen, at exhibitions and by direct mail.

The external house journal, with translated versions for overseas markets, can be an excellent way of educating the market, and a high standard of technical writing, illustration and print production will also enhance the company's reputation.

Public relations techniques will be especially appropriate because there will be need to educate rather than persuade the market. Technical products and services require explanation, and this may be done through case-study reports, pictures, feature articles and videos. The innovator method occurs again here because a client's successful use of a product or service can be demonstrated by the above public relations methods.

Technical articles in the trade press can provide convincing evidence of a product's application in real circumstances which is more credible and substantial than a news release. Public relations articles can be negotiated with editors, and provided they are written as interesting factual accounts of value to readers, and are free of repetitive plugs, they can be more credible and effective than advertisements. The addresses and editorial profiles of thousands of newspapers and magazines will be found in the UK and Overseas volumes of *Benn's*

Media Directory.

Another public relations technique which works well with industrial products is the press facility visit (rather like the innovator method) when trade journalists rather than potential clients are taken on visits and given first-hand experience of a product in use. This could range from a proving flight on a new aircraft to seeing new machinery in operation at a plant.

The seminar, teach-in, demonstration or conference can be another way of educating the market, making use of 'backroom boy' technical speakers rather than salesmen, and supporting the occasion with portable photographic displays, working models and a slide or video presentation. These events can be toured round the country and held at appropriate venues to which clients can be invited.

Mobile exhibitions may be associated with the above events, and these can take the form of a specially designed exhibition vehicle, a converted bus, a caravan, a British Rail exhibition train which stops at selected stations, and for export purposes there have been specially converted exhibition ships and aircraft.

Corporate advertising is used by large companies especially those with back-selling problems of identification or which sell internationally. Such advertisements can be seen in journals like *The Economist* which sells worldwide and this is demonstrated by the excerpts in the facing column from an advertisement for the Dutch chemical company Akzo of Arnhem.

It is about half the copy at the base of a two-page full-colour advertisement in *The Economist*. Most of the advertisement space was filled with pictures of products which contained Akzo materials. They included a shirt, bar of soap, sports shoe, tennis racquet cover, tyre, an aircraft and a motor-car.

Marketers of industrial goods also have the benefit of advertising agencies and public relations consultancies which specialise in indus-

trial accounts. Because space rates are lower and production costs may exceed the cost of space, advertising agencies will usually charge fees on industrial accounts rather than rely on commission from the media.

CREDIT WHERE CREDIT IS DUE

Take a look at your running shoes. You won't see Akzo's name on them anywhere.

Yet it's more than likely that we were responsible for the technology behind the light, bend-where-your-foot-bends uppers.

As well as the rugged, waterproof soles.

In fact we've probably had a hand in every part of the shoe's design. And the next time you're in the car, take a look around you. You won't see our name anywhere.

Yet the chances are that the lightweight materials in the chassis were developed by Akzo. As were the smooth textures of the upholstery. And the sturdy plastics that make up the dashboard ......

EXPORT SALES

Many industrial products and services depend on overseas sales. The home market is usually too small and the goods are specialised. This also has other complications. Products may have to be varied to suit foreign markets. A typesetting system will need to set different characters and alphabets, a combine harvester will have to harvest various crops in different seasons, a bus may need special wheels, tyres, lights, seats and perhaps either heating or air-conditioning for individual countries or regions of the world.

Overseas sales can be organised in four ways: (i) through the company's own travelling salesmen; (ii) through importers and agents in foreign countries; (iii) by licensing arrangements whereby foreign companies manufacture the products, and (iv) by overseas subsidiary companies which may be wholly or partly owned by local interests (either public or local) according to investment legislation.

A popular way of promoting British industrial goods and services in overseas markets is through the trade exhibition or trade fair. To help further exports, the British Government gives official support through the British Overseas Trade Board which organises British pavilions and joint exhibition schemes at special rates. All-British exhibitions are held in some countries, there are Area Advisory Groups, BOTB seminars on export marketing, and country-by-country hints to exporters booklets are obtainable from the BOTB.

Useful overseas publicity can be obtained through the Central Office of Information which distributes information world-wide about products which enhance Britain's international reputation. This information includes news releases, photographs, feature articles, radio tape interviews and documentary videos for use on overseas television. Similarly, the External Services of the BBC broadcast in many languages, especially Arabic, programmes about British industrial products and developments.

Inward and outward trade missions are organised to many countries by the Department of Trade and Industry and local Chambers of Commerce. Businessmen travelling on these missions receive DTI grants of about one third of the cost. These missions provide opportunities to meet prospective buyers. Inward missions consist of foreign buyers visiting Britain to visit sources of supply.

There are also means of distributing news stories overseas by computer and teleprinter by Universal News Services, and EIBIS is a unique London agency which translates and distributes news releases and feature articles to the press of selected countries and has been doing so with great success for many years.

These services are particularly valuable in industrial marketing which depend on exports. Many of the trade and technical journals mentioned in the Media section have international circulations so that PR material in them can also aid overseas trade.

In addition, there are advertising agencies and public relations consultancies with overseas branches or subsidiaries so that export campaigns can be planned and produced in the UK.

SUMMARY

In this chapter, following a definition of industrial goods and services, the differences were distinguished between industrial and consumer marketing. The nature of industrial products and services were also discussed. Business-to-business marketing and back-selling were explained.

The buyers of industrial goods and services were next described, and industrial marketing research was referred to with mention of the use of prototypes. The innovator theory was explained, with a chart.

Next, the chapter went on to consider the media and methods for promoting these goods and services, concluding with a section on export sales and the various Government aids for exporters, plus private overseas news services. It was shown how public relations could be especially relevant to industrial marketing.

PAST EXAMINATION QUESTIONS

Question 9, LCC Series 2, 1988

Discuss the main differences between marketing an industrial product such as machinery, and a consumer product such as a soft drink.

Comment

This chapter contains adequate information on which to base an essay of about $1\frac{1}{2}$ pages, contrasting the market and buyers, media, advertising and public relations methods, marketing research techniques and so on for the two completely different classes of good.

Question 8, LCC Series 2, 1987

This question was quoted in Chapter 12 on Public Relations, is also relevant here, and should be referred to again.

Question 13, LCC Spring 1984

In what ways would the advertising and public relations programme for a technical product sold to industry differ from that for a fast-moving consumer good?

Comment

This question is best answered by dividing the answer into two parts, one part dealing with advertising and one with public relations but preceded by an explanatory introduction of the marketing differences.

Model answer

Qu.13. Technical product sold to industry and a fast-moving consumer good could hardly be more different. The first could cost thousands of pounds and be sold to only a few customers whereas the second could cost only a few pence and be sold to millions of consumers. That is the magnitude of the contrast.

Differences in advertising

In order to reach a mass market with a small unit repeat purchase product such as a food, drink, toiletry or household article that is sold through retailers and in particular supermarkets, the advertising has to be impactive and imaginative. It also has to use popular media. In its creativity and choice of media it will also have to be competitive because there are rival brands.

The creativity will need to be highly memorable like that of Brooke Bond PG Tips, Whiskas cat food, Guinness, Coca-Cola and Nescafe. Press media will include the multi-million circulation newspapers such as *The Sun* and the *Daily Mirror*, general circulation magazines like *TV Times* and the *Radio Times* and big circulation women's journals such as *Woman*, *Woman's Own* and *Woman's Realm*. There will be networked television. Posters may be used, and there will be point-of-sale displays or sales promotion schemes. All in all, the advertising budget will be large, running to several million pounds.

The advertising will not be seasonal but will be continuous across the various media, although television commercials will tend to be used in bursts to obtain a certain number of TVRs, rested and brought back again. The object of the advertising will be to maintain continuous factory output.

The advertising will be conducted by a large advertising agency, and there will be great competition to get the account when a new agency is appointed. Accounts tend to change agencies every three or four years.

The manufacturer of an industrial product will probably use little press advertising and no television advertising. Posters are unlikely. The press advertising will be of two kinds - fairly serious, technical or reminder advertising in the fairly small circulation trade and technical press, and prestige or corporate advertising in the business press, perhaps *The Economist* and the *Financial Times*.

Trade exhibitions and overseas trade fairs, and possibly small mobile exhibitions will be used to demonstrate the product to mainly technical buyers or businessmen. A technical product will probably have a limited home market, and international exhibitions and trade journals with international circulations will be useful advertising media.

Technical literature, catalogues and data or specification sheets will be required by salesmen, for distribution at exhibitions, and direct mail will be a good medium since customers will be comparatively few and easily targetted.

Differences in public relations

Apart from corporate and financial public relations for the company, public relations for a popular consumer product would be aimed at the popular big circulation media. For a food product, women's magazines would be ideal PR media. To reach the domestic market, free sheets could be mailed with news releases.

The public relations campaign would aim to publish news stories and pictures, and feature articles about the use of the product. There would be regular contact with journalists who write on food or domestic subjects. A new or modified product could be demonstrated at a press conference for journalists from the popular press. Press relations would also be aimed at the retailer's trade press, announcing new products, prizes, packs and forthcoming advertising campaigns.

Public relations, like that of Coca-Cola, Schweppes and Benson & Hedges, can extend into sponsorship and so secure wide media coverage on television when events they sponsor are shown to millions of viewers.

But generally, the consumer product will rely more on advertising than on public relations.

Industrial products rely less on advertising, probably using a technical agency and retaining it for many years, and more on public relations. Public relations techniques lend themselves more to an industrial product which needs to be and can be explained in more informative and educational detail. By means of exclusive feature articles in the trade and technical press the uses and benefits of the industrial product can be described. Other articles can be of a case study nature and describe the product in actual use by a customer or number of customers. They can be of genuine reader interest, but must be kept free of plugs since these articles are not advertisements and will be published on their merits.

Similarly, it is possible to make videos demonstrating the use of the product. These can be shown at press receptions, on stands at trade exhibitions, at seminars and to groups of buyers. They can also be distributed abroad through the Central Office of Information.

An external house journal, perhaps with foreign language versions, can explain the product, its uses and actual examples of application, and be distributed to specialist readers such an enquirers, technicians, specifiers, businessmen and others who may influence purchase.

There can be general release of company and product news and pictures to the trade, technical, professional and financial press according to the nature of the product. On the whole, this PR material will be more serious and technical than that for a consumer product, and probably - because of its interest - easier to publish than that for consumer products. In fact, public relations methods will often work better for an industrial product than advertising.

EXERCISE

Your company manufacture bottle filling machinery for the drinks industry. Consider the lively market at home and abroad. Then describe the kind of advertising and advertising media which would be most appropriate, and plan a programme of public relations activities to make both the product and the company known and understood. Consider what Government and other agencies could be used to help inform foreign markets.

Part 5: Consumerism, legal and voluntary controls

In this Part we reach the end of the marketing road. What does the consumer think of our products, services and marketing methods? Sometimes there is antagonism, with organised protests by or on behalf of consumers because products are disappointing, dangerous or too dear.

Chapter 16 discusses the effects that consumerism can have on marketing. It can welcome or destroy companies, and malpractices can lead to codes of practice and laws to protect the consumer.

At one time there were proprietary medicine advertisements for products that were supposed to cure long lists of illnesses. Whole page advertisements for these products appeared in the press. Fortunately, they have long since been banned, largely through the self-regulatory efforts of the advertising business itself. There is nothing wrong with advertising, but it can be abused by rogue advertisers. There are still people who will try to sell you fake University degrees, for instance.

Chapter 17 introduces some of the more recent legislation concerning marketing, while self-regulatory codes of practice - which often work more quickly and effectively than laws - are described in Chapter 18.

16.   How does consumerism affect marketing?

INTRODUCTION

Consumerism and consumer sovereignty will be defined, and after this the nature of consumerism, and whether or not it has any effect on marketing, will be discussed. There will then be descriptions of the ways in which the consumer is protected or is able to voice complaints, with details of the activities of consumer protection voluntary bodies and media investigations. Actual codes of practice and some recent legislation will be discussed in more detail in the next two chapters.

DEFINITIONS

The two expressions *consumerism* and *consumer sovereignty* are defined as follows:

> *Consumerism is the consciousness among the buying public of the price, performance and quality of goods and services.*

This 'consciousness' can be expressed individually, as when complaints are made by customers, or collectively through consumer organisations which give advice and seek to protect consumer interests, or by investigative journalists and television programmes.

> *Consumer sovereignty is the power of the consumer to dominate the market place by making demands which influence the design, production, marketing and distribution of goods and services.*

Awareness of the power of the final buyer to accept or reject a product or service can be a major factor in the marketing process of 'satisfying consumer requirements' as set out in the CIM definition of marketing.

NATURE OF CONSUMERISM

A certain contradiction exists between the concept of satisfying consumer requirements, and thereby also maintaining customer goodwill and company reputation, and the fact that so many voluntary controls and statutes exist and that so many offences against satisfaction occur. Consumerism represents a marketing dilemma, a combination of *caveat emptor* (buyer beware) and the dictum that 'the customer is always right'.

In a society where the profit motive rules, the temptation is to maximise profits. Moreover, in a competitive economy products may be produced down to a price at the expense of quality. We find this in many everyday products where durable metals have been replaced by less durable plastics. The life-span of some modern products such as office equipment is often shorter than it was with former models. It was even found that nylon socks lasted too long, so cotton was added. Rationalisation is another problem where product mixes and ranges of lines may be streamlined to those which are most profitable, a process which can irritate customers who still want to buy the deleted ones. Consumerism and marketing are thus engaged in a tug-of-war, and the question is how to resolve conflict or better still avoid it. Or is it inevitable in an ever-changing world of costs and values?

MARKETING AND CONSUMERISM

Some of the ways in which marketing management can meet consumerism at least half-way are these:

(i)   **Guarantees or promises.** A simple promise that a product will perform properly or be replaced is often superior to a wordy guarantee, usually in small print, hedged about with exclusion clauses. Yet why should a product have only a twelve months guarantee when it should perform well for three or four years?

(ii) **Marketing research** to discover not only preferences but why customers bought or have ceased to buy products. It is surprising how such surveys can detect buying patterns or objections quite unknown to a manufacturer. A simple modification, if found desirable, can overcome problems and increase sales. It has been found, for instance, that the position of a handle on a cooker could make a remarkable difference to sales. There is the classic case of the cake mix which would not sell because housewives thought it would give their husbands the idea that they could not cook - until the magic words "you only have to add an egg" were added to the advertising and the pack!

(iii) **Product pre-testing** can produce similar results. There are motor-car manufacturers who invite a number of people who drive regularly to drive a new car for a few weeks or months, and then to report on its performance. Dislikes are then rectified before the new model goes on the market. In one such case substantial amendments were made to the gearbox. Similar tests were made with a new blend of coffee.

(iv) **Offers of refunds** or **replacements**. These can be made by manufacturers or by retailers, and they help to create confidence. The mere fact that the offer is made creates customer confidence. A number of food and confectionery products carry a 'satisfaction guaranteed' notice on the pack or on a slip inserted in the package. These manufacturers are obviously very jealous of their good reputation.

(v) **Customer services.** Many companies employ a customer services officer, or even have a customer services department, and actually invite enquiries or complaints.

This can be reassuring. The Post Office actually advertises its customer services department in local telephone directories, as do British Gas. This sort of organised link with customers can be immensely important, especially where there are large numbers of customers and inevitably problems will occur. It can be a lifeline to a worried customer. One of the annoying things with some big mail order firms is that they deliberately give no telephone number, which can be frustrating to an aggrieved customer.

(vi) **Quality**. If quality standards are maintained, this can be the best of all answers to consumerism. It can be a matter of pride that a company's products or services are of indisputable quality. The sense of responsibility to the customer, this inherent good public relations, may emanate from top management as it has done for decades with Marks and Spencer. Or a shop may challenge customers to find the same goods priced lower elsewhere, as Currys do.

Quality may, of course, be derived from stringent quality control tests before goods are allowed to go on the market.

It is often the case that goods from countries such as Germany and Japan are superior to British ones. It is no accident that both countries had industries destroyed by war and afterwards created new ones with modern plants including automation and robotics which produce goods of equal quality. Sadly, human labour produces goods of variable quality such as the infamous 'Friday car' of the British motor-car industry before robotics were introduced.

Labour relations are also different in Germany and Japan and again it is no accident that German industry has enjoyed both single industrial instead of many craft unions, plus worker directors, which are disliked by both British Conservatives and

Socialists, and have been virtually strike-free.

The success of the German and Japanese economies revolves around the quality of their products. The Japanese companies which have set up in Britain have single union no-strike agreements, and produce high quality products. These are facts of marketing life, not political argument. Britain's success in the Single European Market after 1992 will depend on its labour relations and the quality of its goods, but this may call for a change of attitude regarding worker participation in management. As a German trade unionist remarked on a David Frost television programme, "we do not kill the cow that gives the milk" because, being represented on the board of directors, they know what is going on.

(vii) **After-sales services.** These are repeated here because they maintain continuity of customer relations by means of repair services, spares, instruction leaflets and service manuals, customer magazines, reminders about servicing and servicing contracts, invitations to showrooms to see new models and other aspects of the after-market. These activities and publications show that the supplier *cares* about his customers and they can do much to overcome customer antagonisms. The customer is always to some extent *remote* from the manufacturer, and this distancing of one from the other can provoke consumerist criticism.

The above seven examples show how the manufacturer or retailer can create a good marketing atmosphere. However, now let us consider consumerism from the point of view of organised consumerism.

ORGANISED CONSUMERISM

The following are some of the ways in which consumerism is organised:

(i) **Naderism.** This is the name given to a series of campaigns over a number of years investigated by the American lawyer Ralph Nader. He pioneered a number of assaults on poor products leading to the passing of the Auto Safety Act, the Wholesome Meat Act, the Coal Mine Safety Act and the Air Pollution Act. The campaigns of 'the crusading lawyer' are best known in the motor-car industry where his criticisms resulted in one motor-car being withdrawn from the market because of bad welding, and Government buying agencies demanding new safety standards in the vehicles they bought.

He campaigned against Union Carbide over pollution; won an order against Chevron Oil to stop advertising that their petrol cleaned engines; had dangerous toys withdrawn from shops; and succeeded in getting the American Dental Association to advise its members to cease taking x-rays on pregnant women because of the risk of miscarriages and birth defects; and criticised the ways in which Lloyds of London conducted insurance in America. His research staff earned the name of 'Nader's Raiders'.

(ii) *Silent Spring* and the Cruel Poisons Act. During the 60s there were many campaigns against the contaminating and dangerous effects of chemicals used for pest control, or against effusions into rivers that killed fish as occurred on the Rhine. In the USA Rachel Carson shocked the world with her book *Silent Spring* which described how plant and animal life was being destroyed by chemical pollutions.

About the same time in Britain a private member's bill was passed in Parliament called the Cruel Poisons Act which made it illegal to use fluoracetamide to kill rats because it caused painful deaths. The substance, first used during the Second World War in the London Docks to preserve food stocks from the ravages of vermin, and then used commercially and by local authorities to clear sewers of rates, was an example of a form of consumerism which went too far. Rats breed plague and spread other diseases, and this chemical was the most effective rodenticide ever produced.

However, such was the consumerism outcry in the 60s that President John Kennedy is often remembered for stating the four basic consumer rights which were:

1. **The Right to Safety** - to be protected against the marketing of goods which are hazardous to health or life.

2. **The Right to be Informed** - to be protected against fraudulent, deceitful or grossly misleading information, advertising, labelling or other practices, and to be given the facts needed to make an informed choice.

3. **The Right to Choose** - to be assured, wherever possible, access to a variety of products and services at competitive prices and in those industries in which Government regulations are substituted, an assurance of satisfactory quality and service at fair prices.

4. **The Right to be Heard** - to be assured that consumer interests will receive full and sympathetic consideration in the formulation of Government policy and fair expeditious treatment in its administrative tribunals.

Kennedy's four principles have universal application but they have to contend with the behaviour of a free market economy when it is fashionable to favour private rather than public enterprise. It is the fine difference sometimes between satisfying customer requirements and doing so profitably.

(iii) **Campaign against lead.** In Britain, Des Wilson headed the campaign conducted by the pressure group Campaign for Lead Free

Air (CLEAR) to have lead eliminated from petrol. This received Government support and today lead-free petrol is on sale. Motorists were slow to take it up because of the cost of having adjustments made to their car engines, but many modern cars will accept lead free petrol. Meanwhile, CLEAR has promoted the fact that the tax differential between leaded and unleaded petrol was doubled in the 1988 budget.

(iv) **Friends of the Earth and Greenpeace.** These and other organisations campaign against products, packaging and effusions of waste which create pollution and harm the environment. Friends of the Earth, for instance, have succeeded in preventing the packaging of milk and some soft drinks in plastic bottles which were indestructible and caused a pollution hazard. There are also animal protection societies which protest against the use of furs and skins for clothing, or against laboratory experiments using animals.

(v) **Consumer organisations.** The National Consumer Council is the official body which aims to protect consumers of retail goods and services, and also the users of public services such as health, education, rail and bus services and council housing.

The Consumers Association is an independent non-profit distributing organisation financed by members' subscriptions to magazines and other services, and by the sale of its publications and research results. The Association researches and tests goods and services, and campaigns for improvements in goods and services. Its publications include *Which?*, *Holiday Which?*, *Gardening from Which*, the *Which? Wine Monthly* and annual guides.

There are also other consumer protection bodies such as the Electricity Consumer Council, the Gas Consumers Council, and the Post Office Users' National Council. The British Safety Council has long campaigned for better industrial and domestic safety, ranging from supporting an anti-jack-knife device for articulated lorries to criticising nightdresses made of inflammable materials.

(vi) **The Advertising Standards Authority and the Committee of Advertising Practice** operate a self-regulatory system of advertising control. As was stated in Chapter 11 on advertising there is nothing wrong with *advertising* but it is a tool which can be used responsibly or irresponsibly by *advertisers*. A hammer is harmless provided it is not mis-used as a lethal weapon. There are deliberate mis-users of advertising, there are over-jealous marketing managers, and there are enthusiastic advertising agency creative staff anxious to please clients.

There are also quite innocent and unintended abuses to which exception is taken as when TVS warned of the low standards of continental satellite television by running an advertisement which illustrated an Italian housewife on an Italian striptease television programme. Protests from Saatchi and Saatchi in Rome revealed that she was a British model, the Italians had long since banned such programmes and that TVS had a financial interest in the Super Channel satellite television! There are times when advertising *people* try to be too clever. The ASA received many complaints about the TVS advertisement, although the *Independent* published a letter saying that if Italian strippers looked like the one in the TVS ad he looked forward to satellite television! Attitudes to advertising range from the prudish and cranky to the serious and concerned.

In the next chapter the contents of the British Code of Advertising Practice will be reviewed, but here it is necessary to understand the relationship between the ASA and CAP. It is the ASA which inserts advertisements in the press inviting members of the public to submit evidence of advertisements (*not* radio and TV commercials) which fail to be *legal, decent, honest and truthful*.

To quote from the CAP leaflet *CAP At Your Service*, "The ASA and CAP share a Secretariat but the ASA is an independent body: every member of its Council serves as an individual and two-thirds of the Council are independent of any advertising interest. Where part of CAP's job is to receive and investigate intra-industry complaints, the ASA is best known for the work it does to investigate complaints about advertisements which come from the general public. The Authority represents the public face of self-regulation and speaks to Government Departments and the like on matters of general principle for seeing that these principles are applied".

The ASA is thus the watchdog of the advertising industry and it has dual aims. The first derives from the original National Vigilance Committee of 1926 and the subsequent Advertisement Investigation Department of the Advertising Association which handed over its work in 1962 to the independent Advertising Standards Authority.

The ASA is financed by a levy of 0.1% on gross advertising rates which is administered by the Advertising Standards Board of Finance. The levy relates to press, outdoor, cinema and direct mail advertising. The first objective, then, is to protect the good name of advertising and encourage public faith in it. The second objective is to protect the public from unscrupulous or misguided advertising.

Commercial television and radio advertising are controlled by the IBA Code of Advertising Standards and Practice which is required under Section 9 of the Independent Broadcasting Authority Act 1973. It goes further than the BCAP, banning cigarette advertising, and banning ads dealing with politics, religion, industrial and public controversy. The IBA Code is particularly protective of children's and young people's interests, e.g. dangerous scenes involving children and encouraging young people to drink alcoholic drinks.

The ASA is responsible for the voluntary control of advertisements other than radio and television, doing so by means of the British Code of Advertising Practice which also contains special requirements concerning the advertising of cigarettes and alcoholic drinks. It also administers the British Code of Sales Promotion Practice. Every month the *ASA Report* is published, and this gives details of the complaints received and the decisions taken. In spite of what was said earlier in this chapter of the reasonable behaviour adopted by leading companies anxious to maintain their reputations, the *ASA Report* regularly contains the names of famous companies. The following are examples from *ASA Report* 157, 158 and 161 of May, June and September 1988.

BRITISH TELECOM

Basis of complaint: A member of the public objected to a magazine advertisement for the MerlinFax HS20 which claimed "There's no special installation needed. Just plug the HS20 into a standard phone socket – either a direct line or one that comes through your company switchboard ..." The complainant objected that on making enquiries, he was advised that the product was not compatible with a BT Merlin switchboard. (B.5.1).

Conclusion: Complaint upheld. The advertisers confirmed that the MerlinFax was not compatible with the complainant's system which they explained was a 4-wire small switching system, rather than the standard 2-wire system complete with a separate switchboard to which the advertisement referred. The Authority did not consider

the distinction would be generally understood and was pleased to note that the advertisers proposed to clarify their terminology in future.

CURRYS LTD

Basis of complaint: Four members of the public objected to a national press sale advertisement which included the offer of "$\frac{1}{2}$ Price Video Tapes. TDK E180 Twin Pack Sale Price £2.00. Maxell E180 Sale Price £1.49". On telephoning several branches the complainants were informed that no stock of the tapes had yet been received. They thus objected to the inclusion of the tape offer in the advertisement. (B.14)

Conclusion: Complaints upheld. The advertisers stated that at the time the advertisement appeared they considered that sufficient stock was held, but in hindsight agreed that this may not have been the case. The Authority noted the advertiser's assurance that in future they would endeavour to make sure sufficient stock was available.

AMSTRAD CONSUMER ELECTRONICS PLC

Basis of complaint: A member of the public objected to an advertisement which offered several personal computer software packages for £69 each and claimed "Any of these Amstrad programs could cost hundreds of pounds from another manufacturer." The complainant understood that the programs were based on discontinued North American editions which had been replaced by more advanced software, and therefore questioned the basis for the comparison. (B.21)

Conclusion: Complaint upheld. The advertisers stated that it was their intention to make a comparison between the advertised products and other software packages incorporating similar features which did cost "hundreds of pounds". The advertisers failed to demonstrate that the advertised software was not of an equivalent specification to the more expensive industry-standard packages currently available. In the absence of such substantiation the Authority concluded that the cost comparison was not supported and requested that the advertisers modify future advertisements to avoid any suggestion of technical equivalence between the advertised software packages and the more expensive alternatives offered by competitors.

BRITISH RAILWAYS BOARD

Basis of complaint: Ten members of the public objected to a national press advertisement addressed to Young Person's Railcard holders which stated "This February, go and see anyone you fancy anywhere in Britain for £10 or less". The advertisement outlined the terms of the offer and invited readers to seek full details from their local station or appointed travel agent. On seeking this further information the complainants found that the offer did not apply to London-bound trains which arrived in London on or before 10.00am Monday to Thursday, nor were they available for travel on Fridays. The complainants considered that the travel restrictions should have been indicated in the initial press advertisement. (B.5.1)

Conclusion: Complaints upheld. The advertisers explained that with any offer of this nature there are a number of caveats and that it was for this reason that they suggested in the advertisement that customers obtain full details from the leaflet available at British Rail stations, or appointed travel agents. The leaflet included full details of all the restrictions and qualifications to the offer. The Authority noted this, and whilst it accepted that it would not be reasonable to expect full travel conditions necessarily to be included in the advertisement, it did consider that some indication should have

been included as to the possible restrictions regarding travel times and destinations. The advertisers were requested to outline major conditions such as these in future advertisements for similar offers.

CITROEN UK LTD

Basis of complaint: A member of the public objected to a national press advertisement for the Citroen AX GT which claimed "The new Citroen AX GT doesn't need go faster stripes. It makes it own", and which featured a photograph of the car with speed-lines in its trail. The complainant considered that the advertisement placed undue emphasis on speed and therefore encouraged dangerous driving. (B.2.2; B.19)

Conclusion: Complaint upheld. The advertisers stated that it had not been their intention to encourage speed or fast driving and that the concept used was merely symbolic: the car was not on the road nor could the driver be identified. The Authority noted the advertisers' comments but was of the view that the combination of the headline and illustration was unacceptable in the apparent condonation of speed, and requested that the advertisers avoid similar presentations in the future in which speed is utilised as a primary platform for the advertisement.

SUNDAY EXPRESS

Basis of complaint: Fifteen members of the public objected to a poster and press advertisement for the Sunday Express story about Lana Turner's daughter which was headlined "Making a killing in Hollywood", and featured a photograph of a young girl wearing a see-through nightdress, wielding a large knife in one hand, and holding a teddy bear in the other. The complainants, some of whom referred to increasing public concern about the use of knives and the incidence of child abuse, objected that both the imagery of the advertisement and the manner in which the girl was dressed rendered the advertisement indecent and offensive. (B.3)

Conclusion: Complaints upheld. The advertisers shared the complainants' concern regarding the subject of child abuse and the use of knives, but stated that they considered that the advertisement did not give any offence or encouragement in this context. The purpose of the advertisement was to represent the stabbing of Lana Turner's lover by her daughter, which was the subject of a three-part serialisation. The Authority accepted that it might be reasonable to use evocative images to promote the story, but considered the presentation of the girl wielding a knife in a see-through nightdress to be unnecessary, and capable of causing offence. It was noted that the advertisers had no plans to repeat the advertisement.

PRUDENTIAL PROPERTY SERVICES

Basis of complaint: A member of the public objected to a local press advertisement placed by a branch of Prudential Property Services which included a feature of four properties flashed "SOLD OVER EASTER". The complainant pointed out that he had purchased one of these houses in November of last year and, therefore, questioned whether any of the properties had actually been sold during the claimed period. (B.5.1; B.1.2; B.5.2.1)

Conclusion: Complaint upheld. The advertisers stated that the advertisement had been prepared locally without company authority and was entirely without foundation. They regretted any misunderstanding amongst readers and assured the Authority that advertisements of this type would in future be prepared at a regional level to ensure the accuracy of advertisement claims.

Nevertheless, the question so often

asked in examinations is worth discussing at this point: *how do voluntary controls compare with legal controls? Do voluntary controls have any teeth?*

The great strength of voluntary controls lies in their self-regulatory preventive effect. By their existence the various codes (and the industry has many) deter advertisers, agencies and the media from offending the public with misleading or dishonest advertising. Although complaints do have to be investigated, and advertisements are condemned, they represent a tiny fraction of the huge volume of advertising which appears daily.

Agencies can lose their 'recognition' and commission rights if they produce advertising which offends against the Code, and no publisher wants to receive complaints from readers about the advertisements he prints. If an advertisement does reach the stage of public complaint, action can be taken swiftly and the offending advertisement can be amended or withdrawn.

The ASA cannot exact any other penalty, other than making public its decision. This 'publish and be damned' role of the ASA is a great advance on the days of the Advertising Association's investigations before 1962 when decisions had to be confidential for fear of a libel prosecution!

While legislation carries penalties, and the existence of legislation does have its preventive effect, it is nonetheless a lengthy and expensive process to prosecute an offender. It may take years for a case to come to court, by which time the harm has been done and it is too late to protect consumers other than by fining the guilty advertiser.

(vii) **Mail Order Protection.** For many years publishers have been anxious to protect both themselves and their readers from either unscrupulous or inefficient mail order traders. Now that this has grown into the vast direct response marketing industry, a number of controls exist to protect the consumer. In many ways, the British Code of Advertising Practice seeks to regulate the advertising of direct response marketing, but other methods include the MOPS scheme which is frequently advertised in newspapers and magazines. See *Fig. 1.*

Shopping by post?

Play it safe

Readers who reply to cash with order advertisements in national newspapers or colour supplements are safeguarded by the National Newspapers Mail Order Protection Scheme. This covers all categories of goods and services with the exception of: those advertised under classified headings, perishable foodstuffs, horoscopes, lucky charms, non durable gardening and medical products.

The MOPS protection guarantees that your money will be refunded if a member advertiser stops trading and does not deliver your order, or refund your payment.

Advertisements covered by the Scheme may include the MOPS symbol or the initial letters MOPS in their layout.

For full details send a 9″ × 6″ stamped addressed envelope to:
The National Newspapers' Mail Order,
Protection Scheme,
16 Tooks Court, London, EC4A 1LB

Play it safe—look for the symbol

THE NATIONAL NEWSPAPER

MOPS

MAIL ORDER PROTECTION SCHEME

Figure 1 Advertisement placed in national newspapers for MOPS.

As the wording of this advertisement explains, readers are safeguarded by this scheme. In the past, problems occurred because some mail order traders advertised lines and did not place orders for stock until they had received orders from the public. Sometimes the suppliers' price had increased in the meantime, and the advertiser lost money and went bankrupt so that his customers lost their money. Today, reputable publishers will not accept direct response advertisements unless the advertiser is properly organised and able to

supply within a reasonable time such as 28 days.

(viii) **Mailing preference Service.** Sponsored by the direct response marketing trade bodies, this service helps members to provide an effective service and to comply with the spirit of the Data Protection Act. Members of the public who do not wish to receive direct mail shots can have their wishes put on a Consumer File which is supplied quarterly in hard copy or tape form to members of the various direct mail and list broking associations

Similarly, names can be added of those who wish to receive direct mail material. This is an important service because many organisations sell their membership or customer lists, while share registers are freely available and privatisation of British Telecom, British Gas and so on had put thousands of shareholders on readily available lists.

(ix) **Investigative journalism.** The media frequently champion consumer causes, and exposures of rackets and malpractices appear in the press with the 'heavies' like the *Sunday Times*, *The Observer* and *The Guardian* being just as sensational as the popular tabloids. There are several current affairs television programmes which explore topics of consumer interest, while Esther Rantzen's *That's Life* has been so provocative that it has produced retaliatory legal actions or protests to the Broadcasting Complaints Commission.

(x) **British Standards Institution.** This is a government-sponsored body which sets standards for specifications and materials which are given BSI numbers. While much of this is to do with industrial products (e.g. printing ink colours) BSI standards are also applied to many goods bought by consumers and so represent a standard of quality, or of the quality of the materials from which consumer goods are made.

From the above examples of organised consumerism it can be seen that the consumer has many friends willing and able to protect his interests. There is also government and legal intervention with more than one hundred laws concerning marketing, selling and advertising. In particular, there are the efforts of the Office of Fair Trading. Some of the more recent legislation is discussed in Chapter 18, although the law is subject to constant change and the reader should be aware of current legislation relevant to marketing. Copies of Statutes can be bought at HM Stationery Offices.

Nevertheless, the consumer may not always be aware of marketing activities which are contrary to his interests. Should, for instance, special lighting be used in butchers' shops and supermarkets to make meat look fresh and attractive, or is this a dubious practice? Should pharmaceutical firms test drugs for a longer time in order to discover side-effects? The cost of research is heavy and the temptation is to market new drugs as soon as possible to recoup development costs and make a profit. Should there be better control of the emission of pollutants, even if this 'social cost' has to be met by increased prices? So often costs and prices conflict with what is best for the consumer and what the consumer is prepared to pay.

The lesson has been learned in the motor-car industry as the volume of sales and traffic has increased. Fifty years ago, safety was regarded by motor-car makers as a negative selling factor, but today it is a positive one.

SUMMARY

After defining consumerism and consumer sovereignty, the nature of consumerism was discussed, bringing out the conflict of interests between producers and consumers. Some of the ways in which marketing management can satisfy consumerism and avoid the antagonism of consumers was analysed, showing how the consumer is protected by voluntary bodies and the media. Actual codes of practice and legal controls were left to the next two chapters.

PAST EXAMINATION QUESTIONS

Question 5, LCC Spring 1983

(i) How important is consumerism in affecting the marketing strategy of a company?

(ii) Give examples of marketing strategies which have been influenced by consumerist pressure.

Comment

The question requires two separate answers for which equal marks are awarded. It is the sort of question which expects the candidate to make intelligent observations in the first part, and to be aware of some practical examples. There is no standard correct answer, but the following will give an impression of the style of answer that is expected.

Model answer

Qu.5.(i) If a company wishes to maintain a good reputation, and to really satisfy customer requirements, it should take notice of the wishes of consumers. These may be expressed in complaints or suggestions made direct to the company, or by way of campaigns conducted by consumerist pressure groups, or by investigative journalists. Consumerist views may not necessarily reveal themselves in marketing research surveys, simply because certain attitudes were not anticipated and appropriate questions were not asked.

Sometimes, the final buyer may not be aware of, say, the danger of a product whether it be a drug in a medicine, an ingredient used in baking bread, or lead in petrol, and awareness is stimulated by a voluntary organisation which has carried out research.

There may, therefore, be problems which make a product unsatisfactory but which were unknown to the manufacturer. When a problem is publicised a company should not pretend that the problem does not exist, but should endeavour to eliminate it. A company could gain credit for being socially responsible.

If complaints and exposures persist they can be very damaging to a company. There could be a chain reaction: consumers would stop buying and retailers would not re-stock; company profits would fall and there would be an adverse effect on share prices; staff could become redundant while some staff might prefer to work for a more reputable company.

The company could earn a bad reputation which would be perpetuated by the media which would continue to refer to the company as one whose product was deficient. It cannot do this if the reason for criticism is removed.

Consequently, consumerism can affect marketing strategy in many ways. These can be drastic ones like curtailing sales, or they can be contributory ones like calling for more product development research, revised formulation or use of components, different packaging, and, if the advertising has been the subject of a complaint to the Advertising Standards Authority, amended advertising.

Qu.5.(ii) Some marketing strategies which have been influenced by consumerist pressures are:

(a) **Breakfast cereals.** In the USA makers of cornflakes were criticised because of the negligible nutritional value of this breakfast food. As a result, cornflakes now have nutritional additives such as fruit.

(b) **Lead-free petrol.** Following the CLEAR campaign, the British government legislated in favour of lead-free petrol and reduced the tax on it. Motor manufacturers now make engines which accept lead-free petrol.

(c) **Safer motor-cars.** As a result of demands from motorists, motoring organisations and motoring correspondents, several motor-car manufacturers have built safer motor-cars. There is the Audi with its crushable front and rear-ends which leave the central body of the vehicle intact, while safety factors have been featured in TV commercials for the Volvo 340.

(d) **Aerosols.** The outcry about the effect of chlorofluorocarbons on the ozone layer has led not only to the advertised non-use of this material in some aerosols, but to the promotion of roll-on and stick deodorants as alternatives to aerosol products.

(e) **Inflammable plastics.** Publicity about the fire hazards of plastic foam materials has led to the manufacture of furniture with non-inflammable upholstery.

(f) **Plastic pollution.** The Friends of the Earth claimed that if milk was supplied in plastic bottles there would be enough discarded indestructable plastic milk bottles for them to reach from the earth to the moon. They also dumped plastic soft drink bottles outside Schweppes offices. In both cases, glass bottles were retained.

(g) **Pesticides.** Fears and protests about residual pesticides on fruits and vegetables have led to stores like Tesco negotiating with suppliers over the pesticides used. In continental supermarkets warnings are displayed about pesticides on the skins of citrus fruit. Samples of fresh fruits and vegetables are subject to random tests by local Public Analysts on behalf of the Ministry of Agriculture. The British Agro-Chemical Association, representing the manufacturers of pesticides, issues warnings to growers about excessive spraying.

(h) **Diet.** Advice on dietary and healthy eating has made customers reject products containing undesirable ingredients, and manufacturers today use less sugar and salt, and - like Coca-Cola - use and advertise their use of substitute sweeteners. The fats industry now produce special margarines containing sunflower oil, or spreads like Gold which are neither margarine nor butter.

(N.B. Different answers are likely to be given to this question but the above is an example of an answer which depends not only on the information given by lecturers, but also on the extent to which the candidate is aware of the marketing environment. The sort of examples quoted above have all been reported in the press and discussed in television current affairs programmes. Some of them are evident in television advertising.)

EXERCISE

Your company manufactures a famous brand of toothpaste, but sales have fallen due to rival products containing additives which have improved their cleaning or tooth-decay resistance qualities. A new improved and re-packaged version of your brand is now to be marketed. Devise a sales promotion scheme to launch the improved product, together with a supporting advertising campaign announcing the additive which gives better protection against tooth decay. This campaign can exploit the health advice being published about the effect of modern foods on dental decay.

17. Legal controls affecting marketing

INTRODUCTION

Law is a big subject in its own right and there are so many laws affecting marketing that it is impossible for the student to be familiar with them all. Moreover, new legislation is continually appearing on the Statute Book. Some laws apply to particular industries such as the various Acts and Regulations concerning food and drugs and their labelling and the requirements of hire purchase agreements. In this chapter Common law and Statute law will be defined, some of the most applicable aspects of common law will be explained, followed by an introduction to some of the more recent and important Acts and Regulations to do with marketing. The student is not expected to be a lawyer but he should be aware of the marketing implications of legal controls.

COMMON LAW - DEFINITION

Common law consists of contracts and torts or civil wrongs, for which an aggrieved party or plaintiff can sue for redress or damages in a civil court.

Neither the police nor the Public Prosecutor are involved, and there are no criminal charges, nor can imprisonment be imposed as a penalty. Cases are usually judged on who is the greatest loser, the plaintiff or the defendant, and some loss or injury has to be proved. These are personal cases between an injured party and whoever has caused the injury. An injury could be loss of good character, breach of contract or loss of business.

Common law is unwritten law based on precedent, and the claims and decisions in previous cases are often cited in court as part of the case presented by each side.

STATUTE LAW - DEFINITION

Statute law consists of Acts of Parliament, or Regulations issued by a Minister, and offenders against these written laws are liable to prosecution, fine and/or imprisonment following criminal proceedings conducted by the Crown, through the Public Prosecutor, and the accused.

Complaints may be laid by the public or the police, and if the Public Prosecutor or similar appointed authority such as the Director General of the Office of Fair Trading or the local weights and measures authority considers that there is a case to be answered, and that there is a reasonable chance of success in the courts because of the strength of the evidence, the offender will be prosecuted. The accused is entitled to engage his own legal defence, hence the term 'defence lawyer'. A judge will hear the pleas of the prosecution and defence counsel and witnesses may be called by both sides.

It is an expensive procedure, and it may take months, even years, for a case to come to court. On the other hand, the provisions of the Act lay down behaviour that should be observed, and it is implicit upon everyone to obey the law whether or not they are aware of it. Where laws concern aspects of marketing, it is essential that those responsible for marketing are familiar with these laws and take legal advice whenever necessary. Ignorance of the law is no defence. This also applies to those providing outside services such as advertising agencies and designers of packaging.

LAW OF CONTRACT

In case of dispute it is wise to have a contract in writing. When a written offer, such as a quotation for print, is received it should be accepted by repeating the terms of the offer. If there is any amendment this becomes a reverse offer and a new contract is created which requires acceptance by the supplier. Verbal contracts, such as telephone orders for the purchase of advertisement space, can be legal provided they are carried out, even if nothing is stated in writing. Some contracts occur simply by shaking hands, as often happens in a cattle market.

There are four important elements which make a contract valid, that is, legal:

(i)   There must be an *offer*.

(ii) There must be an *acceptance*.

(iii) There must be a *consideration* - both sides must make a sacrifice, e.g. one side makes payment and the other side supplies a good or provides a service. There is an exchange.

(iv) *Consent* must be genuine, and not be obtained by fraud or unfair means.

The contract can be invalidated if there is a *mistake* or *misrepresentation*. It must not be made for an *illegal* purpose, and the parties to it must have *contractual capacity:* not be under 18 years of age, not be insane or drunk.

Certain contracts must be *written* if they come within certain legislation such as the Law of Property Act 1925, the Hire Purchase Act 1965, the assignment of a copyright, or when a guarantor supports payment for a purchase. A contract of service between an advertising agency and a client could include an assignment of copyright (usually subject to the client having paid his bills!).

A distinction needs to be made between an *invitation to treat* and a contract. Goods displayed in a window constitute an offer to treat, not an offer for sale. The shopkeeper does not have to sell his displayed goods however willing people are to buy them. However, if a customer picks up an item and takes it to the cashier, that is an offer to buy, and if the cashier takes the money in exchange for the item, that is an acceptance and a contract has been completed.

SLANDER OF GOODS

This can occur when one party denigrates another party's goods, and if as a result loss of trade can be proved damages may be awarded by the court. However, this is also covered by the British Code of Advertising Practice where the slander (known as 'knocking copy' or 'ash-canning') occurs in an advertisement.

Associated with this is personal *defamation,* the spoken or transient form called *slander,* and the published broadcast or permanent form being known as *libel.* Defamation can occur in advertising when a statement is falsely attributed to someone. This has occurred when a person of the same name has been misquoted. Testimonials have to be vetted very carefully. People in pictures should not be given quoted remarks unless they have actually made them.

PASSING OFF

Damages may be claimed when business has been lost because a rival product has been packed or named in such a way that customers have purchased it in mistake for the original. In some countries there have been deliberate attempts to do this, as when a local product has been given a similar name and 'get up' as a famous imported one. There are also goods imported from the East (e.g. jeans and skirts) which bear the fraudulent labels of well-known British brands.

The deception may be introduced by means of the company or brand name, lettering or typography, colour scheme, labelling or packaging or in an advertisement. There was the case of Zeiss binoculars. The name was famous, but the binoculars were made by an entirely different firm of the same name. The product was advertised by a mail order firm.

DATA PROTECTION ACT 1984

According to the Act "'Data' means information recorded in a form in which it can be processed by equipment operating automatically in response to instructions given for the purpose." This generally means that it is held on a computer. The Act also says "'Personal data' means data consisting of information which relates to a living individual who can be identified from that information (or from that and other information in the possession of the data user), including any expression of opinion about the individual but not any indication of the intentions of the data user in respect of that individual". The object of the Act is to safeguard individuals from the mis-use of personal information held on computers, and to provide individuals with the means of obtaining information about such information which is held about them.

This applies to marketing where, for instance, personal details are contained in mailing lists held on databases, many of which are sold or hired to other direct mail users. Holders of such data have to register the fact (in some detail) via the Data Protection Registrar. Registered data users must comply with the following seven data protection principles:

Personal data shall be:

1. Collected and processed fairly and lawfully.

2. Held only for lawful purposes described in the register entry.

3. Used only for those purposes and only be disclosed to those people described in the register entry.

4. Adequate, relevant and not excessive in relation to the purposes for which they are held.

5. Accurate and, where necessary, kept up-to-date.

6. Held no longer than is necessary for the registered purpose.

7. Protected by proper security.

More than 200,000 registered organisations are on lists which are held in 171 British libraries. A fee of up to £ 10 has to be paid to obtain a print out of personal details held on a business computer. However, it is not always easy to know who is the original holder of the information, nor on which or on how many lists the information may be held. It may be very expensive to obtain the required data, and some people object to having to make such payment. For example, a person may dislike receiving direct mail shots, but their name and address may be obtained from a list broker, or be on a list sold to other users. The sender of the direct mail shot may not hold the original data, nor know its source.

Nevertheless, the British List Brokers Association publishes its *Implications of the Data Protection Act for Direct Marketing / Direct Mailing*. The Advertising Association publishes its Code of Practice covering the use of *Personal Data for Advertising and Direct Marketing Purposes*.

The Mailing Preference Service (described in the previous chapter) enables people to have their names deleted from mailing lists and links with the data protection system.

TRADE DESCRIPTIONS ACT 1968

This is one of the most important statutes concerned with marketing, coupled with the more recent Consumer Protection Act that *inter alia* repealed the Trade Descriptions Act 1972 (which largely concerned the countries of origin of products especially when goods bearing British names or marks were made abroad).

The 1968 Act contained the following requirements of a trade description which is an indication, direct or indirect, given *by any means whatever,* of any of the following matters with respect to goods or parts of goods:

(a) quantity, size, gauge;

(b) method of manufacture, production, processing or reconditioning;

(c) composition;

(d) fitness for purpose, strength, performance, behaviour or accuracy;

(e) any physical characteristics not included in the preceding paragraphs;

(f) testing by persons and results thereof;

(g) approval by any person or conformity with a type approved by any person;

(h) place or date of manufacture, production, processing or reconditioning;

(i) person by whom manufactured, produced, processed or reconditioned;

(j) other history, including previous ownership or use.

This is a very extensive list and it can cover any statements made in advertising or sales literature. Its provisions range from, say, a description of a hotel in a holiday brochure (and there have been several convictions in this area) to a small classified ad for a second-hand motor-car.

CONSUMER PROTECTION ACT 1967

Probably one of the most important statutes to do with marketing, it amends or repeats a number of the earlier Acts and is far-ranging in its provision to protect the consumer. In particular, there are Parts on Product Liability, Consumer Safety and Misleading Price Indications, from which the following explanations are quoted:

3.   Meaning of "defect"
(1) 'Subject to the following provisions of this section, there is a defect in a product for the purposes of this Part if the safety of the product is not such as persons generally are entitled to expect: and for those purposes "safety", in relation to a product, shall include safety with respect to products comprised in that product and safety in the context of risks of damage to property, as well as in the context of risks of death or personal injury.

(2) In determining for the purposes of subsection (1) above what persons generally are entitled to expect in relation to a product all the circumstances shall be taken into account, including:

(a) the manner in which, and purposes for which, the product has been marketed, its get-up, the use of any mark in relation to the product and any instructions for, or warnings with respect to, doing or refraining from doing anything with or in relation to the product;

(b) what might reasonably be expected to be done with or in relation to the product; and

(c) the time when the product was supplied by its producer to another;

and nothing in this section shall require a defect to be inferred from the fact alone that the safety of a product which is supplied after that time is greater than the safety of the product in question.

10.   The general safety requirement
(1) A person shall be guilty of an offence if he:

(a) supplies any consumer with goods which fail

to comply with the general safety requirement.

(b) offers or agrees to supply any such goods; or

(c) exposes or possesses any such goods for supply.

(2) For the purposes of this section consumer goods fail to comply with the general safety requirement if they are not reasonably safe having regard to all the circumstances, including:

(a) the manner in which, and purposes for which, the goods are being or would be marketed, the get-up of the goods, the use of any mark in relation to the goods and any instructions or warnings which are given or would be given in respect to the keeping, use or consumption of the goods;

(b) any standards of safety published by any person either for goods of a description which applies to the goods in question or for matters relating to goods of that description; and

(c) the existence of any means by which it would have been reasonable (taking into account the cost, likelihood and extent of any improvement) for the goods to have been made safer.

21. Meaning of "misleading"

(1) For the purposes of section 20 above an indication given to any consumers is misleading as to a price if what is conveyed by the indication, or what those consumers might reasonably be expected to infer from the indication or any omission from it, includes any of the following, that is to say:

(a) that the price is less than in fact it is;

(b) that the applicability of the price does not depend on facts or circumstances on which its applicability does in fact depend;

(c) that the price covers matters in respect of which an additional charge is in fact made;

(d) that a person who in fact has no such expectation:

(i) expects the price to be increased or reduced (whether or not at a particular time or by a particular amount);

(ii) expects the price, or the price as increased or reduced, to be maintained (whether or not for a particular period); or

(e) that the facts or circumstances by reference to which the consumers might reasonably be expected to judge the validity of any relevant comparison made or implied by the indication are not what in fact they are.

(2) For the purposes of section 20 above, an indication given to any consumers is misleading as to a method of determining a price if what is conveyed by the indication, or what those consumers might reasonably be expected to infer from the indication or any omission from it, includes any of the following, that is to say:

(a) that the method is not what in fact it is;

(b) that the applicability of the method does not depend on facts or circumstances on which its applicability does in fact depend;

(c) that the method takes into account matters in respect of which an additional charge will in fact be made;

(d) that a person who in fact has no such expectation:
(i) expects the method to be altered (whether or not at a particular time or in a particular respect); or

(ii) expects the method, or that method as altered, to remain unaltered (whether or not for a particular period); or

(e) that the facts or circumstances by reference to which the consumers might reasonably be expected to judge the validity of any relevant comparison made or implied by the indication are not what in fact they are.

(3) For the purposes of subsections (1)(e) and (2)(e) above, a comparison is a relevant comparison in relation to a price or method of determining a price if it is made between that price or that method, or any price which has been or may be determined by that method; and

(a) any price or value which is stated or implied to be, to have been or to be likely to be attributed or attributable to the goods, services, accommodation or facilities; or

(b) any method, or other method, which is stated or implied to be, to have been or to be likely to be applied or applicable for the determination of the price or value of the goods, services, accommodation or facilities in question or of the price or value of any other goods, services, accommodation or facilities.

The above quotations provide samples of the legislation, and are sufficient to indicate the vigilance required by those responsible for marketing, whether they be producers or distributors. In most cases, the enforcement authority is the local weights and measures authority, or the district council in Northern Ireland. Briefly, a person found guilty of an offence due to a faulty product can claim for damages; if it is a case of consumerist safety the penalty can be imprisonment not exceeding six months or a fine; and if the offence is about a misleading price there can be a fine.

Broadly, the Consumer Protection Act covers product liability, consumer safety and misleading prices. Producers, importers and own labellers are made liable for unlimited damages for defects which cause injury or death, without proof of either negligence or contractual relationship. This requires a general duty to sell safe products, and this responsibility is additional to existing safety legislation. All earlier legislation on prices is repealed, and the Act imposes more stringent controls on bogus price offers.

Traders have to be especially careful about buying foreign goods. In the past, products such as electric-light bulbs and Christmas tree lights have proved to be defective and dangerous. Similarly, manufacturers have to be careful about electrical, electronic and mechanical products which are assembled from imported components. In the past, several well-known firms have had to recall products such as domestic appliances which have been found to have faulty parts or wiring.

CONTROL OF MISLEADING ADVERTISEMENTS REGULATIONS 1988

This is a short but significant piece of consumer protection legislation the title page of which is headed 1988 No 915 CONSUMER PROTECTION. The Regulations are what are termed a *statutory instrument*, being issued by the Secretary of State.

By definition, in these Regulations, *"advertisement" means any form of representation which is made in connection with a trade, business, craft or profession in order to promote the supply or transfer of goods or services, immovable property, rights or obligations.* However, the Regulations do not apply to investment and financial advertisements.

A further interpretation within the Regulations is that "an advertisement is misleading if in any way, including its presentation, it deceives or is likely to deceive the persons to whom it is addressed or whom it reaches and if, by reason of its deceptive nature, it is likely to affect their economic behaviour or, for those reasons, injures or is likely to injure a competitor of the person whose interests the advertisement seeks to promote".

Complaints may be made to the Director General of Fair Trading, unless they are broadcast ones which should be considered by the IBA or the Cable Authority. If the Director General considers an advertisement, about which a complaint has been received, is misleading he can bring court proceedings for an injunction. "An injunction may prohibit the publication or the continued or further publications of an advertisement."

The Regulations provide the IBA and the Cable Authority (except regarding advertisements transmitted originally by the IBA) with the power to refuse to broadcast a misleading advertisement.

The Regulations implement Council Directive No 84/450/EEC (OJ No L 250 19.9.1984, p17) relating to misleading advertising, and are an example of the harmonising of Common Market legislation under the European Communities Act 1972.

Very interesting is the reference on the Explanatory Note at the end of the Regulations which says that "Before he considers a complaint the Director may require the person making the complaint to satisfy him that appropriate means of dealing with the complaint have been tried and that, despite being given a reasonable opportunity to do so, those means have not dealt with the complaint adequately. (Such means might include complaining to a local authority trading standards department or to a self-regulatory body, such as the Advertising Standards Authority."

Thus, the Regulations are not set up in competition with the long-established voluntary control by means of the British Code of Advertising Practice, as administered by the ASA and described in both the preceding and the following chapters. The Regulations provide a legal last resort.

In such a book it is impossible to consider all the legislation affecting marketing. In fact, in the past, three excellent books have been published on the law of advertising, only for them to go out of print and not be repeated because of the constant change in legislation. In this chapter emphasis has been placed on the Consumer Protection Act 1987 which is the most modern and comprehensive piece of legislation in this field. Some additional points will be raised in the Model Answer at the end of this chapter.

SUMMARY

In this chapter a big subject has been introduced briefly with a comparison being made between common law in which a plaintiff sues a defendant privately, and legislation where prosecutions are made by the Crown against offenders, perhaps through the agency of the Office of Fair Trading or a local weights and measures authority. Under the first heading was discussed the law of contract and slander of goods (with reference to Passing Off). Under the second heading, the Data Protection Act 1984, the Trade Descriptions Act 1968, the Consumer Protection Act 1967, and the Control of Misleading Advertisement Regulations 1988 were discussed with relevant passages being quoted from the Statutes and the Statutory Instrument. Copies of the Statutes and Regulations can be purchased from the various shops of HM Stationery Office or through booksellers.

PAST EXAMINATION QUESTIONS

Question 7, LCC Series 2, 1987

The following practices are illegal in some countries.

(i) Explain each of these malpractices.

*(ii) State how and why they have been made
       illegal, in a country of your choice.*

(a)   Inertia selling
*(b)   Failure to state the origin of a
        wine*
(c)   Subliminal advertising
(d)   Passing off.

Comment

There are two parts to the question, each part
being given equal marks. The question is worded
for the benefit of candidates sitting in different parts of the world where particular laws
apply. The following Model Answer is based on
British law.

Model answer

Qu.7. (i) (a) INERTIA SELLING. This mal
practice occurs when goods are supplied
which are unsolicited, that is not ordered
by the recipient. The system operates on
the assumption that the recipient will not
bother to return the goods, and will therefore feel obliged to pay for goods which
are retained. But what happens if the recipient is annoyed at having received unwanted goods and destroys them or merely uses
or keeps them? Supposing the goods are
perishable like cream left on the doorstep
by a milkman?

Qu.7. (i) (b) FAILURE TO STATE THE
ORIGIN OF A WINE. Wines usually have
a special country of origin like champagne,
port and sherry. However, similar styles of
wine are produced in countries such as
Australia, Britain, Cyprus, South Africa
and the United States. It is therefore
necessary to label them as, say, Cyprus or
South African Sherry, or British Port-type
wine.

Qu.7. (i) (c)   SUBLIMINAL ADVERTISING.
This applies to cinema and television
commercials in which the selling message

occupies so few frames of the film or
second of the videotape that while the mind
accepts the message the eye does not record
it. The classic case was of the American
cinema-owner who used such a commercial to
promote soft drinks, and members of the
audience actually got up and bought drinks
without being aware that they had been
persuaded to do so. In one of the Columbo
detective films a murder was committed by
this method, the killer being urged to
commit the crime while watching a film.

Qu.7. (i) (d) PASSING OFF. This occurs when
a product is so named as to resemble an
existing product, e.g. Koca Kola, or when
the packaging is of such a design or colour
that it could be mistaken for another. This
is a practice often found in Third World
countries where an indigenous product is
made to look like a famous import, and
illiterate or unsophisticated people are
hoodwinked into buying the deceptive product. At one time the Japanese were noto-
rious for look-alike products such as sup-
posedly Ronson lighters. Pirated editions
of books and videos are other examples.

Qu.7. (ii) (a)   INERTIA SELLING is controlled
by the Unsolicited Goods and Services Acts
1971, 1975. The Acts set out the rights and
duties of those who receive unsolicited
goods or services, including charges for
unauthorised directory entries (relieving
them of the obligation to make a payment),
but requires the recipient to keep unsolicited goods in good condition and wait for
collection.

Qu.7. (ii) (b)   FAILURE TO STATE THE ORIGIN
OF A WINE. The legal requirement to
state the origin of a wine is covered by
the Trade Descriptions Act 1968 which
requires that the place of manufacture must
be stated.

Qu.7. (ii) (c)   SUBLIMINAL ADVERTISING is
illegal under the Independent Broadcasting
Authority Act 1974 and the IBA Code of

Advertising Standards resulting from this Act.

Qu.7. (ii) (d)   PASSING OFF is a tort or civil wrong when there is deliberate imitation of another product in order to delude buyers that it is the original product, usually by its "get up" or packaging but also in advertisements. If the perpetrator is sued in court it is necessary to show that there is a likelihood of confusion in the minds of the buyers, and a strong case can be made out if it can be shown that the ruse has caused a loss of business.

EXERCISE

Consider the many ways in which an unscrupulous manufacturer can pass off a product so that customers may be easily deceived into believing that the product is actually a well-known brand. Consider all aspects such as the company name, brand name, lettering, typography, trade mark, slogan, colour, shape or style of the container and/or packaging such as a carton or wrapper. Take a famous product and devise a get-up which could pass off a rival product as the original one. Then consider what legal action, and on what grounds, the original manufacturer can seek protection or redress.

18. Self regulatory controls affecting marketing

INTRODUCTION

This chapter will be devoted to the principal codes of practice which apply to marketing, namely the British Code of Advertising Practice and the British Code of Sales Promotion Practice, together with the codes of the British Direct Marketing Association, the British Direct Mail Producers Association, and the Institute of Public Relations and the customer protection services offered by publishing houses. This will supplement some of the information already given in Chapter 16 on How Does Consumerism Affect Marketing? These self regulatory controls will be contrasted with the legal controls described in the previous chapter, and the chapter will begin by re-iterating the value of self-regulatory controls already touched on in Chapter 16.

VALUE OF SELF-REGULATORY CONTROLS

The value of self-regulatory controls lies in their preventive effect, the ease with which complaints can be made, and the speed with which they can be investigated and resolved.

In the first instance, industry codes of practice not only impose discipline on those who conduct marketing, advertising, sales promotion and public relations, but they represent the public relations of marketing communications. The Chartered Institute of Marketing, incidentally, publishes a code which is an amalgam of the various codes. Quite apart from protecting the consumer, codes set out to protect the credibility and professionalism of their sector of marketing communications. For instance, it does the advertising business no good if people are sceptical of the honesty and reliability of advertising. Public relations is often criticised (even by marketing people) but the Institute of Public Relations is proud of the standards set out in its code to which all members are required to adhere. An advertising agency's reputation will be at stake if it offends against the BCAP, and a recognised agency could lose its right to commission if it operated against the provisions of the BCAP.

Thus, codes act as double watchdogs, protecting the reputation of the industries and professions involved, and protecting consumers and others against abuses. However, in an imperfect world there will be outsiders who are not bound by codes, and there will be those who commit offences unintentionally or because they are over-zealous in competitive situations.

Some examples from the ASA *Reports* were quoted in Chapter 16. Most of the cases investigated were not evil: more often they resulted from carelessness, poor liaison between those responsible, poor taste or perhaps an excess of enthusiastic selling. The days when proprietary medicines were advertised in the popular press with long lists of illnesses they could not possibly cure were ended by the investigative efforts of the Advertising Association long before the BCAP and the ASA were ever heard of. The AA's original code dealt only with medicines and treatments.

The ASA invites complaints from the public (see *Fig 1*) and makes no secret of its work to stamp out misleading advertising. Thus, the self-regulatory system is more accessible than legal control where a complainant has to go to considerable trouble to secure a prosecution, not to mention having to appear in court as a witness perhaps.

There is an effective linkage of interests. The media do not wish to lose faith with their readers by publishing misleading advertisements. Advertising agencies do not want to lose their commission, and in their own interests they can resist attempts by clients to be unethical. The public are made aware of the system through ASA advertisements. Many publishers use the ASA ads as 'fillers' when they have unsold advertising space. The public are free to submit complaints, and they do so often quite frivolously because they dislike certain advertisements. For instance, teetotallers complain about any alcoholic drink advertisement.

Moreover, the BCAP is supported by 22 industry organisations which expect their members to adhere to the code, while the Committee of Advertising Practice has four standing committees on mail order, health and nutrition, financial advertising and sales promotion. Additional consultant experts are also engaged, and there is also the CAP Copy Panel made up of advertising experts. CAP also monitors advertisements quite independently of those complained about and deals with intra-industry complaints when one advertiser complains about another's advertising. Before 1962, when the ASA was set up, the Advertising Association could be sued for libel if it criticised advertisements, but today those investigations and decisions are published.

From these remarks it will be seen that the voluntary self-regulatory system of control of advertising is well organised, sincere and largely very successful. Against this it is only fair to recognise the huge volume of advertising, the vast number of advertisers, and the fact that there are some 12,000 publications in the UK. Media also extend to posters, cinema, direct mail and door-to-door mail drops, plus hundreds of sales promotion schemes. The opportunities for abuse are many, but only a fool or a rogue would deliberately risk sacrificing his reputation because of disreputable advertising. That advertising should be *legal, decent, honest and truthful* is a responsibility of an advertiser to himself as well as to the public.

BRITISH CODE OF ADVERTISING PRACTICE

The BCAP is administered by the Advertising Standards Authority, and this is published by the Committee of Advertising Practice, Brook House, 2-16 Torrington Place, London WC1E 7HN. The 8th edition (December 1988) is a 100-page booklet, available free of charge from the above address.

Part C of the Code sets out *Rules Applying to Particular Categories of Advertisement.* Section CI deals with health claims; CII with hair and scalp products; CIII with vitamins and minerals; CIV with slimming; CV with cosmetics; CVI with mail order and direct response advertising; CVII with financial services and products; CVIII with employment and business opportunities; CIX with limited editions; CX with children; CXI with media requirements; CXII with alcoholic drinks; and there is an Appendix on cigarette advertising.

These rules are specific as to what may or may not be included in advertisements. For example, no advertisement may claim or imply the *cure* of any ailment, illness or disease; in mail order advertisements the true name and address of the advertiser must be given; and regarding children they should not be encouraged to enter strange places or converse with strangers in order to collect coupons, wrappers or labels. These brief examples indicate the wide-ranging nature of the Code. It is *specific* unlike some professional codes which refer to broad principles of professional behaviour.

It is therefore the responsibility of the marketer (and his outside agencies) to be familiar with the stipulations regarding this business. A great deal of consumerist activity would be redundant if the relevant contents of the code were understood before a product was packaged, advertised or in any way promoted. In fact, a valuable part of the self-regulatory system consists of advertisers or their agencies seeking the advice of the CAP Committee before publishing advertisements for products or services covered by the CAP. Many an advertisement has been modified as a result of such caution.

Most advertisements are legal, decent, honest and truthful. A few are not, and, like you, we want them stopped.

If you would like to know more about how to make complaints, please send for our booklet: 'The Do's and Don'ts of Complaining'. It's free.

The Advertising Standards Authority.
We're here to put it right. ✔

ASA Ltd., Dept. Z. Brook House, Torrington Place, London WC1E 7HN
This space is donated in the interests of high standards of advertising

Figure 1   ASA advertisement as inserted in the press.

INDEPENDENT BROADCASTING AUTHORITY CODE OF ADVERTISING STANDARDS AND PRACTICE

This code is a legal requirement of the Independent Broadcasting Act 1973, and although the IBA has the legal power to ban a television or radio commercial from the air, it is included in this chapter on voluntary controls because it is set out in the form of a code and not a statute. Reference was made to it in the previous chapter under the Control of Misleading Advertisement Regulations 1988.

In many respects the IBA Code resembles the BCAP but it goes further and bans cigarette advertising, and commercials dealing with politics, industrial and public controversy and religion. It is especially protective regarding the effect of commercials likely to be seen by children; e.g. children must not be seen doing something it would be dangerous for them to copy. Control is achieved by the vetting of all advertisements by the IBA and the Independent Television Association (ITVA) before transmission. Even then, complaints are sometimes received from viewers, and they are dealt with painstakingly. Again, as a sensible precaution proposed commercials are often discussed with the IBA before videos are completed.

BRITISH CODE OF SALES PROMOTION PRACTICE

Like the BCAP, the code is published by the CAP Committee and administered by the Advertising Standards Authority. The code is contained in a detailed booklet similar in style to the BCAP. It covers "promotional products which the consumer receives, or may receive, as a result of participation in a sales promotion. (For example, premiums, prizes, gifts, etc.)"

In its Basic Principles the Code states that "sales promotion should be so designed and conducted so as not to cause avoidable disappointment." There have been sales promotion schemes which disappointed because gifts or premiums received were inferior to expectations, or delivery was delayed, or they were poorly packed and damaged in transit.

Another Basic Principle states "Neither the design nor the conduct of a promotion should be such as to conflict with the public interest. In particular, promotions should contain nothing which is likely to provoke, or may appear to condone, violent or anti-social behaviour, damage to property or the causing of nuisance or injury to any member of the public". In the past some treasure hunt promotions caused damage and nuisance.

In the General Guidelines Applying to All Forms of Sales Promotion, recommendations are laid down concerning protection of privacy, children and young people, safety, presentation, quality and suitability of promotional products, exaggeration, terms of the promotion, conditions governing participation, availability of promotional products, and administration. Emphasis is placed on giving prominence to any requirement for additional proofs of purchase and the closing date of the scheme. Moreover, when a promotion is advertised on a pack, wrapper or label, any terms or conditions must be visible by a consumer *prior to purchase*.

There are then recommendations on How The General Guidelines Apply in Particular Cases, and they refer to free gifts, charity-linked promotions, and promotions and the trade. The free gifts section also deals with competitions, free draws and games of chance (e.g. Bingo), and typical criteria for entry instructions are set out consisting of:

(i) the closing date;

(ii) any restriction on the numbers of entries or prizes which may be won;

(iii) any requirements for proof of purchase;

(iv) description of prizes;

(v) any age, eligibility or geographical restrictions;

(vi) notification of winners and results (see Section 6.2.3);

(vii) the criteria for judging entries;

(viii) ownership of copyright in entries;

(ix) if entries are returnable by the promoter, how they are to be returned;

(x) how participants may obtain any supplementary rules which may apply;

(xi) whether a cash alternative to any prize is available;

(xii) any permissions required, e.g. from parent or employer.

BRITISH DIRECT MARKETING ASSOCIATION CODE OF PRACTICE

This code deals with the conduct of direct marketing (formerly known as mail order trading) and it supplements the BCAP and BCSPP described above. An interesting addition to this code is the BDMA's Guidelines for Telephone Marketing Practice. The Guidelines set out stipulations on disclosures of the identity of the direct marketing company, honesty in statements made on the telephone, the making of calls at reasonable hours, courtesy and procedures during telephone conversations, and restriction of contacts. The latter point is aimed at curbing the malpractice of generating calls by random or sequential dialling manually or by computer.

DIRECT MAIL PRODUCERS ASSOCIATION CODE OF PRACTICE

The object of this code is to promote the use and improve the status of direct mail as an advertising medium and in so doing to uphold the BCAP and the BCSPP. Members are expected not to mail, or produce for mailing, literature or material which may be regarded as vulgar, dishonest, illegal or likely to cause offence in any way to recipients or to any other persons.

INSTITUTE OF PUBLIC RELATIONS CODE OF PROFESSIONAL CONDUCT

The IPR code (and the similar one of the Public Relations Consultants Association) is less specific than those concerning advertising and sales promotion. They are concerned with the professional behaviour of individual practitioners or, in the case of the PRCA code, with that of public relations consultancies. Complaints are receivable from members and not from members of the public.

Typical clauses concern undisclosed business interests, rewards to holders of public office, dissemination of information, confidential information, conflict of interests, disclosure of beneficial financial interests, payment contingent upon achievements, employment of holders of public interest, injury to other members and respect for other professional codes. Members may complain to the Professional Practices Committee, and a serious breach of the code would be considered by the Disciplinary Committee which can reprimand or suspend a member if found to be in breach of the code.

PUBLISHERS MAIL ORDER PROTECTION SCHEME

The MOPS scheme is described and illustrated in Chapter 16. There are also reader protection schemes run by individual publishers such as the one illustrated here which is taken from the *TV Times*.

MAIL ORDER ADVERTISING
British Code of Advertising Practice

Advertisements in this publication are required to conform to the British Code of Advertising Practice. In respect of mail order advertisements where money is paid in advance, the code requires advertisers to fulfil orders within 28 days, unless a longer delivery period is stated. Where goods are returned undamaged within seven days, the purchaser's money must be refunded. Please retain proof of postage/despatch, as this may be needed.

Mail Order Protection Scheme

If you order goods from Mail Order advertisements in this magazine and pay by post in advance of delivery, TV Times will consider you for compensation if the Advertiser should become subject to bankruptcy proceedings or go into liquidation, provided:

(1) You have not received the goods or had your money returned, and

(2) You write to the Publisher of TV Times summarising the situation not earlier than 28 days from the official on sale date of TV Times and not later than three months from that date (please retain proof of payment)

Please do not wait until the last moment to inform us. When you write, we will tell you how to make your claim and what evidence of payment is required.

We guarantee to meet claims from readers made in accordance with the above procedure as soon as possible after the Advertiser has become subject to bankruptcy proceedings or gone into liquidation. (Claims may be paid when the above procedure has not been complied with at the discretion of TV Times, but we do not guarantee to do so in view of the need to set some limit to this commitment and to learn quickly of readers' difficulties.)

This guarantee covers only advance payment sent in direct response to an advertisement in this magazine (not, for example, payment made in response to catalogues etc.) received as a result of answering such advertisements. All display advertisements are covered. Advertisements as loose inserts are not covered.

For further details contact Advertisement Department, Independent Television Publications Ltd, 247 Tottenham Court Road, London W1P 0AU.

Figure 2 Announcement published in TV Times.

SUMMARY

In contrast to Chapter 17, this chapter has dealt with voluntary or self-regulatory controls, and it complements references to them in Chapter 17. The British Code of Advertising Practice and the British Code of Sales Promotion Practice, as administered by the Advertising Standards Authority and the IBA Code of Advertising Standards and Practice are discussed. The first deals with advertisements in the press and cinema and outdoor, the second with sales promotion schemes, and the third with commercials broadcast by independent television and independent radio stations. Reference was also made to the British Direct Marketing Association and the Direct Mail Producers Associations codes of practice. A further reference was made to the reader protection mail order schemes operated by the press, this being illustrated by an announcement published in *TV Times* which complements the MOPS scheme described and illustrated in Chapter 16.

PAST EXAMINATION QUESTION

Question 9, LCC Autumn 1986

Explain the functions of:

    (i) The Advertising Standards Authority
    (ii) The Office of Fair Trading
    (iii) The Consumers' Association
    (iv) The IBA and its Code of Advertising Standards and Practice.

Comment

The question is in four parts with equal marks for each part. All four have been described in Chapters 16, 17 and/or 18. This information can be consolidated and amplified along the lines of the following model answer.

Model answer

Qu.9. (i) The Advertising Standards

Authority administers the British Code of Advertising Practice and conducts the self-regulatory control of advertisements in newspapers, magazines and on posters or in the cinemas. It is not concerned with television and radio commercials which are controlled by the Independent Broadcasting Authority.

The ASA is an independent body, but it is financed by a levy on advertisements collected by the Advertising Standards Board of Finance. There is an independent chairman and a council representing many aspects of society.

Complaints are invited in writing from the public, and ASA advertisements with their familiar 'tick' symbol appearing frequently in newspapers and magazines. If the complaint is well-founded, the advertiser is contacted and asked to either amend or withdraw the advertisement. Decisions are published in the monthly *ASA Report* which is issued free of charge, and often quoted in the press. In addition, the ASA conducts its own monitoring of advertisements, special attention being paid to categories such as children, alcohol and slimming.

Qu.9. (ii) The Office of Fair Trading administers the Fair Trading Act 1973 which aims to make illegal certain acts of unfair competition. It is an official consumer protection body, dealing with consumer trade practices such as advertising, salesmanship, packaging and payment.

The OFT has concerned itself with monopolistic professional practices, and was responsible for the change in the advertising agency commission system which had formerly guaranteed 'recognised agencies' certain rates of commission from the media. Such rates are now negotiable between individual agencies and the media.

The OFT is also responsible for administering the Control of Misleading Advertisements Regulations, which provides legal protection if a complainant has failed to receive satisfaction from a voluntary body such as the ASA.

If a practice is condemned as a result of an OFT investigation, the law may be changed, two examples being orders on mail order transactions and business advertisements.

Qu.9. (iii) The Consumers' Association is an independent non-profit-making organisation which provides unbiased reports on products and services. These reports are called *Which?* reports, published on general or specific subjects like motoring and money, and sold by subscription. Comparisons are made between rival products and best buys are recommended.

The Association conducts research for these and more specialised subjects. It has become a recognised authority, and its spokesmen often appear in television programmes, such as Esther Rantzen's *That's Life,* giving advice on controversies regarding products or services.

Qu.9. (iv) The IBA's Code of Advertising Standards and Practice is a legal requirement under the Independent Broadcasting Authority Act 1973. In many ways it resembles the British Code of Advertising Practice, except that it goes further and bans advertising for cigarettes and gambling, and for ones dealing with politics, religion or industrial and public controversy. Thus, unlike the press, advertisements are not accepted for political parties, religious denominations or sects, or on behalf of the protagonists in strikes or take-over bids.

The Code covers commercial television and radio (ITV and ILR), but not cable television which has its own code concerning non-IBA programmes.

Television commercials are jointly vetted by the IBA and ITVA representing the television companies. It is sensible to discuss possibly sensitive commercials with the IBA before they are completed, even perhaps at the script and storyboard stage.

EXERCISE

Obtain an free loan a copy of an explanatory ASA video from Viscom Film and Video Library, Unit BII, Parkhill Road Trading Estate, London SE21 8EL, telephone: 01-761 3035. There are at least three ASA videos available, and leaflets about them can be obtained from the Advertising Standards Authority Ltd, Brook House, 2-16 Torrington Place, London WC1E 7HN.

Also, obtain from the ASA a free copy of the British Code of Advertising Practice, preferably sending a large stamped addressed envelope.

View the video, and then select cases from the *ASA Report* and consider the interpretation of the Code references given at the end of each statement of *Basis of Complaint*. This will demonstrate how breaches of the code have been claimed, and whether or not the criticised advertisement did in fact breach the Code. The decision contained in the *conclusion* will then show whether or not the ASA decided that there had been a breach and, if there had, what action took place.

ADDRESSES OF ORGANISATIONS

Advertising Association, The
    Abford House, 15 Wilton Road, London SW1V
    1NJ

Advertising Standards Authority Ltd,
    Brook House, 2-16 Torrington Place, London
    WC1E 7HN

Association of Independent Radio Contractors,
    Regina House, 250-269 Old Marylebone Road,
    London NW1 5RA

Association of Media Independents Ltd
    34 Grand Avenue, London N10 3BP

Audit Bureau of Circulations,
    13 Wimpole Street, London W1M 7AB

British Association of Industrial Editors,
    3 Locks Yard, High Street, Sevenoaks, Kent
    TN13 1LT

British Direct Marketing Association Ltd,
    1 New Oxford Street, London WC1A 1NQ

Broadcasters' Audience Research Board Ltd,
    Knighton House, 56 Mortimer Street, London
    W1N 8AN

Communication, Advertising & Marketing Education
Foundation Ltd,
    Abford House, 15 Wilton Road, London W1V
    1NJ

Consumers Association,
    2 Marylebone Road, London NW1 4DX

Direct Mail Producers Association,
    34 Grand Avenue, London N10 3BP

Incorporated Society of British Advertisers,
    44 Hertford Street, London W1Y 8AE

Independent Broadcasting Authority,
    70 Brompton Road, London SW3 1EY

Independent Television Association,
    Knighton House, 56 Mortimer Street, London
    W1N 8AN

Institute of Marketing,
    Moor Hall, Cookham, Maidenhead, Berks SL6
    9QH

Institute of Practitioners in Advertising,
    44 Belgrave Square, London SW1X 8QS

Institute of Public Relations,
    Gate House, St John's Square, London EC1M
    4DH

Institute of Sales Promotion,
    Arena House, 66-68 Pentonville Road, London
    N1 9HS

Joint Industry Committee for National Readership
Surveys,
    4 Belgrave Square, London SW1X 8QS

Joint Industry Committee for Radio Audience
Research,
    44 Belgrave Square, London SW1X 8QS

London Chamber of Commerce Examinations Board,
    Marlowe House, Station Road, Sidcup, Kent
    DA15 7BJ

Market Research Society,
    175 Oxford Street, London W1R 1TA

Public Relations Consultants Association,
    10 Greycoat Place, London SW1P 1SB

Royal Society of Arts Examinations Board,
    Murray Road, Orpington, Kent BR5 3RB